Paid Work and Housing

A comparative guide to the impact of employment on housing and support for people with learning disabilities

Jenny Pannell and Ken Simons *with* **Margaret Macadam**

Norah Fry Research Centre

Pavilion

JR
JOSEPH
ROWNTREE
FOUNDATION

RESEARCH *INTO* PRACTICE

RESEARCH *INTO* PRACTICE

Paid Work and Housing

A comparative guide to the impact of employment on housing and support for people with learning disabilities

Jenny Pannell and Ken Simons with Margaret Macadam

Published by:

Pavilion Publishing (Brighton) Ltd
8 St George's Place
Brighton, East Sussex BN1 4GB

Telephone: 01273 623222
Fax: 01273 625526
Email: pavpub@pavilion.co.uk
Website: www.pavpub.com

In association with:

Joseph Rowntree Foundation
The Homestead
40 Water End
York YO30 6WP

and

Faculty of Health & Social Care
University of the West of England, Bristol
Glenside Campus
Blackberry Hill, Stapleton
Bristol BS16 1DD

and

Norah Fry Research Centre
University of Bristol
3 Priory Road
Bristol BS8 1TX

First published 2000

ISBN 1 84196 007 1

Editor: Liz Mandeville
Cover and page design and layout: Stanford Douglas
Printing: Paterson Printing (Tunbridge Wells)

Paid Work and Housing

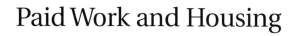

The Joseph Rowntree Foundation has supported this project as part of its programme of research and innovative development projects, which it hopes will be of value to policy makers and practitioners. The facts presented and the views expressed in this report, however, are those of the authors and not necessarily those of the Foundation.

Acknowledgements

First we must thank the Joseph Rowntree Foundation, particularly Alex O'Neil. We would also like to thank members of our Advisory Group: Rob Greig, Morag McGrath, Denise Northover, Philippa Rudge, Neil Shearn and Peter Singh.

Second, we would like to thank our many contacts in France, including the directors, staff and users in CAT Le Castelet Avèze, CAT Albi-Jarlard and CAT S.I.T.E.S. (Nîmes) and the IRTS du Languedoc Roussillon in Montpellier. Hosting researchers who work in a different language is hard work, yet everyone was unfailingly helpful and patient. We hope we have done justice to their views and experiences.

We often had very little time with people in the UK projects, but all the following organisations were quite exceptionally helpful and co-operative:

- Antur Waenfawr
- Cleansweep and Bristol PATHWAY
- Co-options
- Denbighshire Employment Opportunities
- Food and Futures
- Gillygate Wholefood Bakery
- Menter Fachwen
- SHAW (Sheltered Housing and Work) Projects
- South East Wales PATHWAY
- WISE.

SWALLOW also deserve our thanks, particularly Kim Hawkins, Jane Murdoch and Edward Scott, and Christine Fisher and David Holmes who supported them in the fieldwork. They were great partners and they added much to our work. We can only hope they got half as much out of it as we did.

We should also thank our long-suffering colleagues in the Norah Fry Research Centre and the University of West of England, in particular Linda Holley (who provided her usual efficient secretarial and administrative services) and Margaret Macadam (our loss and New Zealand's gain!).

Finally, we are forever in the debt of Alison Wertheimer, who helped reduce the original report by half to enable publication.

Jenny Pannell and Ken Simons

Contents

Chapter One
Setting the Scene

This report is a much abbreviated version of an earlier document. The latter had already led to a published report which focused solely on the wider social policy issues (Simons, 1998). However, for the purposes of formal publication, drastic pruning of the original text was required. For those interested, the full original report is available from the Norah Fry Research Centre website at no charge. The address is: www.bris.ac.uk/Depts/NorahFry/

How this project came about

This report is the result of the serendipitous experiences of two researchers.

Jenny Pannell, then a senior lecturer at the University of the West of England, knew from her experience as a service provider that the normal provision for adults with a learning disability was residential care and a day centre. As the mother of a teenage daughter with learning disabilities, she was concerned about the lack of choice when making the difficult transition from school to adulthood. Holidaying in the village of Avèze in Southern France, Jenny noticed several people with learning disabilities working in the bakery. The villagers seemed to know them well and it turned out that the village had a CAT – *Centre d'Aide par le Travail*.

The CAT was providing a range of work opportunities for people with learning disabilities; it also employed support staff, enabling some of the workers to live in 'ordinary' rented housing. The French system allowed workers to combine their CAT wages and social security benefits up to the level of the French minimum wage.

Jenny was keen to explore the French system further, to see what lessons we might learn in the UK. After visiting the CAT in Avèze, she approached the Joseph Rowntree Foundation and SWALLOW with an outline research proposal. SWALLOW suggested that she contact the Norah Fry Research Centre, where Ken Simons, a researcher, had recently completed a study of innovative housing and support schemes which helped people to live in their *own* homes (Simons, 1995). During this study he had met Ronald Smith, a man with learning disabilities. Ron and his new wife, Kirsten, had moved out of a group home and bought their own home with a mortgage. They were able to do this because they worked for SHAW, an organisation involved with housing and employment, including horticultural nurseries (see **Chapter Ten**). There is nothing special about a horticultural scheme. What is unusual is that Ronald and Kirsten earned enough to buy a home. For most citizens in the UK, their level of earnings determines the kind of housing they can access. However, the opposite is true for the vast majority of people with learning disabilities; their housing and support arrangements determine whether or not they can work – and in many cases these arrangements preclude more than a toehold in the workplace. At the same time, while some people are being supported to live in their own home, this typically happens *'despite the system not because of it'* (Simons & Ward, 1988).

The result of Jenny and Ken's shared interests was a joint proposal from University of the West of England and the Norah Fry Research Centre to compare the French and UK systems, focusing on exploring the extent to which they facilitate opportunities for people with learning disabilities to access work and housing.

Should we be copying CATs? The aims of the study

From the start it is important to emphasise that we never envisaged that CATs should be a model to be replicated in the UK. Rather, we set out:

- to describe a range of CATs

- to examine the context in which they function, in particular the relationship between the benefits system and the minimum wage, and the way that supported housing and work are combined

- to identify and describe a range of employment-related projects in the UK, and explore how they deal with similar issues

- to identify wider lessons for UK policy, particularly the potential impact of implementing a minimum wage.

We undertook relatively short fieldwork visits to talk to a range of people directly involved (including people with learning disabilities) and see for ourselves what was involved. We also explored the formal rules on funding and benefits.

We did not formally evaluate the services. Our enthusiasm for particular organisations was generally due to the principles people were trying to articulate. This was not the same as 'getting it right'; indeed, as is often the case, services struggling to be innovative tended to be the most self-critical.

Finally, imminent major changes to the benefits system and regulation of housing and support services were likely to affect people with learning disabilities. The new Labour Government was about to institute a wide range of social policy reforms, including the introduction of a national minimum wage. There was a widespread assumption that such a step would be beneficial (Beckett, 1997). However, an important reason for the study was that reforms of this kind are often introduced with scant regard for people with learning disabilities. We wanted to ensure that their issues were firmly on the agenda.

An introduction to CATs

The CAT is the dominant service model in France. CATs deliver support and employment to over 80,000 disabled people, most of whom have learning disabilities. A key feature is their dual role: they provide 'social care' but are also quasi-commercial, providing real jobs. CAT workers' wages and benefits are combined, giving them an income significantly above the French equivalent of Income Support – a key factor in opening up housing choice.

CATs often span the gap between day and residential services, providing support and housing services as well. Housing includes hostels and also supported tenancies in social or private rented housing.

Employment for people with learning disabilities in the UK

There is no UK equivalent to CATS, and the majority of people with learning disabilities are not employed. However, over the last decade there has been increasing interest in 'supported employment' (see **Chapter Seven**). This involves finding ordinary jobs for individual people with learning disabilities, and supporting them in the workplace, enabling them to earn a wage that reflects their contribution to the company.

Even during some difficult economic times, supported employment has succeeded in finding *'real jobs with real wages'* (Pozner *et al.,* 1993; Lister & Ellis, 1992; Wertheimer, 1992a, 1992b). Most users have been people labelled as having mild or moderate learning disabilities, but some have had much greater support needs.

However, only a tiny minority of people with learning disabilities have access to supported employment. The initial growth has slowed down (Beyer *et al.,* 1997), provision is patchy and piecemeal, and many schemes are small and fragile with little long-term funding (Beyer, 1993). Similarly, largely as a function of the benefits system (see **Chapter Eleven**), many people using supported employment work fewer than 16 hours per week and retain at least some of their incapacity benefits.

There is considerable potential for further developing supported employment. But we were also interested in exploring other UK initiatives (McGrath, 1995) that have some echoes of the CAT system, including community businesses (**Chapter Eight**) and worker co-operatives (**Chapter Nine**). We were particularly interested in whether they could provide sufficient secure, stable employment to give people the confidence to work full-time, while not foreclosing the option of moving into more integrated settings.

Despite our reservations about segregated settings, we also felt it worth exploring sheltered workshops, as they could enable people to earn a reasonable income, so we visited SHAW (see **Chapter Ten**).

The significance of work

Many people would take it for granted that work is a desirable activity for people with learning disabilities. There is significant evidence that many people with learning disabilities want paid work (Flynn, 1989; Simons, 1993; Mental Health Foundation, 1996), though that does not necessarily mean that everyone who wants to work also wants to abandon day centres completely (Simons, 1993; Shanley & Rose, 1993).

The idea of paid work has great significance for a number of reasons, including the following.

- **The stigma of being unemployed, or even worse 'unemployable'**
  'I wanted to work for my family's sake as well [as mine]. *Then you could say you have got somewhere in your life'* (self-advocate, quoted by Simons, 1993)

- **Wanting to contribute**
  'There was satisfaction you had a job for the week... You could say "I've done that"' (woman who had undertaken contract work in a day centre, quoted by Simons, 1993)

- **Being part of a wider world**
  'You get outside and meet people' (Simons, 1993)

● **Escaping poverty**

Most people with learning disabilities are poor (Davis *et al.*, 1993) and many want to work to escape poverty. In the words of one man:

'If I had a job… I'd be singing "That's living all right"' (quoted in Booth *et al.*, 1990)

We have tried to bear these points in mind when exploring the different models, so our criteria for assessing them included the extent to which they:

● opened up a range of employment and housing options

● increased opportunities for inclusion, both at home and at work

● gave people valued roles and status within their community

● increased people's income.

Addressing concerns expressed by the UK self-advocacy movement, we were also concerned with the degree to which these initiatives:

● opened up access to all people with learning disabilities, regardless of degree of disability, gender or ethnicity

● increased the extent to which people with learning disabilities participate in decision-making in the services they use.

Ronald (see page 1) illustrates the difficult choices people face. SHAW, which provides sheltered *and* supported employment, offered to try and get Ronald a job in an ordinary setting. He turned it down, because although the nursery where he worked was segregated, it offered **secure employment**. Aware that if he lost his job he would risk losing his house, he accepted some segregation at work, in exchange for totally 'desegregated' housing (Simons, 1995).

Some trade-offs are inevitable, but also work means different things to individuals, so, for example, we have tried not to assume that financial reward is the sole, or most important, reason for entering the workplace.

The fieldwork

We carried out individual interviews and group discussions with:

● 100 people with learning disabilities

● 150 professionals.

We also talked to a smaller number of families of people with learning disabilities, customers of the businesses in which they work and employers.

We had contact with 16 organisations, including:

● three CATs

● a college which trains professionals working in CATs and support services

● two alternatives to CATs, providing support in housing and employment

● two supported employment schemes (WISE and South East Wales PATHWAY)

● four community businesses: (Menter Fachwen, Antur Waenfawr, Co-options and Denbighshire Employment Options)

● a co-operative development agency (Food and Futures)

● two worker co-operatives (Gillygate Wholefood Bakery and Cleansweep)

● SHAW Projects (Northumberland).

Organisations were selected because they were potentially interesting, for pragmatic reasons (eg located near each other) and because they give a broad indication of what is happening in the UK and France.

Field work was carried out in 1996 and 1997, and the original report was completed in 1998. We have contacted most of the organisations and have commented on major changes but not on matters on detail. Figures are also from that period. Changes are bound to occur, and how an organisation responds will determine whether it survives and develops. As René Bouschet, Assistant Direct at CAT Avèze said recently:

> *'Changes are always happening in CATs. We have to modify, improve, change direction and search for new areas of work. That's what makes working in a CAT so interesting – we have to respond to the changing environment. For example, snails weren't selling, so we stopped production, and grew more vegetables – but if demand for snails increases, then we'll go back to snail farming.'*

There have also been developments in the French systems described in **Chapter Two**, but no major changes which impact on CATs.

Figures quoted in **Chapter Two** to **Five** are for 1996–7.

The role of SWALLOW

We wanted to include people with learning disabilities in our research team, reflecting the increasing involvement of service users in training, consultancy, research and evaluation. We invited SWALLOW to assist us, as we knew they were becoming interested in employment issues.

SWALLOW (South Wansdyke Learning and Living our Way) is committed to user involvement at every level. Over half of management committee members are people with learning disabilities or other disabilities, and they employ two people with learning disabilities.

Members of SWALLOW helped us in two ways. One member of the project joined our Research Advisory Group, and three people (with support) worked with us as evaluators at CAT Avèze (**Chapter Three**). The views of SWALLOW members have also more generally helped to shape our thinking.

Chapter Two

The French Service and Benefits System: an overview

Introduction

This chapter describes the origins of the CAT system, its legal basis, key features, and relationship to other services for people with learning disabilities. It also outlines the benefits system and housing and support options. The French systems are complex and vary between regions, but our descriptions have been simplified, focusing on their impact on CAT workers. For a more detailed picture, see Thornton & Lunt (1997). The **Glossary** lists the numerous acronyms used in the French system.

How did CATs start?

CATs started in the early 1960s, in response to parental concerns about their children's futures. By 1970, 173 CATs were providing 7,000 places and were largely occupational in approach. The 1975 Law (see right) established a funding régime which led to rapid growth and by 1980, 688 CATs provided 44,500 places. In the 1980s, CATs became much more commercial, developing links with local industries, and this was underlined by the provisions of the 1987 Law (see overleaf).

Voluntary organisations and key professionals formed a powerful lobby, attracting significant state funding for CATs. This powerful coalition is now lobbying to protect existing services from threatened cuts.

The legal framework

The 1975 Law *en faveur des personnes handicapées* [in favour of disabled people], provides the statutory basis for the AAH benefit for disabled people and the government assessment agency COTOREP. Article One reflects the holistic approach of the legislation.

> *'La prévention et le dépistage des handicaps, les soins, l'éducation, la formation et l'orientation professionnelle, l'emploi, la garantie d'un minimum de resources, l'intégration sociale et l'accès aux sports et aux loisirs du mineur et de l'adulte handicapés physiques, sensoriels ou mentaux constituent une obligation nationale.'*

[There is a national obligation to provide for the prevention and screening of disabilities, care, education, training and vocational guidance, employment, the guarantee of a minimum income, social integration and access to sport and leisure opportunities for children and adults with physical, sensory or mental impairment.]

The Law acknowledges the rights of people with disabilities to full citizenship, including employment, a guaranteed minimum income and integration.

The other key legislation is the Law of 10 July 1987, which replaced previous legislation on employing disabled people with a range of options for employers and created the state funding organisation, AGEFIPH (see pp9–10).

Who runs CATs?

Nearly all CATs are run by voluntary not-for-profit organisations, financed by their trading activities, grants from central and local government and occasional fundraising activities. Many are run by regional groups affiliated to large national voluntary organisations formed by parents and/or professionals, notably ADAPEI (which runs 60% of CATs) and l'APAJH; both are somewhat similar to MENCAP. Other CATs are smaller, local organisations, sometimes linked historically to local businesses or benefactors. A few are run by public authorities, usually based in institutions such as long-stay hospitals.

We visited one CAT run by ADAPEI, one by l'APAJH and one by a smaller organisation.

What sort of work do they do?

CATs provide full-time employment in sheltered or semi-integrated settings. Work includes agriculture, horticulture and grounds maintenance, factory work, services such as catering, postal deliveries and laundries, and shops such as local bakeries.

Key features include:

- contact with the local community
- involvement in the local/regional economy
- making available a variety of tasks and jobs
- providing opportunities for developing autonomy and personal growth.

A survey found that CATs activity (measured by turnover) was evenly split between:

- CATs' own manufacturing, production (35%)
- sub-contracting work for other organisations (34%)
- provision of services (31%).

The average number of disabled workers per CAT is 70, but as most have different sections and work teams undertaking different tasks, often in different locations, the organisations do not necessarily feel as large as these figures suggest.

Disabled workers are supported and supervised in their work by staff known as *moniteurs/monitrices,* who have usually worked previously in the type of employment being carried out, and had additional training to work in a CAT. They lead a small team of CAT workers, devise aids and techniques to assist individual workers, and allocate tasks according to the workers' skills, experience and developmental needs. Some also seek out work for their team, contact clients and provide estimates or specifications for the work. The extent to which they also work alongside the CAT workers varies according to the type of job. In specialist areas such as a bakery or metal workshop, they carry out a number of the tasks, but in more routine work like packaging their role is confined to supervising, training and encouraging the CAT workers.

Who uses CATs?

Most people working in CATs are classified as *handicapé mental*, a term which has replaced the more offensive terms used previously, such as *débile* and *arriéré* (retarded). There are also some people with a history of mental illness, and some with multiple disabilities; very few workers have only a sensory or physical disability.

Men outnumber women: 61% men and 39% women (Samoy, 1992). Half are under 30 and 36% are in their 30s. However, there is now a growing debate about what happens to people nearing retirement (often at a younger age than usual because of ill-health or premature ageing).

Housing, care and support

Housing options for CAT workers include hostels, social housing (rented from HLMs, the French equivalent of housing associations or local authorities), private rented housing or living with parents. Employment is in segregated but not isolated settings, and much of the housing is integrated, so CATs are quite different from 'village communities'. Also, unlike sheltered workshops, CATs deliver a very wide range of goods and services.

A 1993 national survey of CATs (*Insertion et Travail Adapté*, 1994) found that 21% of workers were living independently, 38% in hostels and 42% with their families. Since then, many CATs have developed independent living arrangements and housing support. In the three CATs we visited, a high proportion lived independently, and only one had hostel accommodation.

CAT workers living in the community usually have their own tenancies and pay rent from their benefits and wages. Some share in groups of two to four (rather like UK 'group homes'), but most prefer individual studio or one-bedroom flats. Many live as couples, and

there are some CATs where workers have children (though this is unusual). Some are home-owners and at least one CAT has developed shared ownership housing for its workers (*Insertion et Travail Adapté*, 1994).

Support services, funded by local government, are usually (though not always) provided by the same voluntary agency which runs the CAT, through the *Service de Suite* or *Service d'Accompagnement*. Like housing support services developed in the UK, this includes help with budgeting and liaison with bureaucracy, accessing services such as home care and medical attention, social activities and counselling. Two surveys found that over half of all CATs had support services linked to them, although there were great regional differences, no doubt reflecting social as well as funding differences.

Services de Suite or *d'Accompagnement* (whether linked to CATs or not) employ professionally trained support staff. Known as '*éducateurs/éducatrices specialisé(e)s*', or '*moniteurs-éducateurs/monitrices-éducatrices*', they provide a full range of support services including training, social support, partnering people on activities, liaising with bureaucracy and advising on budgeting and benefits. They assist with tasks such as shopping as part of their training and support role, although housework or personal care is accessed through the social services. A contact is usually provided for overnight, weekends and public holidays.

It is our impression that people with high support needs are more likely to remain in hostel-type provision.

Income and benefits

Most adults under pensionable age work at CATs. The system is geared to people working full-time, and as benefits criteria do not appear to create the same problems as in the UK, most work full-time. All the figures quoted here are for single people working full-time. The position of part-time workers and couples is more complicated. Disabled people living as couples or with children receive different levels of wages and benefits. Different arrangements also apply to disabled workers in open employment or *ateliers protégés* (sheltered workshops).

CAT workers receive their income from three main sources:

- wages direct from the CAT
- a wages supplement (*complément de rémunération*) paid through the CAT but provided from central government
- AAH (*Allocation aux Adultes Handicapés*) – a disability benefit.

These combine to produce an income similar to the SMIC (or minimum wage), currently FF 1478 (£164) per week gross for a 39-hour week, and FF 1163 (£129) per week, after deducting national insurance contributions.

As in UK residential care homes, CAT workers living in hostels have to pay for their board and lodging and are only left with 'pocket money'. Unlike their UK counterparts, though, they are able to work full-time if they wish.

CAT workers living independently are entitled to Allocation de Logement (equivalent to Housing Benefit). This goes towards their rent and is paid in addition to disability benefits and wages. The actual amount varies according to rent levels and the worker's income, but rarely covers the full rent.

CAT workers living at home also keep the full amount of wages and benefits.

Marie is a CAT worker who lives on her own in a flat rented from a private landlord. She has the following weekly income and expenditure:	
Net wages + government wages supplement	£72
Plus disability benefit (AAH)	£47
Sub-total before housing costs	£119
Plus 'housing benefit'	£24
Sub-total	£143
Less rent	£44
Disposable income	£99

The AAH benefit is awarded according to level of disability. Full (100%) rate is FF 3392 (£337) per month and most CAT workers receive between 60% and 80%. AAH is means-tested, so although Marie (see box) is assessed at 80% (= £70 per week) she receives less. People who work in CATs save the state money because of this cap on their AAH benefit.

Workers' wages are paid out of the income from CAT trading activities. The legal minimum is 5% of the SMIC, the maximum is 50%, and the average paid to all workers in the CAT must be at least 15% of SMIC. Less than a third of all CATs pay more than 15% of SMIC (Marie is paid at 15%). Wage levels vary because of differences in CATs' profitability and types of work undertaken.

In addition to AAH, CAT workers also get a *complément de rémunération* (wages supplement) from the state, intended to bring their total wages near to the SMIC.

The combination of wages and benefits for a CAT worker produces a figure significantly higher than RMI (equivalent to Income Support). RMI is FF 2375 (£264) per month for a single person. Marie gets nearly £120 per week before housing benefits and costs. Her income is a little less than the net SMIC figure of £129 per week, because her net wages include deductions for her weekday lunches at the CAT, and a voluntary insurance payment (*mutuelle*).

A CAT worker cannot receive wages and benefits above 110% of the SMIC, a cap introduced when it emerged that some workers were getting well over the SMIC.

How do people get assessed for benefits and access to CATs?

Access to CATs and to disability benefits are assessed separately by the government organisation, COTOREP. The percentage of disability for people with both physical and mental disabilities is assessed using the following categories:

- below 50% disability = low level = not needing special support

- 50–75% disability = moderate = will need some support

- 76–90% disability = significant = will need high level of support

- over 90% disability = severe = will need constant support.

COTOREP recommends whether someone is suitable for a CAT, usually on the basis that they have less than a one-third ability to work in normal employment but are physically capable of working and have expressed the desire to work. The person can choose whether or not to follow COTOREP's recommendation, and this does not affect their disability benefits entitlement.

People with very severe learning disabilities and multiple disabilities who are assessed as incapable of work, are likely to be recommended to a specialised home (*maison d'accueil spécialisée*) which resembles a UK nursing home, or to a *foyer occupationnel*, a hostel or day centre with occupational therapy but no proper work. People with a lesser disability may be directed towards an *atelier protégé* (sheltered workshop), though

there are few places in these compared with CATs because the latter have been more generously funded.

While it is difficult to gauge exactly people's 'level' of disability, our impression was that CAT workers had similar levels of disability to people in UK day centres and supported employment.

Measures to promote employment opportunities for disabled people

As with the UK quota system, France previously required employers to hire a percentage of disabled people, but this was difficult to enforce and widely ignored. The key legislation now is the 1987 Law, a radical reform which sought to change attitudes by replacing obligation with a social partnership (Schmitt, 1995). Employers are encouraged to contribute to social wellbeing, an approach also supported by the trade unions (Thornton & Lunt, 1997). The 1987 Law is also important because all organisations employing more than 20 employees must provide work for disabled people, through a range of options including:

- direct employment of disabled people to a quota of 6% of the workforce

- entering into a programme agreement to provide employment or training to disabled people

- paying a voluntary contribution to the government funding and regulatory body, AGEFIPH

- sub-contracting work to CATs and *ateliers protégés*

- employing CATs or *ateliers protégés* on a contract basis (such as grounds maintenance, catering or postal services)

- using CATs or *ateliers protégés* to provide labour on the employer's premises (a small work team in a factory, for example).

If the employer chooses the CATs/*ateliers protégés* options, this reduces the direct employment obligation option to a quota of 3% of the workforce. Employers who do not meet their obligations can be required to pay a fine to AGEFIPH.

The 1987 Law is important for CATs because it encourages employers to contract with CATs. During 1992–94, 12% of employers met their obligations by sub-contracts only, and 22% by sub-contracts and other means. Between 1988 and 1994, the number of employers contracting with CATs and other sheltered work increased from 6,900 to 18,100. The larger the employer, the more likely they were to sub-contract (Velche & Ravaud, 1995).

AGEFIPH has also been able to use the 'fines' paid by employers to provide financial support to a range of employment initiatives and support services, including CAT projects and individual help to employers and companies.

In the first six years, however, 400,000 disabled people had benefited from AGEFIPH funding but only 10% had learning disabilities or mental illness (figures combined). Approximately half of all employers chose to pay the 'voluntary contribution', and AGEFIPH's total income from this source amounted to around FF 16000m (£177m) per year (*Insertion et Travail Adapté*, 1995).

The funding of CATs

CATs' employment activities are financed mainly by income from their commercial activities and national government funding.

CATs employ around 20,000 staff at a ratio to workers defined by government. They are public sector employees and their full salary costs (about 65% of CATs' total running costs) are paid by government grant. The Government is obliged to meet an agreed deficit and the CAT can appeal if it disagrees with the amount offered.

CATs are under pressure to increase their commercial activities and reduce their reliance on government funding. There are also pressures to increase the size of individual CATs to between 80 and 120 workers and carry out more sub-contract work (considered more profitable than CATs' own businesses). Their parent voluntary organisations are also under pressure to develop supported employment projects to place people in open employment, and many are doing so.

Most CATs are run by voluntary organisations which can fundraise and pass income on to the CAT, but a CAT cannot fundraise directly. None of the CATs we visited received charitable money from their parent organisation (although those that do tend to be funded for new projects). All three stressed that they were run on business lines, providing high quality goods and services to their local communities.

Funding for hostels and support services is paid by local government at a day rate per resident, and from board and lodging payments paid by hostel residents out of their benefits and wages. Unlike the UK, support services are funded quite separately from 'bricks and mortar'; housing benefit contributes to housing but not care and support costs.

Chapter Three
CAT Le Castelet, Avèze

The distinctive feature of this CAT is its role as a community business in a rural economy (which has parallels with the community businesses described in **Chapter Eight**). CAT Avèze is one of three CATs managed by a voluntary organisation established by the works council of a bank.

Origins

The voluntary organisation running this CAT had previously run a home for children with learning disabilities and the CAT was set up in 1980 for young people leaving the home. When the home closed in 1985, the whole site was taken over by the CAT and its linked hostel.

Location and facilities

The CAT's main site is in the centre of the village and includes two workshops, the bakery, the gardening team's base, a canteen, the hostel and a shared practice flat for up to six people.

The CAT also owns a market garden about 1km away, and the baker's shop in the main street, over which there is an office base for the floating support staff, and a flat where people 'practise' living on their own.

Current activities

The organisation now comprises:

- the CAT employment project (with a number of different workgroups)
- the floating support service SAVS
- the hostel.

At the time of our visit, the workgroups included:

- the contract gardening team
- the market garden/snail farm
- the bakery unit
- the village baker's shop and a mobile shop
- two packaging workshops.

Like the Welsh community businesses (**Chapter Eight**), the workshops were originally based on the local economy, but like much of Wales too, rural depopulation means the local economy now depends heavily on tourism. Many of the gardening team's customers are holiday cottage owners, and the bakery's customers include local hotels, plus people staying at the campsite and in holiday homes.

Until recently the packaging was mainly for local hosiery factories, but competition from abroad has led to decline and these contracts have been replaced by new contracts, including assembly and packaging for a manufacturer of lamps and other home decorations.

The contract gardening/minor works team, market garden and packaging workshops all started in 1980. There was also a laundry and carpentry workshop, but they were not economically viable and closed. The CAT then bought the local bakery, built a modern bakery unit and set up a mobile shop. In 1995 the market garden diversified into producing, cooking and bottling snails. The CAT is now considering alternative options for one of the sub-contract workshops.

The range of work provides a variety of tasks, depending on individual abilities and choices. They start with a six-month trial. Workers can ask to move to another work-group (except for the bakery, which requires specific skills and some autonomy because of unsocial hours). Workers may also be asked to move temporarily because of seasonal factors or commercial demands.

The *moniteurs/monitrices* in charge of workgroups see their role as both educational and commercial. The two *monitrices* in the packaging workshops see their main aim as developing the abilities of the CAT workers, although this could conflict with the need for the workshop to pay its way. They have been aware of an increasing need for profitability in recent years.

Some workers had started in the packaging workshops and moved to the bakery.

'People who stay with us are either less capable, or need more supervision and structure in their lives.'

Both *monitrices* had previously worked in the hosiery factories, and then received block-release training for working in the CAT.

A *moniteur* in the contract gardening team saw his role as twofold: contact with clients (drawing up estimates, organising work and invoicing), and training and supervising the CAT workers, which he described as follows.

'The first step is [establishing] a relationship based on respect for these men and women who have some difficulties adapting to society. Then comes an evaluation of the worker's physical and intellectual capabilities so that we can suggest tasks at which he/she can succeed. This idea of success is essential… it's quite common to find workers succeed with tasks they thought were too difficult – success is very motivating… The moniteur has constantly to encourage and reassure the workers, and lead them on to do things on their own initiative so that they become more independent in their work…

'We mustn't forget social interaction, either, because we have to make sure that there are good relationships in the work team based on respect, courtesy and mutual aid. More than this, we have the aim of developing the workers' social skills, because organising their working time and being in contact with new people (such as clients) are also experiences which help them integrate into the normal world of work.'

Housing support and the hostel

We interviewed the director of care and support, attended a staff meeting, and visited one person in her flat (as well as one hostel resident). Others did not want us to visit and we welcomed this sign of their self-confidence and assertiveness.

The hostel is a purpose-built block of 24 self-contained studios. Residents were proud of their very large studio flats and most had bought their own furniture.

The first supported housing got off the ground in 1989 and comprised three flats in the village arranged as clusters of bedsits. However, workers preferred living alone or as couples, so the flats were replaced with 28 studio or one-bed flats in Avèze and the local market town, Le Vigan. Four couples now live together, and others have a relationship but don't live together. The CAT was considered very progressive in letting people live as couples, or have boyfriends/girlfriends to stay:

> 'this has worked out really well...
> In the flats, people can do as they please'.

A formal contract between SAVS (*Service d'Accompagnement à la Vie Sociale*, or Service of Social Life Support) and residents sets out each party's rights and responsibilities, and is accompanied by an individual plan and the name of the person's keyworker. SAVS and hostel staff (*éducateurs/éducatrices*) work evenings, weekends and holidays when people are not at work. Hostel staff are also on duty in the mornings and a sleep-in person is on call.

SAVS/hostel staff organise some optional activities during evenings and weekends but residents are encouraged to make their own choices about how they spend their free time.

Both residents and staff saw advantages and disadvantages in being in the town or the village. The village is a 'safer' environment, nearer to the CAT, and villagers keep a neighbourly eye on residents (although this could also be seen as over-protective). People living in Le Vigan are more anonymous and there are more leisure activities. However, they have to be able to get to themselves to work, whether by scooter, on foot or by service bus. One man who is rather a loner found the noise and bustle of town life rather upsetting and he was trying to arrange a swap with someone in the village.

SAVS helps to find flats, but residents hold tenancies, manage their money, hold bank accounts and pay their own bills. Most also do their own shopping and housework, although SAVS staff help with organising this and some have home help. SAVS staff also help with administrative tasks such as claiming benefits, budgeting for bills and liaison with landlords.

Apparently landlords welcome CAT workers as tenants. The flat we visited was on the ground floor of a large old house, with a sizeable kitchen-living room and a large bedroom-living area. Rents in Avèze and Le Vigan are less than in larger towns in the region: FF 1200–1700 (£133–139) per month (excluding fuel costs) for a bedsit or one-bedroom flat.

Residents can just about manage on their wages and benefits with careful budgeting, though holidays can be a problem for those without family support. After paying rent and essentials, and saving about £25 a week towards major items, residents were only left with about £13–14 a week. Hostel residents could end up with more spending money than those living independently, and some people chose to return to the hostel as it was less demanding than living in the community.

Aims, objectives and procedures

The Director, Joël Neuville, describes the CAT's primary aim as *l'épanouissement* (opening out, flowering, blooming) of people's lives, each person growing to their full potential in their personal and working lives – though he felt that the former was often more difficult to achieve. He saw the CAT as having both a social and an economic role:

> 'Our social mission is to ensure the maximum integration in civil society, but our economic mission makes it almost like a commercial firm, subject to the pressures of the marketplace. There is growing pressure because of state funding cuts to emphasise the economic at the expense of the social.'

The CAT's mission statement includes enabling people to move out into ordinary employment, but with the recent recession this has been difficult to achieve, though it does occur. While we were there, one man was trying out work in the less sheltered setting of an *atelier protégé*, and since our visit, a bakery worker has moved to the local hospital's bakery, though he maintains links to the CAT and is not yet on a normal salary, having retained his status as a 'disabled worker' because of the support he needs from CAT staff. In the Director's opinion:

> '*about a dozen of our 52 CAT workers would in theory be capable of working in less sheltered employment, but the problem would be their inability to live more independently and look after themselves outside working hours*'.

There used to be no other support service in the area, but since our visit, a new support service has been set up, in addition to SAVS, which includes people in supported and open employment (similar to SAVA in Nîmes).

Of 52 people, 2 were of North African origin, 3 of Spanish origin and one of South East Asian origin. People have to be French citizens (or, in theory, EU citizens) to gain access to a CAT through COTOREP, so migrant workers' adult children without French nationality would be excluded.

The views of SWALLOW members

SWALLOW members spent three days visiting the CAT and working alongside French people with learning disabilities. There was also plenty of time for social activities, including SWALLOW members preparing English afternoon tea at their holiday home for eight CAT members and an *éducateur*, visiting the Le Vigan market (including the CAT stall), lunching with CAT workers and staff in the canteen, and informal chats during break times. SWALLOW members told the French workers about their experiences in England and compared the different systems. The researchers, the SWALLOW support worker

and partners facilitated the visit and acted as interpreters. One SWALLOW member who kept a diary has allowed us to use extracts.

The three SWALLOW members were in their 20s and 30s. Two lived with their parents and one lived in a shared house with visiting support from SWALLOW. One had a part-time paid job, one went to a day centre which was exploring work opportunities for its users, and one was a part-time volunteer.

The first day was spent looking round the CAT work activities and facilities such as the hostel and 'practice flat'. SWALLOW members then chose activities for the other two days. Wherever possible they worked alongside CAT workers. Jane spent a morning in the bakery shop.

> '*Today I have been working in the bakery and it was on the till, also I was helping stacking the shelves and even counting the takings at the end of the morning. I thoroughly enjoyed serving the customers and trying to talk in French* [with the researcher's help]... *The favourite part... was talking to the people and working on the till... it was the best thing I have ever done in my life*' (Jane's diary).

Jane felt that working the till at her day centre's coffee bar had helped her with working in the bakery shop.

In the afternoon Jane and Kim worked in the packaging workshop, packing tights and stockings and medical supplies. Jane worked alongside one of the CAT workers, with help from the *monitrice*; both took great care, showing her what to do and helping her get it right.

> '*This afternoon I was putting things* [stockings and tights] *in boxes, it was great fun helping out... then the* [work was] *finished when the boxes goes on the lorries* [back to the factory]*'* (Jane's diary)

The *éducatrices* commented on Kim's ability to fold and pack medical items with great dexterity, a skill which she herself attributed to working in a nursery in England where she helped the children with games and puzzles. She preferred packing the more complex medical supplies rather than the hosiery, but would also prefer to rotate jobs in the workshop.

> *'You can get tired from working at one thing all the time... some people did the same thing all day... the long-haired girl who came to tea did the socks in the morning and she was doing them again in the afternoon.'*

The next day Jane and Kim followed the mobile shop and then:

> *'after that we went to the snail garden and did a tour around the garden... and* [saw] *how they grow the potatoes as well as the vegetables, like the onions for example'* (Jane's diary).

Edward went on the mobile shop round, talking to customers, explaining why we were there, and helping the CAT worker and staff member. He spent a morning working in the bakery; some of this was quite heavy work, while other tasks required manual dexterity. All the work involved standing and Edward observed that this could become quite tiring after a time.

Edward also went out with the contract gardening team. Discussing this later, the SWALLOW members, support worker and researchers observed that the gardening team workers were using machinery such as a strimmer, a petrol mowing machine and a hedge-cutter. SWALLOW members were anxious about the idea of using machinery, but one of the CAT workers told them he had been nervous to start with, but felt very

confident once he got used to it. SWALLOW members also commented on how the *moniteur* encouraged the CAT workers to get on with things.

Thinking about the difference between services in France and the UK, SWALLOW liked the idea of work opportunities.

> *'It's important to keep a person occupied during the daytime because it can get boring... you need something to get you out of the house to do things.'*

They really approved of the availability of paid work, and being able to combine wages and benefits up to the minimum wage so you could live somewhere independently with support. They contrasted this with the UK system which finds housing, and then

> *'... gosh, what are they going to do all day?'*

They commented that if people are employed 9 to 5, then it isn't a problem because their free time is much more valued, and they probably do more with it anyway. As someone said, in supported housing there can be a lot of 'sitting around', so people *think* they need more support just to be taken out somewhere, or organised into doing something.

They also liked the way that more able workers were encouraged to get on with things on their own, while there was also always something for less able workers to do. In the packaging workshop, for example, numbered spaces helped a worker who couldn't count, to put the right number of tights into the box. The help was given in a subtle way so that there was no obvious distinction between the more and less able.

They also commented on the team spirit among the CAT workers, with people helping each other rather than always seeking help from the *moniteurs/monitrices*. They noticed that it was all very friendly and helpful and the atmosphere seemed very relaxed.

On the housing side, SWALLOW was only able to visit the hostel and the practice flat, but there was plenty of informal discussion with CAT workers about housing and leisure activities, especially at the tea.

SWALLOW members compared the hostel and the practice flat with hostels they knew, and the SWALLOW base house (where people practise independent living skills). From their brief visit and talking to residents, their impressions of the hostel were favourable.

> *'It was very nice, very bright, as soon as I walked in I could sense there was a very happy atmosphere in the building.'*

They also thought it compared well with hostels known to them.

> *'At* [X hostel in UK], *it's very strict, there's no happy atmosphere... over here, they can choose what they do a bit more, it's not as strict as other places* [hostels in UK]*.'*

However, the support worker found it very institutional, especially compared with SWALLOW housing.

There was a lot of discussion about the fact that housing and work were linked. SWALLOW members were realistic in their assessment of the problems of having to travel to work if you lived elsewhere, but on balance separating work and housing was better.

> *'Living on top of where you work – even though it's quick and easy to get to where you work, you'd still lose a little bit of that independence you could have gained – it would be better to live a bit further away.'*

Overall, members enjoyed their visit.

> *'It's all very interesting, talking to the French people.'*

> *'It's been terrific... it's been good for us* [seeing projects in another country]*.'*

They weren't sure how it would work out trying to do something similar involving employment in England, because:

> *'with SWALLOW we just go for the houses... SWALLOW just do the housing side at the moment so we haven't had the chance to see if it would work... though they seem to have got it quite good over here... from what I've seen they all enjoy what they do'.*

They were also concerned at the risk of losing their benefits if they were in paid work in a similar sort of project in the UK.

Chapter Four

CAT Albi-Jarlard

Introduction

CAT Albi-Jarlard is one of several centres run by the ADAPEI Les Papillons Blancs. It is one of a new wave of CATs developed in the 1980s which sought to achieve integration by basing themselves in the world of industrial estates and council housing. Albi CAT's Assistant Director, Anny Tournie, contrasted these with the 'golden ghettos' – institutions in large houses or chateaux.

Origins

CAT Albi-Jarlard was the brainchild of *éducateurs/éducatrices* in a school run by Les Papillons Blancs, responding to the young people who wanted a life outside institutions and their immediate family circle.

A conscious decision was taken to keep the CAT small (30–35 workers), rather than replicate factory-style CATs employing hundreds of workers. They also decided to take only people with moderate to severe learning disabilities (though they now have a few workers with mental health problems).

At the time of our visit, Bernard Dourel had recently been appointed Director. Coming from a larger CAT and having also worked in industry, he was particularly keen to ensure that the CAT benefited from modern techniques of work design, could improve productivity, maintain health and safety and provide job satisfaction.

Location and current activities

The CAT rents premises on the Jarlard industrial estate and, at the time of our visit, its five workgroups were:

- a picture-framing workshop
- a painting and decorating team
- a contract gardening team
- a packaging sub-contract workshop
- an industrial sub-contract workshop.

This combination of direct production, sub-contracted work and services provides a range of jobs catering for varying abilities, and spreads the CAT's financial risks.

Some CAT workers are in supported employment with a *charcuterie* producer, a fruit wholesaler and a factory producing animal identification products (such as ear-tags for cows). At the time of our visit, five were working in the factory. The initial high level of support from *moniteurs* had been reduced and was now provided only as and when needed.

Workers use service buses and go to two or three different canteens in central Albi for lunch. This was part of the CAT's philosophy of rejecting institutional arrangements such as minibus pick-ups or providing lunch at the workplace.

Two of the 33 workers were of Algerian origin and two of Spanish/Portuguese origin. Staff felt that North Africans were probably under-represented, perhaps because the North African population is less aware of the

COTOREP system and may prefer to keep disabled relatives at home.

Housing and support

A building in central Albi provides a central office and coffee bar/meeting place for residents and *éducateurs*, with a shared flat for four workers and an *éducateur* upstairs.

Twenty people were living in six shared flats rented from HLMs (Habitations à Loyer Modéré – Housing at Reasonable Rents). To avoid too great a concentration of people on one estate, they have two flats each on three estates. Unlike the other CATs we visited, the tenancy is between the CAT and the HLM, so CAT workers are legally sub-tenants.

We visited one flat and talked to residents and the *éducatrice* on duty. The flat was on a typical council estate: three-storey blocks with rather bleak communal areas. It was a hot evening and the neighbours' music was noisy. The residents saw this as a disadvantage of living there, but were clear about their rights and assertive in asking for help to deal with such problems.

Some CAT workers live as couples, but the larger shared flat we visited was more like a UK small group home, with a sleep-in room/office for an *éducatrice*. One CAT worker owns his flat, having saved up and used money he inherited. Another three rent individual flats. Ten CAT workers live at home with parents. Occasionally, CAT workers are housed in the *foyers de jeunesse*.

The decision to rent HLM flats was deliberate. HLMs are for low-wage workers, and as CAT workers earn around the minimum wage, they can live within their means. However, social housing of this kind accommodates many disadvantaged people, life on the estates is not easy and the Assistant Director was frank about integration:

> *'Our residents are no more or less accepted than other minorities, whether they are North Africans, families in difficulty, people with disabilities…'.*

Residents are not generally rejected by their neighbours, but are only accepted at the level of saying 'hello' rather than having friendships. Thus the aim to encourage integration by living on the HLM estates has had only limited success.

User involvement and links with families

There is no user representation on ADAPEI's management committee, although the CAT itself has a *conseil d'établissement* (forum) which meets formally twice a year. Forum membership includes two parents, two members of staff and three CAT workers. Jean-Louis is one of the worker representatives and told us that he approved of the forum and found it useful.

The CAT encourages workers to be confident and assertive. We certainly observed this and the following story illustrates this well. A famous professor visited CAT workers to ask about their sexuality and relationships. After he had asked them some very personal questions he was visibly taken aback when one of the CAT workers turned round to him and asked: '*Et la vôtre?*' ['And what about *your* sex life?'].

Chapter Five
CAT S.I.T.E.S., Nîmes

Introduction

This chapter covers the CAT we visited in the city of Nîmes (population 130,000). As in previous chapters, we provide a description of the CAT's employment and housing/support services, together with details of its management arrangements. The distinctive features of this CAT which we explore are its commitment to being a CAT 'without walls', with workshops/workgroups out in the community, and its commitment to user involvement.

Origins

The CAT we visited in Nîmes is one of three in the city managed by the *département* [county] voluntary organisation L'APAJH in Gard.

S.I.T.E.S. (*Structure d'Intégration par le Travail, l'Economique et le Social*) was established when the Gard L'APAJH was already running other traditional-style CATs and *ateliers protégés*. The objective was to create workshops/workgroups which were more like ordinary businesses and which would encourage integration.

The idea came from staff observations of how people worked in another large L'APAJH CAT, la Bastide, based in a large house on the outskirts of the city. This had developed teams working outside in a municipal plant nursery and carrying out contract gardening work for the city council. Staff had observed that the sort of interpersonal conflict and behavioural problems displayed by some workers within

the walls of the traditional CAT were much less among the teams working 'outside the walls'. They concluded that this 'outside the walls' model had much to offer, and founded S.I.T.E.S. in the early 1980s.

CAT S.I.T.E.S., Nîmes

Management organisation: L'APAJH, *département* [county] of Gard. This also runs a more traditional CAT and a new CAT based on supported employment principles.

The L'APAJH network of voluntary organisations was started by professionals who were opposed to segregation of disabled children in the French education system. There is a strong, somewhat left-wing ethos, based on citizenship rights rather than charity.

L'APAJH associations vary between *départements*; some run projects such as CATs, others only provide services for old people or children, and others again are pressure groups which confine their activity to campaigning and do not provide services themselves.

There are over 400 L'APAJH projects for people with different disabilities and across all age groups in most parts of France.

Location and facilities: work activities

CAT S.I.T.E.S. has an administrative office and one workshop based in a semi-suburban, semi-industrial area of Nîmes, and other workshops/workgroups based in the city and the surrounding area. The housing and

social support service SAVA (*Service d'Accompagnement Vers l'Autonomie*) is also managed by L'APAJH, but is completely separate, working with clients from this and other CATs and also people who are not in CATs (see below). For this reason there is no direct link between the CAT and any housing provision.

About half of S.I.T.E.S. workers live at home with their families, while the other half live in their own rented flats, with support from SAVA. Of the thirty-four workers, just over half (eighteen) have a learning disability, fourteen have mental health problems and two have multiple disabilities. A few workers work only part-time because, for health or other reasons, they are unable to work full-time, but we were told that this caused great problems with the wages/benefits system, which was based on an assumption of full-time work and penalised people who could only work part-time.

At the time of our visit, the workshops/workgroups comprised:

- the metal workshop, manufacturing metal gates, fences, grilles and other decorative metalwork for organisations and individuals to order (in the same location as the offices)

- the *élévage* (animal and bird farm), raising small domestic pets such as budgerigars, canaries and rabbits for both direct sale and wholesale supply to pet shops, and also mice and rats for feeding zoo animals and reptiles (at a farm site in the countryside south of Nîmes)

- the phone-box cleaning team, with contracts to clean telephone kiosks in Nîmes all year round, and in a nearby coastal resort in the summer only (based on an industrial estate in Nîmes)

- the hotel services team, providing catering and domestic services at a residential training centre which runs short courses for people with visual impairments (based at the residential training centre)

- the contract gardening team, providing gardening services to public and private clients, including maintenance of nearby motorway service areas (based in the town of Sommières, about 20 miles away, and the only workshop we did not visit).

Because the work activities are scattered and the workers live all over the Nîmes area, transport to work was a potential problem. Traditional CATs have often used minibus pick-ups to collect their workers and return them home at the end of the day. This collection service was rejected by S.I.T.E.S. and workers use either their own transport or public transport. Nîmes residents get free public transport if they are disabled, but those living in the surrounding area do not, so if necessary the CAT subsidises the cost.

Some workers had developed high-level skills; for example, in the metal workshop, workers were cutting metal, welding and soldering. Some had attended short courses at college to acquire the necessary skills. One had recently left to work in open employment, using the skills acquired at the CAT metal workshop. Another had found employment in his local village and the CAT had put his new employer in touch with AGEFIPH for financial assistance (see **Chapter Six** for more details of AGEFIPH role). Two more former CAT workers were now employed as office cleaners by Nîmes City Council, in a supported employment-type arrangement set up by the CAT staff.

The hotel and catering services team was interesting, because it is a partnership between two voluntary agencies. The CAT had been contracted to provide hotel and catering services by another voluntary agency which ran the training centre. People with learning disabilities working at the centre came into contact with, and expressed their concern for, others with disabilities different from their own.

The CAT was set up to encourage integration, but in the workplace this was somewhat limited. The pet farm was in an isolated position in the countryside, and although some customers did visit, there was little opportunity for contact with the wider population. The residential training centre for the visually impaired was situated in a quiet suburban area, and there was limited contact with training-centre clients and staff. The telephone-box team did get out and about around the city (and to the coastal resort), but there was only limited opportunity for social interaction with the general public. The same applied to the contract-gardening team. More social interaction took place within the teams and with the CAT moniteurs.

Housing and support services

We made a particular effort to observe the support service in Nîmes, and spent more time with this than on the work activities. SAVA, the *Service d'Accompagnement Vers l'Autonomie* (Support Service to Develop Independence), is based in an office near the centre of Nîmes, where clients call in to see the support staff in the evenings. We observed a drop-in session and chatted to residents. The ethos is strongly focused on *accompagnement*. SAVA staff describe this as working alongside the service user, encouraging them to make their own decisions, rather than deciding for them.

We observed five aspects:

- the office base, which offers a drop-in surgery with information, support and mediation with employers, colleagues or families

- helping to arrange or find leisure and holiday activities (on an individual or small-group basis)

- help with budgeting and managing money

- liaison with health and social services (by using existing services such as GPs and duty social workers)

- help to find and keep rented housing.

SAVA was funded to support 95 people, the majority having learning disabilities and a few having mental health problems. L'APAJH has a contract with the DDSS, the social services of the *département* of Gard, which pays the full cost. Clients do not have to pay out of their benefits or wages. Clients have to be recognised by COTOREP as disabled, and live in Nîmes city or its surrounding districts, but they don't have to be working in CATs (although most do). We were told that some of their clients have in fact rejected traditional hostel-type housing, and the more institutional CATs, for a variety of reasons.

From feedback in our interviews with service users and our observation of staff and clients, users seemed to appreciate the subtle and sensitive support they received. There was an easy, relaxed atmosphere between users and staff and users seemed very confident and assertive in seeking advice and support. As well as the usual keyworker arrangements and individual plans found elsewhere, there were also detailed outcome-based monitoring systems in place; in fact the contract with the *département* required detailed monitoring and reporting of results, and SAVA was the most sophisticated organisation of the three case study visits.

SAVA uses a variety of housing providers, including private landlords and HLMs. Private flats ranged from FF1,400 to FF 2,000 per month (£155–£222 per month or £35–£51 per week). SAVA had access to sixteen individual and shared cluster flats through links with an institutional landlord and one HLM, and helps other residents find their own private rented or HLM flats. Some residents receive help with housework and personal care; this is accessed by SAVA staff but provided by social services. We heard about some of the problems in shared flats. One woman told us her post went missing, and she had had some neighbour problems which she had asked SAVA staff to help her with.

Mohammed lived with his wife in a house in a nearby village. He was buying his house from a relative, under an arrangement facilitated by SAVA staff. Guy had moved to his own rented flat (with help from SAVA) after his father died and his mother became ill. After living with parents for some years, he said he was enjoying the freedom of being able to do what he liked and come and go as he pleased.

Because French employer organisations above a certain size have to pay a sort of housing 'tax', L'APAJH also has nomination rights to an HLM for housing constructed using the 1% housing tax. We visited a couple in one of these '1%' flats. Paulette and Jacques had recently moved from a less desirable private rented flat into a very smart HLM block not far from the city centre. They had a spacious one-bedroom flat with a large living room, kitchen and balcony. They told us the rent was higher than others we had seen: FF3,300 per month (£366 per month or £84 per week) although they received housing benefit towards this. They had had no problems with their neighbours, and SAVA

helped them organise their finances. They were a very independent, self-assured couple and had travelled widely on their own, visiting most of the tourist destinations in Southern Europe. Both felt that their jobs at the CAT were important, otherwise the days would be too long and they would be bored.

User involvement

There is a great emphasis on user involvement in this CAT; this happens at a number of levels. There is a monthly meeting with user delegates, which also runs a sort of credit union that makes small loans to individuals.

There is also a formal council for the CAT that meets three times a year. Elected members keep their place for three years. The council has nine members:

- three CAT workers
- two staff members
- two members of the L'APAJH voluntary organisation
- two representatives from families (but we were told that as only one of these places is filled, a fourth place is in fact given to another CAT worker).

Thus, like SWALLOW, nearly half the members were service users. We were told that staff members help the CAT worker-members prepare for the meetings so that they can play a full part.

Chapter Six

The French CAT System: reflections and conclusions

Introduction

As explained in **Chapter One**, we did not expect to recommend that CATs should be replicated in the UK, because systems cannot be transported across borders and because, like any system, they have weaknesses as well as strengths. Neither have we carried out a formal evaluation. What follows are some general observations, based on three visits and a brief literature review.

We shall return to our recommendations for the UK in the final chapter, after describing and discussing the projects we visited in the UK. But before that, this chapter reflects on what we can learn from the French system and picks out some themes, many of which are also echoed in the chapters looking at UK projects. We have drawn not only on the visits, but also on wider literature about CATs and related services, to show how the CATs we visited fit into a wider picture.

CATs are greatly valued by their supporters for offering:

> 'both productive employment and the necessary social support to make such employment rewarding; indeed, they may be the only means of protecting people with severe mental disability from being eliminated from the labour market' (Thornton & Lunt, 1997, p109).

First we draw together the views of service users from all three CATs.

CAT workers' views: the advantages of working

When we spoke to CAT workers, both formally and informally, they were very clear about the importance of work. When we first introduced the research and explained that most people with learning disabilities in the UK do not work, there was general surprise.

> 'You mean they don't have CATs? Well, what do they do all day?'

> 'How boring!'

> 'What about earning money?'

Workers we met at all the CATs were realistic about their likes and dislikes over working. They liked working for a number of reasons.

Earning money

Everyone thought the money mattered, and they were very clear about how they could save up their wages and buy things. Furniture, clothes, paying for holidays and buying stereo systems and mopeds were all mentioned.

> 'It's better to work than to be unemployed... it's important to work to earn money.'

> 'I like to work... you need to work for the pennies.'

Something to do during the day

Some of the workers had experience of not working, while waiting for their place in the CAT or when unemployed.

'*It's boring being at home.*'

'*I don't know what I'd do all day if I wasn't working.*'

The alternatives offered by the French system were either day centres or being at home. It is worth remembering that one of the factors needed for a COTOREP referral to a CAT is that the person not only has an aptitude for work, but has also expressed a desire to work. The educational system for children and young people with learning disabilities is generally segregated, and we gather that it acts as a preparation for working in a CAT, so this becomes the 'expected outcome' for young adults with learning disabilities. Thus, by definition, one may expect CAT workers to express such a view.

Comradeship with colleagues in the workteam

Companionship and teamwork were important, too. We observed the friendship and banter between CAT workers themselves, and with the *moniteurs*. Generally, the atmosphere appeared relaxed and helpful.

'*Oh yes, she* [the monitrice] *helps us a lot. She's really nice.*'

We, and SWALLOW, also noticed how much CAT workers helped each other. For example, at Albi one of the workers in the picture-framing workshop told us he liked the sense of teamwork in their workgroup.

'*I really like working with him* [indicating his colleague].'

A member of Albi's painting and decorating team said he found the same in his team.

Job satisfaction and a place in the community

The work at all three CATs demanded a wide range of skills, and people took real pride in showing us what they did, and in helping SWALLOW members work alongside them at Avèze.

For example, at the pet farm at Nîmes, one man, who appeared quite large and potentially clumsy, was most adept at tasks which required great dexterity, such as ringing baby birds. Another worker showed us the computer records of births, deaths and dates.

Workers also expressed pride and satisfaction when they had produced something for sale, or completed a task. They liked driving round in the company van with its logo: for example, a CAT worker who collected and delivered the work to and from the stocking and tights factories in Avèze. At Nîmes, workers liked having *un travail sérieux* (a 'real job'), which was recognised in the community.

At Avèze, one of the *moniteurs* summed it up.

'*"Bonjour, boulanger!"' I heard a passer-by say, when he saw one of our CAT bakery workers on his way to work. It takes something like this to make you realise how far we have come from the negative image which people still have of learning disability.*'

Learning new skills

Both workers and CAT staff talked about the positive side of learning new skills, and how this linked to home life as well.

'Everything is linked… if you learn to fill in a cheque or answer the telephone, it's useful for work and for your home life… it's part of integration to learn how to present yourself.' (Assistant Director, Nîmes)

Workers in the Avèze gardening team were proud of using machinery, even though they'd been anxious at first, as were the Albi picture framers. One of the workers at the Nîmes pet farm, unusually among the people we met, could write, and he showed us how he counted and recorded the rabbits' breeding results. Staff commented that CAT workers needed to keep using such skills, otherwise they would lose them. We were told that some CAT workers who had lacked or lost such skills had been able to learn or regain them through needing them in their work.

Because they were 'proper workers'

One man told us that it was a dishonour not to work and that society expected it.

'Work is very important for us French people… if someone doesn't work, they're a bad person and they're looked down on… it's hard for people who aren't in work, like the unemployed.'

This theme of being a 'proper worker' was reflected in a number of comments at all three CATs. It included pride in having a pay slip, paying tax and national insurance contributions (in principle, at least!), wearing work clothes such as the traditional blue overalls of the French working class or with the CAT logo, and having a role in society.

CAT workers' views: the disadvantages of working

Although people had many positive views about their jobs, there were things they didn't like, too.

The pressures of working

The main thing people disliked about working was how tired they became. This was especially the case when they felt they were being pushed hard to finish things when they were busy. As in interviews in the UK, this was a particular problem for people whose physical or mental health was not robust.

'They push us to work harder, to go faster, to work as fast as we can… there's not much rest during work time.'

'After work, I'm too tired to go out in the evenings, so I just stay at home and rest.'

People working in the sub-contracting workshops were very clear about the demands made by the factories which send them work. When asked who decided about the work to be carried out in the workshop, they told us:

'the factory decides'.

This was confirmed by the *moniteurs/monitrices.*

'The factories put pressure on us to get things done quickly and well, therefore there are pressures on us to give the most difficult tasks to the most able, even though everyone would be capable of doing the tasks if we had enough time for them to learn how to.'

We had a question for workers in our interview schedule which asked 'What would you do or change if you were the boss?'. They suggested employing more workers to help when they were too busy.

Dirty, unpleasant or boring jobs

Some workers commented that the work is boring at times.

> *'Sometimes I get fed up with the work... but it happens to everyone.'*

We noticed that some tasks seemed very repetitive, although in these cases workers were often chatting to each other. On the other hand, this is a feature of 'real jobs', and we observed the same problem in some of the UK fieldwork.

There were other things workers did not like very much, including dirty jobs like cleaning out the animals at the pet farm. Some had found some of the animals distasteful. One young woman had hated working with the mice to start with, but did not mind them now; however, she was still not keen on the rats.

People not pulling their weight in the team

When asked their views on how they would run the CAT 'if they were the boss', some workers said they would sack people who did not pull their weight and give the place to others who wanted to work.

At one workgroup, we observed an episode which reflected this problem. One worker had been persistently late and this meant that others had to cover for her. Following previous warnings, she was disciplined by being laid off for a few days and suffered a loss of wages for this, with the threat of sacking if she did not come to work on time in the future.

Remuneration is based partly on work performance, so lateness, absenteeism or poor performance (unless due to the nature of the person's disability) could result in slightly lower wages (though this is more of a gesture because of the interplay with benefits).

Workers' rights

A significant disadvantage of the CAT system is the fact that CAT workers have the status of *travailleur handicapé* (disabled worker), which means they are 'placed' by COTOREP, and are not employed under a contract of employment. They have none of the rights of other workers. As one of the senior staff explained:

> *'disabled people working in the protected sector seem like workers who are separate. While it is true that they work in a sheltered environment, they are still working in a productive capacity. However, they remain outside workers' organisations and the world of the trade union movement'.*

In contrast, workers in *ateliers protégés* or open employment in theory have such rights, but they are rarely exercised.

> *'There are many reasons for this non-participation. Disabled people who are working may not have the necessary confidence... their life in institutions, often from early childhood, hasn't accustomed them to stand up for themselves... and the trades unions have tended to ignore the existence of sheltered employment and disabled workers, thus reinforcing the marginalisation of these workers.'*

Although staff raised this point with us, none of the many workers we spoke to raised it as an issue, and it appeared that they thought of themselves as 'proper workers'. They also have access to greater support (in both work and personal/social life) than workers in open employment.

Family relationships

We met only one parent during all the fieldwork, who was visiting her son. She told us she was very happy with the CAT he was now in, although he had moved from another CAT which hadn't suited him.

UNAPEI recently surveyed over 12,000 parents, 43 per cent of respondents having adult children in a CAT. The idea of people with learning disabilities being able to work and earn wages seems to be deeply enshrined. Ninety per cent of respondents felt that work was the preferred means towards personal growth and independence; ninety-three per cent were satisfied that disabled workers received at least the SMIC. However, there was dissatisfaction with the low level of pocket money for those in hostels. There was concern about the future, over 80% giving as their greatest worry the future of their adult child after their death (*Vivre Ensemble*, 1995).

Family involvement was very slight in all three CATs we visited, partly because of the strong commitment from the professionals to user independence. One staff member commented that people with learning disabilities in a family situation often found life quite easy and undemanding, whereas the CAT had much greater expectations of them, which made life less 'comfortable'. In one CAT, staff were now seeking a little more family involvement, while still keeping a distance.

This was a theme which recurred at all three CATs: how to encourage autonomy and independence for adults with learning disabilities, while maintaining an appropriate level of family contact. We were told of some parent-led CATs where family involvement was constant and intrusive, perhaps discouraging risk-taking and autonomy. We gained the impression that this was more likely to occur with parent-led voluntary organisations, especially where they also ran establishments for children and young people. One director told us:

'the majority of voluntary organisations [and CATs] *managed by parents put all the accent on protection… they make sure their children have benefits, housing, work, but above all they remove all the obstacles from the way of the disabled person and make for them an ivory tower'.*

There is a general tendency in a lot of the French material (and with some CAT staff during our visits) to describe adults with learning disabilities as *les jeunes* (the young ones), even though they may be in their 20s, 30s or 40s. Some of the CATs workers we interviewed also used the same terminology when referring to other CAT workers. One CAT worker referred to her moniteur in the same family terms.

'She's like my mother.'

In contrast, many staff stressed that they always referred to the workers as *hommes* and *femmes* (men and women), as a conscious rebuttal of this old-fashioned attitude. Staff generally addressed workers by their first names, but workers equally used first names to staff (though this did not usually include the senior staff such as the Director).

User choice and equal opportunities

The way workers were selected for a place in the CAT differed. In at least some CATs it depended on their expressed preference for a certain type of work. For example, Yasmin had particularly wanted to work in the countryside with animals and had not had to wait too long for her place at the pet farm.

In other cases, people could seek a placement in another team for a change, or try something different to see if it suited them. For example, one of the workers in the Avèze CAT packaging team had tried working in the bakery, but didn't like it. A member of the painting team at Albi was helping out in the picture-framing workshop during our visit.

There was a fairly even gender balance among the CAT workers, but there appeared to be some gender stereotyping of tasks at all three CATs. We noticed the same problem in the UK. All the workers in the metal and picture-framing workshops were male, as were most in the gardening teams. Everyone in the hotel and catering services was female, as were most of the workers in the packaging workshops and the bakery. Other teams had a mixture, such as the pet farm and the telephone kiosk team. However, this would be likely to follow from the decision to place people in their preferred occupational roles. It is also our impression that gender stereotyping is even more prevalent in France than in the UK, and perhaps particularly so in the South; women staff members at the CATs confirmed this view.

Formal procedures

We were interested in formal procedures for such issues as complaints, equal opportunities and performance-monitoring. The UK interest in formal procedures for complaints was not reflected in France in the projects we visited, nor in our literature review and discussions at the college.

There were formal systems with rules and contracts for both social support and work. The formal contract between each resident and the S*ervice de Suite/d'Accompagnement* or the hostel includes rules over such matters as not causing noise nuisance to neighbours. There is a specific clause forbidding discrimination or violence against other residents/workers. At one CAT, the contract actually states that this will be punished by

immediate expulsion, without any formal appeal mechanism. However, we were told that in practice there would be a case conference and if the resident/worker did not stay in the CAT, another placement would be found. Decisions rest with the Director; the management committee has no involvement in matters of this sort. There is an implied right of appeal to the DDASS (as the funding body).

There was no formal equal opportunities policy for the whole organisation covering both service delivery and employment, although the contracts (above) refer to discriminatory behaviour between residents. The staff equal-opportunities policy is enshrined in the employment agreement drawn up by the employers' federation.

Interior rules cover such issues as confidentiality of information, and corporal punishment is absolutely forbidden. Staff can be sacked for infringing such rules and this had happened on one occasion.

All the CATs' support services had full and detailed documentation setting out their mission, objectives and action plans. Performance-monitoring is required by the funding bodies. A review of literature produced a crop of articles on performance monitoring similar to that found in the UK.

Economic links and entrepreneurial skills

We were struck by the entrepreneurialism shown by the CATs we visited, as in the community businesses in **Chapter Eight**. They were willing to take hard decisions if necessary, closing down loss-making sections and seeking new areas of work.

We consider that this close relationship with the local economy, while not without risks, is one of the strengths of the CAT model. It also helps to provide a wide range of jobs, demanding different skills and different levels of ability, as SWALLOW remarked.

In our literature review we came across an enormous range of work carried out by CATs because of this determination to be implanted into the local and regional economy. The following examples are all of the CATs' own direct production (rather than sub-contract work).

- Near Montpellier, a CAT runs a fish and shellfish farm and carries out commercial fishing

- In the Doubs area, near the Swiss border (North East France) there is a CAT which manufactures watches

- In the Bresse region, near Geneva, a CAT produces the renowned Bresse chickens (which carry their own *appellation controllée* trademark)

- In South West France, Burgundy and the Bordeaux area there are a few CATs which produce wine

On the sub-contract side, major international companies such as Kodak and Peugeot use CAT teams (in their own factories as well as CAT workshops) to carry out production and packaging work.[1]

Like some of the UK examples discussed in later chapters, CATs have to be entrepreneurial and seek new avenues when old ones close. At Avèze, for example, they had to close down the laundry and the carpentry workshops because they did not pay. However, they seized the opportunity presented to them by the retirement of the local baker, to diversify. The Cévennes climate is not ideal for growing vegetables, so the market garden has now diversified into snails; the bakery produces seasonal items such as chocolate eggs and chickens for Easter. The decline in the packaging work has led to a

team going out to work in a nearby factory, while the waiting list for full-time places has encouraged plans for a new part-time service.

However, this degree of entrepreneurialism also needs a 'critical mass' of size, financial stability and staff expertise. This would be more difficult to achieve in a very small organisation, like some of the UK co-ops discussed in **Chapter Nine**. To give one example of the advantages of a larger organisation, at all three CATs the separate workshops keep their own budgets and aim to make a profit, but, because each CAT had some workshops which were less profitable, with less able workers who would not be very productive elsewhere, other workshops effectively subsidise them.

We were also struck by the stable staff teams and the impact of the French professional training and career structure. Compared with some small voluntary agencies in the UK, which often suffer from high staff turnover and a loss of expertise, the CAT staff seemed well established, with clear training programmes and career paths. This may be at least partly due to the (relatively) high salaries paid to *éducateurs* and *moniteurs*, compared with salaries for similar posts in the UK.

The entrepreneurialism displayed by CAT and voluntary agency staff does not only apply to seeking new work activities, it also extends to developing new services. These have included:

- CATs 'without walls'

- housing support services for people in their own tenancies instead of hostels

- a number of variations on the supported employment theme

- part-time employment options.

---

[1] Data obtained from *Insertion et Travail Adapté* and *Vivre Ensemble*, various volumes, 1993–96

Although CATs still provide most of the work opportunities for people with learning disabilities, there have been a number of recent new initiatives which provide alternatives to the CAT system. These are usually funded through AGEFIPH. The main alternative is a form of supported employment service called EPSR, which translates as 'specialist team for rehabilitation', usually focusing on both employment and social support. Such teams have often been set up by the same voluntary organisations which run CATs. Many cater for people recovering from mental illness as well as people with learning disabilities.

We visited one such EPSR in Montpellier, run by the voluntary organisation L'APAJH. It provides shared housing on an HLM estate and tries to find work opportunities, but this was difficult given the depth of the recession in France in 1996. Some CATs themselves also provide variations on the supported employment theme, as described above and in the chapters on our visits to Albi and to Nîmes.

Community involvement and social skills

We have discussed economic links; social skills and links with the local community are also valuable and important. This is a more complex issue, because even if a CAT worker is not in regular contact with the public during their working day, they still contribute to the life of the community and have status as workers.

CAT staff often commented to us how work skills also encourage social skills; they often noticed that there is an improvement in, for example, care and pride over dressing and personal care (such as shaving and hair) when workers start at the CAT. We certainly observed that CAT workers were well-presented, and did not display the odd clothing, hairstyles and so on which so often characterised people who had been patients in long-stay mental handicap hospitals in the UK.

Staff told us about one worker who was very sensitive, and had had an aversion to anything to do with death. He had overcome this aversion and was now much more robust in his personal life as well, through having to come to terms with death by dealing with dead animals at the pet farm.

From our observation, we also noticed workers from the Avèze CAT around the village and the local town, in shops and the market and the streets (although because they did not stand out, we only noticed them as we got to know them better). We did not spend long enough in the other CATs to notice this, and it may apply less in larger towns.

However, when we asked about friendships between CAT workers and their neighbours and local communities, all three CATs told us that most contact with the wider community was at a very limited level, and most friendships were between the CAT workers.

Rights and responsibilities

A major advantage of the French model is that the overall system is based on a concept of clearly defined rights for disabled people from the 1975 Law. This runs alongside duties imposed on employers, based on the 1987 Law. These laws have led to the creation of organisations to support their implementation, particularly COTOREP and AGEFIPH.

Although COTOREP's decisions are often criticised, it does provide a national system of assessment for benefits and planning for future placements. There are clear criteria, which have been improved recently, and an appeal system. Any benefits system has its disadvantages, and the French system was criticised by our interviewees, especially for discouraging part-time working and for its perverse effects on couples. One worker we met in Nîmes liked the work but found it difficult to manage on his wages and benefits because he had a girlfriend living with him who received no income; this was one of a number of complications we came across when talking to couples.

The benefits situation with couples is complex, depending on whether one or both are in the CAT, or disabled, or getting other benefits. Some could be better off than if living alone, like one couple we met in Avèze where both are working in the CAT; others were worse off, like the man in Nîmes.

The 1987 Law and AGEFIPH have achieved a number of positive outcomes:

- comprehensive programmes for employment and integration in large companies

- encouragement for companies to contract with CATs

- a source of additional funding for new employment initiatives.

A number of major employers have been encouraged to develop comprehensive programmes for the employment of disabled people. For example, EDF-Gaz de France (the national electricity and gas company) entered into one of the first such programmes in 1989. Between 1989 and 1996, it created direct employment for 550 disabled workers. It also contracts with CATs for grounds maintenance, laundry and postal services to the value of FF50m (£5.5m) per year, providing work for another 450 CATs workers with learning disabilities. The programme also includes a partnership leading to the employment of five CAT workers, accompanied by a *moniteur*, in

the print-room at the Gaz de France research centre. The CAT workers use the canteen and belong to the table-tennis club, encouraging integration.

AGEFIPH can also use the 'fines' paid by employers to fund a range of employment initiatives, including new initiatives by CATs:

- an ADAPEI-run CAT in Var, in Provence, which now has 70% of its workers in outside employment, using AGEFIPH funding for training and support

- AGEFIPH funding for new assembly lines to enable CAT workers to work in teams in more open employment in factories

- paying for a CAT to install packaging equipment to package fair-trade coffee for a Dutch company

- new equipment for a sawmill to create posts for workers from the local CAT

- helping to establish a bauxite mine employing 13 CAT workers and another 8 disabled workers alongside 21 professional miners, extracting bauxite for aluminium production.[2]

Although the legislation is important, CATs have found that smaller companies (with fewer than 20 employees) excluded from the legislation are often easier to work with than larger companies. For example, the ADAPEI des Pyrénées-Atlantique (in South West France) manages eight CATs and a linked project providing both supported employment and housing support to people living in the community. It prospected 250 companies in the area over two years and observed that:

'paradoxically, it is often the companies not subjected to the 1987 Law which give us the greatest welcome' (Vivre Ensemble, 1993).

---

[2] Data obtained from Insertion et Travail Adapté, various volumes, 1993–6

However, the AGEFIPH funding can still be useful in these smaller companies to finance supported employment, plant and machinery, or training.

A survey of employers (Labourdette *et al.*, 1990) in the area around Troyes (East of Paris) found that only 29% of local companies employed any disabled workers. Four out of five companies knew about their local CATs. Of those interested in working in partnership with a CAT, only 29% wanted to sub-contract work out to a CAT, and 51% preferred the CAT to send a team of workers into their premises. Companies already working in partnership with a CAT were highly satisfied (96%). They gave three main reasons for working with a CAT: 57% in order to provide work for disabled people, 40% because sub-contracting to a CAT was cheaper than other means (because of the effective government subsidy), and 24% for tax reasons, especially to avoid having to pay the AGEFIPH voluntary contribution or fine.

This suggests that the 'stick and carrot' approach adopted in France can be effective, although, as stated in **Chapter Two**, most of the funding has gone to other groups, especially people with physical disabilities, rather than to people with learning disabilities.

How much integration?

The question of segregation versus integration is crucial. A disadvantage of the CAT model is that much of the work remains in segregated or semi-segregated settings. This can be mitigated to some extent where workers live in ordinary housing in the community, but the working day may offer little opportunity for social interaction with non-disabled people other than the *moniteurs*. For CATs workers who both live and work on-site, as did a few of the workers at Avèze, the CAT remains very institutional.

Some CAT workers are relatively integrated in that they are in a form of supported employment, outposted in factories (Albi, Avèze), or offices (Nîmes) with visiting support from moniteurs (which has some similarity to the role of job coaches in supported employment in the UK – see **Chapter Seven**). Workgroups such as the painting and decorating team (Albi), the telephone box cleaning team (Nîmes) and the contract gardening teams have some contact with the public and with clients, and they are working away from their CAT base.

Sub-contract workers and those in CAT enterprises such as the picture-framing workshop (Albi), the bakery workers (Avèze) and the metal workshop (Nîmes) have very little outside contact during their working day. Newer developments described above, such as the small teams placed in large organisations like EDF/Gaz de France, Kodak or Peugeot, or the bauxite mine and the sawmill, overcome this to a degree, but literature from the USA suggests that separate gangs or enclaves are less successful than supported employment (Beyer, 1995).

All the workers have a (typically French) long lunch break of one and a half to two hours. In Nîmes and Albi, this gives them time to go to worker canteens which are used by workers from a range of workplaces in the vicinity. The ones we visited provided a good, well-balanced three-course meal at modest cost, ensuring a healthy meal in the middle of the day (another bonus of working, as we also found in some of the UK models). However, we observed that they appeared to eat with their colleagues rather than mixing socially with people from other workplaces (but then this too is 'normal' in that most people would eat with people they know). Avèze village and the local town are too small to provide such an opportunity, so workers eat in the CAT canteen.

French research has shown considerable regional differences between the number of disabled people who are offered placements in sheltered work environments. Four out of five of such placements are to CATs, the other one in five being to *ateliers protégés* (as there are fewer of these). The regional disparity appears to relate to two factors: local economic conditions such as unemployment rates, and the number of CATs in the region. This means that regions with high unemployment (such as Nord-Pas de Calais, the Northern French industrial region) have a much higher rate of referral to CATs. More prosperous regions (such as Ile de France, around Paris) have fewer CATs referrals.

Some of the literature suggests that CATs have been looked on as a cheap alternative to the 'asylum', where disabled people can be put to productive work to offset their cost to the state. The title of the key text (Zafiropoulos, 1981) bears this out: *From the Asylum to the Factory*. We heard of some very large, factory-style CATs which sounded very different from the small-scale workshops and workgroups we visited, where the focus was very much on the individual. There must be a danger of CATs, especially large ones, becoming 'warehouses' for large numbers of people with learning disabilities, rather than leading to the 'flowering' and individual personal growth and development described by the Director in **Chapter Three**.

The CAT system has also been criticised for not moving people on into open or less sheltered employment.

Studies of CATs show under 1% of workers moving on into sheltered workshops or open employment. A number of reasons have been cited, including parental desire for security and CAT management incentives to keep productive workers (Labourdette *et al.*, 1990). Since 1990, there has been a move for 25% of CAT places to give priority for progression to open employment, but problems remain,

especially over financial incentives and wage supplements (Zibri, 1995).

Funding systems have also encouraged voluntary organisations to develop CATs rather than other provision. Many CAT workers, and particularly parents, like the security of the CAT system. Other new initiatives such as supported employment options offer more scope for integration, but are limited by a number of factors, including the work (or lack of it) available in the locality.

This point was raised by **Pierre**, who was working on one of the CAT-sponsored supported employment projects in a local factory. He lived with his parents and travelled into work by bus. He told us he had previously worked in a large factory-style CAT in another town, which made a wide range of products including leather goods such as rodeo saddles, and decorative items such as Christmas decorations. He had left the CAT for open employment in another factory, but had lost his job when it closed down. He was very clear that he now preferred the security of his supported employment through the CAT, even though he got less money than in open employment. He was happy living at home in a nearby village, using public transport to get to work each day. He had no desire to live in HLM housing in town. Like the man at SHAW described in **Chapter One**, he was willing to accept a lower income for what he perceived to be greater security.

Of course, as we have already noted, the CATs were not immune from economic pressures. Indeed, there has been some debate about the whole future of CATs. Senior staff at all three CATs talked about the need to continually re-invent their organisations to deliver new services and change their provision in the light of changes in both

demand and funding. One director felt the
future lay in larger, more productive and
profitable CATs. He doubted whether many
of the workers in his CAT could survive in
open employment, even with support.

Another director had doubts about
whether the present system can continue,
given the problems with the French economy
and the cost of their social systems.

*'The ideal would be not to need a system
like CATs so that the disabled person could
go to work in an ordinary business… we
need something more flexible. I believe
that the CAT system is finished. These days,
innovation means doing things which cost
as little as possible. The future will surely
be more integration with the least possible
public funding.'*

Chapter Seven
Supported Employment

Introduction

We felt it was important to provide the UK reader with adequate background about the wider system in France (hence **Chapter Two**). Space precludes an equivalent for the UK. We therefore plunge straight into a description of the first of the four kinds of UK project we visited – the supported employment agencies. For those interested, the original full report has an extensive discussion of the issues.[1]

Supported employment: a definition

This report uses the term 'supported employment' in a very specific way. However, over the last decade the term has increasingly been used to refer to any form of 'assisted employment' for disabled people, often involving very different contexts and approaches. The resulting confusion has not been helpful.

For example, the following might be referred to as 'supported employment'.

- **Sheltered workshops** Often set up by local authorities (and organisations such as Remploy) in the immediate post-war years, these small factories or workshops are designed specifically to employ disabled people. Although most pay some sort of wage, they are segregated settings. Because of this we only feature one in this report (SHAW, **Chapter Eleven**)

- **the Sheltered Placement Scheme (SPS)** which provides a subsidy for employers taking on disabled workers. Since workers continue to be paid by a sponsoring agency (usually a local authority or voluntary organisation), they tend to have rather a different status from their co-workers

- **Integrated paid employment** obtained with the assistance of a supported employment agency. The function of supported employment agencies is to help disabled people find and *maintain* paid employment in integrated settings. A key feature of the approach is what Beyer (1995) characterises as 'place and train'. It is based on the principle that the best way to help a person become an effective and valued employee is first to find them a job which reflects their individual strengths (if necessary getting employers to adapt the

---

[1] Available on the Norah Fry Research Centre Website: www/bris.ac.uk/Depts/Norahfry/

job), then helping the individual not just to learn the specific task required, but also to adapt to the context of that particular working environment.

In practice there is considerable variation in how supported employment agencies work, but most would emphasise helping workers:

- to negotiate the proper 'rate for the job'
- to develop positive relationships with co-workers
- to carry out work that is of genuine value to the employer.

Throughout the rest of this report, this is the specific sense in which we use the term supported employment.

There are now well over 200 UK employment agencies which work to the definition of 'supported employment' as provided (see page 35). As part of this research we visited two such organisations in South Wales: WISE (Welsh Initiative for Supported Employment) and South East Wales PATHWAY (one of the supported employment initiatives fostered by MENCAP). Both concentrate solely on employment; neither provides housing or support outside the workplace, although job coaches may liaise with other support services and are often involved in benefit issues. Funding has been mainly through social services and from the European Social Fund, although since our field work, there is increasing funding from the Employment Service.

The projects were selected because, unlike many supported employment schemes, both have a significant number of clients in full-time work. In a few cases this has enabled people to broaden their housing choices.

Both projects have placed people with learning disabilities in a wide range of jobs including office work, cleaning, retail, catering, gardening and data-processing. Employers have included large retailers such as super-markets and chain stores, local authorities, hospitals, golf clubs, factories, nursing homes and restaurants.

WISE

WISE is a voluntary organisation, founded in 1985 by parents wanting their sons and daughters to access employment. Staff include employment consultants (who find jobs), a training consultant who trains and supervises the job trainers, and job trainers who train and support people in the workplace.

WISE supports over 80 people in jobs, including about 30 in the Supported Placement Scheme. Some clients have held down their job for over ten years and most work full-time (defined under the benefits system as more than sixteen hours!). Nearly everyone lives with their parents, though a few have their own flats and one couple is buying a council house.

Prospective clients must be referred through social services, have expressed a clear desire to work and have support for this from parent(s) or carer(s). People who have not worked much or are unsure what they want to do usually have one or more unpaid work placement(s). Some are also advised to work on specific skills such as literacy or numeracy. When people are clearer about the sort of job they want, WISE helps them try to find work, though clients are warned that WISE mainly finds entry-level jobs in catering, cleaning and retailing. Sometimes employers 'job carve', creating a post by combining elements of several jobs. WISE expects employers to pay the going rate for the job and provide the same terms and conditions as for other workers.

WISE staff always carry out a 'better-off' calculation to look at the effect of working on their clients' benefits, and their *Jobseekers Pack* spells out the implications very clearly for clients and parents/carers.

'If you are lucky enough to be offered a job and you enjoy the work, you will need to discuss the benefits situation with your Employment Consultant and your parents or carers. Sometimes you may have to choose between keeping all your benefits or working in a job you enjoy.'

Sally had worked full-time in a solicitor's office for the past six years. Her job included photocopying, filing and delivering legal documents. She caught the bus to work and enjoyed the social contact with people in the office. As well as her wages, she received Disability Living Allowance (DLA) and Disability Working Allowance (DWA).

David had been shelf-stacking and collecting trolleys at a local supermarket for a couple of years. He usually worked three afternoons a week, which kept his wages below the therapeutic earnings limit, and although he thought full-time work might be too tiring, would like to have worked some additional hours. He preferred the security of remaining on benefits, having previously been laid off from a job in a DIY store. David received SDA, Income Support and DLA, and lived in a flat attached to his parents' house. He liked the social contact at work, and being out of the house.

James was very interested in computers and had acquired good keyboard skills at college. He had previously worked for short periods inputting data at the university and for the council, and WISE was looking for another part-time, paid job for him. Meanwhile, he was working at the museum, analysing reasons that visitors gave for their visit. He found this particularly interesting, and enjoyed the social contact. James originally received SDA, Income Support and DLA, but even though the museum was only reimbursing his bus fares and lunch costs his benefits had been stopped until his GP confirmed that the voluntary work was

'therapeutic'. Meanwhile James's parents were keeping him; had he lived on his own, there could have been a serious problem.

PATHWAY

South East Wales PATHWAY is unusual because more than half of the 80 people it supports in the workplace are either full- or part-time workers but earning well over the therapeutic earnings limit. Most live at home with parents, a few live in registered care homes, and some live on their own, usually in rented flats.

Referrals come through social services, but there are also links with day centres and disablement employment advisors. About a third of clients work in factories which are the main local source of employment. Factory work offers plentiful opportunities for chatting, the routine nature of factory work can be easier for people to cope with, and once someone has learnt a task they can carry on with it.

Simon and **Mark** work in a large electronics factory run by one of the South East Asian companies which have moved into the valleys. Both work five mornings a week and receive DWA and DLA. As they live in the same street (with their parents), they travel to work in a shared taxi. Both felt it would be too tiring to work more hours, but still thought work was *'better than hanging about the house'* or being at the day centre. Their main task is sweeping up – an essential task, as electronics manufacturing requires a clean, dust-free environment. The personnel manager feels that supported employment has a positive impact on workplace morale.

Four PATHWAY clients work in a cardboard box factory whose manager says they are *'some of our most productive workers'*. He was particularly enthusiastic about the training and support given by job coaches. The four are paid the same hourly rate as other workers. However, they cannot do overtime because of being paid through the Sheltered Placement Scheme, which was quite a bone of contention with one worker who would like to have earned more.

Paul, who had done a horticultural course, worked as a groundsman at a local golf club. He lived on his own, in a house inherited from his parents, and a home care assistant visited weekly. He worked full-time, and received DLA and DWA. Paul loved the job except when bad weather meant there was not much to do. He used garden machinery (grass cutters, strimmers, cultivators) with confidence and worked as a member of a team of six grounds maintenance staff.

The argument for supported employment

Supported employment has a number of benefits: real jobs, real wages and an integrated setting. We found that it was welcomed not only by people with learning disabilities but also by participating employers.

> *'His work is a little slower than average, but he more than makes up for it by his effect on office morale'* (office manager, WISE employer)

> *'Our employee... rarely, if ever, misses a day's work or fails to attend punctually. He takes great pride in being considered equal to other employees'* (building company, WISE employer)

According to staff, some parents or carers were initially apprehensive and often underestimated their son's or daughter's employment potential. However, the parents we met were enthusiastic, commenting on the benefits of working, including increased self-confidence, a sense of worth and savings for clothes, holidays and the future. One

couple commented on the importance of their daughter being *'a valued member of the workforce'* and had arranged a personal pension plan for her.

People living at home seemed to have the best chance of being better off by working, though some parents appeared to control their wages and benefits. Some people knew exactly what they received, but others said they just handed it all to Mum. Both agencies agreed that working was very difficult for anyone in residential care unless they kept their earnings below the earnings disregard (by limiting their hours or receiving a very low hourly rate).

People living independently could be slightly better off by working and claiming Housing Benefit, but this would depend on the HB rates, eligibility for other benefits such as DWA, and access to adequate support services in the community. Job coaches could be involved in crisis situations, but this was not feasible on a long-term basis.

Even though they were earning the going rate, most clients were on relatively low wages. However, one man at PATHWAY earns over £15,000 a year and is thinking of buying his own home – a realistic choice at his income level. Others had inherited the family home.

Social contact appeared to be limited to official events such as Christmas parties, rather than meaningful friendships with colleagues. Most people we met had more social contacts at Gateway Clubs and similar provision.

Staff and employers commented on the healthier lifestyle engendered by working; there was more structure to the day, less opportunity for eating snacks, more physical exercise and often access to good cheap food in canteens. At least one rather overweight worker had lost weight due to increased exercise and improved diet.

Supported employment agencies have sometimes been accused of 'cherry-picking' more able people, and though some clients had come from day centres, they were probably at the more able end of the spectrum (though definitions are difficult). Agencies had to meet funders' targets, and were constrained by the need to 'deliver' and by the availability of referrals and jobs. They also felt they were not funded to provide continuing and/or high levels of support.

At the time of our visits, there was concern that supported employment services were funded almost entirely by social services, usually on a short-term basis. Staff felt that more funding should come from mainstream employment sources. Since our fieldwork, this has increased.

Agencies were surprised to find that smaller employers were often easier to work with, even though large companies often had inclusion policies. With larger organisations, co-operation had more to do with the attitude of local management than with company policy. Staff and employers liked the French 'stick and carrot' model of encouraging employers to offer opportunities by a combination of incentives and 'fines'.

There was some concern about the impact of the minimum wage at the time of our fieldwork, with fears that it might be more difficult to persuade employers to create posts. Because many employers were already paying close to the minimum wage, this has not caused a problem. The difficulties have arisen because of the need to keep within the disregards (see discussion in **Chapter Eleven**). Both organisations have had problems over this. Some clients have reduced their hours to keep below the £15 disregard. Many employers have also expressed their concern about needing to keep within the law, and the limits this places on people's hours.

Chapter Eight
Community Businesses

Community business: an introduction

In the context of this report we have defined community businesses (now more often described as **social firms**) as businesses developed with the main aim of providing opportunities for people with learning disabilities to undertake meaningful work in the local community.

Individual community businesses vary in the extent to which they:

- **are commercial organisations**, some generating income primarily through commercial activities and others relying more on subsidies, though we would expect all to trade to some degree

- **have links with the communities in which they are based**, some growing out of a particular community, and the business's contribution to that community being an important part of their raison d'être, others being simply another local business

- **emphasise inclusion**, some focusing on ensuring that people with learning disabilities work alongside non-disabled people, or have significant contact with the general public, others concentrating more on the work itself.

Local context

The community businesses we visited are on the North Wales coast, a rural area with high unemployment and heavily reliant on tourism. The area has a high proportion of Welsh speakers and Welsh is the first language for many people.

Antur Waunfawr

Antur Waunfawr was not set up simply to provide employment for people with learning disabilities. Its founder, R. Gwynn Davies, believed that people with learning disabilities would not live 'normal lives' without *'considering society as a whole'*. Antur Waunfawr is about community regeneration and is driven by a vision that inclusion will come about by enabling people with learning disabilities to play a visible and valued role as contributors to that community.

The business is funded through a variety of sources. Social services provide a core grant. A £2,000,000 lottery grant helped establish the recycling project, along with £20,000 from Environment Wales and £50,000 in kind from the local authority. A three-year grant from the European Social Fund provided substantial funding. At the time of our visit Antur Waunfawr was planning an application to the European Regional Development Fund. Finally, the businesses generate an annual turnover of around £250,000.

Antur Waunfawr currently employs 20 people with learning disabilities and 20 people from the local community. All activities focus on the village and include the following.

Renovating buildings

Concern runs deep about incomers purchasing second homes, resulting in a lack of affordable housing for local people. Over a number of years, Antur Waunfawr has successfully renovated a cottage, a flat and a shop, the latter providing a retail outlet for their products. As Menna Jones, the Chief Executive, points out, this gives them a very visible presence in the village, and the involvement of Antur Waunfawr workers in the renovation has definitely changed local attitudes towards people with learning disabilities.

Environmental services

Garden design, tree planting, drystone wall repairs and maintaining a seven-acre nature park have provided resources for the village and enabled Antur Waunfawr to build strong links with other local organisations like the Urdd (Welsh League of Youth).

Community management services

These include caretaking for the village chapel, providing firewood, cutting grass, and gardening for older people.

Shop and café

The shop in the village also runs a small café.

Fruit and vegetable garden

The produce grown in the garden supplies the café and is sold in the shop.

Community recycling

Antur Waunfawr has established a community recycling business in partnership with Gwynedd Council based in Bangor.

Carpentry workshop

Antur Waunfawr also has a more conventional workshop, making wood products and concrete paving slabs.

Housing and support

Antur Waunfawr has become a specialist provider of housing and support to local people with learning disabilities, reflecting to some extent the lack of alternative providers. The renovated cottage and flat houses three people with learning disabilities, supported by Antur Waunfawr. It also bought two ex-council houses on an estate in nearby Caernarfon and, with the help of a local authority grant, renovated them to a high standard. Three people live here, again supported by Antur Waunfawr.

The local Inspection Unit insisted on registration (probably because Antur Waunfawr is landlord and care provider), so people are not eligible for Housing Benefit, and have licences rather than assured tenancies. Like many other providers, Antur Waunfawr has had to conform to standards they do not see as particularly appropriate (such as keeping files in people's homes).

Antur Waunfawr anticipates an expanding need to support people either in their own tenancies, or in homes inherited from the family.

Menter Fachwen

The headquarters of Menter Fachwen is a small cottage in the village of Llanberis. The organisation was set up to provide:

- employment for local people
- work opportunities for people with learning disabilities, including people with more complex needs – indeed,

Menter Fachwen has now developed a reputation for being able to support people with very challenging behaviour.

A separate organisation (Agoriad) specialises in supporting people into open employment and some people move on from Menter Fachwen.

Menter Fachwen runs two types of business.

- **Works canteens** The four canteens, based in local factories, provide 'real' work settings. According to Christine Jones, one of the Menter Fachwen team, they are '*... busy, pressured environments. They provide an essential service to the workplace*'.

  Although they are in a minority in each staff team, people with learning disabilities are essential members of the team, and, if ill or on holiday, have to be replaced

- **Environmental projects**

  – two contract gangs, doing gardening and grounds maintenance in the local community

  – a team renovating a large walled garden in the grounds of a local agricultural college

  – a team maintaining eight acres of woodland with a wildlife centre and seasonal cafe

Unlike the canteen teams, environmental project workers generally have less inter-action with the wider public. However, Menter Fachwen has opened a visitor centre, and shop work and 'wardening' offer more direct contact with the public. Like the CATs, Menter Fachwen finds that environmental projects enable a few individuals with more severe disabilities/challenging behaviour to be productive in a work environment.

The business is funded by a combination of grants, contracts and commercial activities. The local authority provides a core grant of about £35,000, and social services fund a number of individual placements. Although some individuals require two supporters at any one time, Menter Fachwen's per capita costs are lower than those of many equivalent local services. The organisation has a three-year grant from the European Social Fund to cover training costs. Finally, the commercial activities give the business a turnover of around £250,000 a year.

One staff member had worked in the local Citizens' Advice Bureau so has a good knowledge of the benefits system. The organisation would like to do more benefits advice work, but currently lacks the funding.

Many of those who work for Menter Fachwen live with their families, although one person is still in the local long-stay hospital, and two are in the house renovated by Antur Waunfawr.

Co-options

Co-options' headquarters is based in a local enterprise centre in Rhyl, reflecting the fact that it is more commercially oriented than the other two community businesses.

Co-options started in 1989 on a co-operative basis. A group of people with learning disabilities visited Food and Futures (see **Chapter Nine**) and wanted to do something similar, so a local co-operative development worker became involved.

Supported living opportunities were already well established, but the local strategy for learning disability had only just begun to consider work opportunities. An initial bid to local employers having failed, employment opportunities had to be created. From the start, Co-options made a big effort to include people labelled as 'most disabled', focusing on individualised supports. Some early success led to more support for individualised work opportunities, within services and among families. This in turn led to considerable expansion.

When we visited, 62 people with learning disabilities were being supported through the community businesses (plus 165 in various forms of supported employment). Co-options has a significant strategic role locally, but the focus is still on individuals, and trying to find opportunities that match their strengths and interests.

Co-options' structure is described as a 'community co-operative'. It is a limited company without shares, operating on a non-profit basis, and with unpaid directors. It is a complex organisation with a wide range of attached projects and services as well as the core businesses, so the following account is inevitably selective. The elements that make up Co-options extend well beyond community businesses and include the following.

Tangible Dream Bike Shop

Started as a project recycling bikes and wheelchairs, this is now a specialist mountain bike shop. A group including people with learning disabilities obtained European funding to visit a project in Portugal. This led to the shop's promoting specialist mountain biking holidays in that area, through specialist magazines.

People with learning disabilities maintain and repair mountain bikes, as well as doing cleaning and stock control. In many instances they have direct contact with customers.

Scoffs (originally called Café Ciao Bella)

This café, located in the enterprise centre, is staffed by people with learning disabilities working alongside people from the local community. It also does external catering and has a sandwich round.

Mosaic

Mosaic's main products are handmade pottery and other craftwork. Its base in a large room in the enterprise centre can feel rather like a day centre, but it is a business, although the emphasis is on high quality work rather than mass production. Everyone with learning disabilities who works in Mosaic requires considerable assistance and has one-to-one support. This is well in excess of what might be found in local day services, but is achieved within the standard level of fees because of the income generation (plus a small subsidy from other parts of Co-options).

The employment services

These include a range of training and assessment services (Co-options is an NVQ assessment centre specialising in the employment of staff in community care settings), a payroll service, and recruitment and administration services.

Supported employment programme

Job coaches are supporting people in a wide range of ordinary worksites.

Co-options parallels the co-operative development agencies (**Chapter Nine**) in 'floating off' a number of businesses that have become private companies operating on a purely commercial basis. These include the following:

Magic Toy Box Nursery

With increasing interest in early learning and childcare for working parents, this business started at just the right time, when there was not too much local competition. Its modest capital requirements meant it was able to keep costs down.

Paraphanalia (formerly Essentially Celtic)
Aromatherapy oils are produced, using local products.

Some workers with learning disabilities have continued to play a significant role in these businesses but this has varied, according to the commitment of those who take over the business and their economic circumstances.

Initial funding for Co-options came from the EU Horizon Fund. In two years the resources for Co-options went from nil to £550,000, which required a 'very steep learning curve'. As EU money tailed off there had to be a lot of restructuring, just to break even. However, things are now on a more even keel. The current annual turnover for Co-options is about £481,000, made up of a combination of local authority contracts, EU funding and income generation.

Denbighshire Employment Opportunities

This initiative combines supported employment and community businesses, including Popt'yr Garn. This started as a basic training unit within the Henllan day centre, but as people with learning disabilities started moving out it was refitted as a commercial catering unit and began supplying cakes to local shops. Then, as the Centre emptied further, part of the premises was converted into a conference centre. Popt'yr Garn now caters for the conference centre as well as continuing with the cake business and some off-site catering.

Seven people with learning disabilities are employed part-time (usually three or four on any one day), working alongside two full-time staff. Like many in community businesses, most workers combine this work with college or employment.

When we visited, Bethan and Nerys, both of whom have learning disabilities, were working alongside two-co-workers. They were clearly proud of their kitchen and Bethan particularly enjoyed making coconut creams, for which she was totally responsible.

The women workers had been away for a weekend together. For Nerys, not only was this her first trip without her parents but she was able to achieve her ambition of enjoying a pint, just like her brothers.

Issues arising from visits

The views of people with learning disabilities

All the people with learning disabilities we met were very positive about their employment and many were very clear about how much they valued what they were doing. Regardless of how much they earned, for some, the job provided a clear sense of identity and place.

> '*I feel part of things. I've got my job and the church.*'

The rationale for community businesses

The idea of 'contributing' and the significance of 'community'
The community business ethic is consistent with and reflects the nature of these Welsh villages. Their relative isolation has fostered a particularly strong sense of self-reliance and community, coupled with the collectivist traditions that grew out of the local slate-mining industry, once the mainstay of the local economy. Interestingly, all three organisations also provide local supported employment services.

Paul

Paul had led a very sheltered life, living with his mother until her death triggered a number of changes, including a move to his own flat and getting a job. He lives in a small village which had lost its local shop and garage. This decline could well have continued but, with EU money, the villagers bought and re-opened the shop and garage and started running them as co-operatives. Paul is now effectively a shareholder in these businesses, playing an active part in decision-making and attending shareholder meetings where, as he says, '*I always listen carefully to what they say*'.

Paul started work cutting the grass outside factory units on an industrial estate. This would normally be seasonal work but employees in one factory decided, on their own initiative, that Paul could also do indoor work. Now, as well as cutting the grass, he keeps the factory free of rubbish, keeps the tea machine and restroom clean and cleans gearboxes.

Paul was supported initially by a job coach but since his employer suggested he no longer needed that much help, most of his support comes from a co-worker, with occasional visits from the supported employment agency.

An incident during our visit illustrates the value of additional workplace support. Blizzards meant Paul had no electricity for two days. His co-worker, Berwyn, knew that the supply would probably be re-established that evening but that the clocks on Paul's night storage heaters would be out of sync when the power came back on. Concerned that Paul could run up a large bill, Berwyn was trying to arrange for someone from the local community living team to go round and sort this out.

Paul was very at home in the workplace and particularly enjoyed the social events. He is occasionally the butt of jokes by his workmates but seems to take this in his stride and, as Berwyn pointed out, '*He is very well liked. We wouldn't do without him*'.

These community businesses do little traditional fundraising, which they felt was not consistent with enabling people themselves to make a valued contribution.

'*We don't want it to be "Ah bechod"* [ah, shame].'

Antur Waunfawr has 250 local shareholders, with 20 directors from the area. Menter Fachwen has a Senedd (council), consisting mainly of people from the local community. These structural links ensure that the communities feel a sense of ownership for the projects, although organisations have to work hard to foster this. Antur Waunfawr, for example, does not simply provide services to the village but also arranges social events. Even so, it is possible to over-romanticise the nature of these local connections. As Menna Jones from Antur Waunfawr puts it:

'*People will still go to shop in Safeway, rather than support the local shop*'.

The community businesses have to provide services that are valued and which meet the needs of the communities. They also have to market their services, and charge realistic prices for the work they do.

Flexibility

Co-options differed from the other organisations described in this chapter. Although involved with supported employment, it had still chosen to put time and energy into developing community businesses. Co-options remains very committed to supported employment, but had concluded that it could not *always* deliver work options that particular individuals either wanted or needed. It is possible to influence people, but existing attitudes in the workplace facilitate or limit what can be done. To some degree, the worker with learning disabilities has to adapt to the workplace.

In contrast, community businesses bring the possibility of adapting the work environment to the person. The most vivid example of this is an idea that Co-options was still only exploring. **Ted** has a physical impairment as well as a learning difficulty. He has no speech, and Co-options members spent a lot of time getting to know him and developing his ability to communicate. They explored many possibilities and recently arranged an assessment for a Liberator speech pack.

Although Ted had left special school with no obvious achievements to his name, Co-options staff felt that he probably had hidden skills. Gradually his strong interest in computers emerged and he was supported to take part in a mainstream basic computing course.

Co-options has begun thinking about how Ted could be involved in an environment where computers feature significantly. There were no suitable potential local employers, so Co-options was exploring the idea of opening a Cybercafé which Ted could help to manage. The area has an unusually large older population, there is considerable local interest in the University of the Third Age and Co-options considered it likely that there might be interest in the Internet among the local retired community. There was, therefore, a potential customer base for a Cybercafé that was 'pensioner-friendly'.

The need for entrepreneuralism

Community businesses have to strike a balance between the needs of people who may not be very productive and financial viability, and, most importantly, they need an entrepreneurial streak, seizing commercial opportunities when and where they arise. This approach can be hard to find in a local authority context. For example, the success of specialist mountain biking holidays convinced Co-options that there was scope for developing cycle tourism in the area. The attractive local hills are not too steep, and the roads are very quiet. However, the response from the local planning department was not very positive.

Effective niche marketing is required in areas where there are not too many local competitors. For example, to call Tangible Dream a 'bike shop' is a massive under-statement – people come from as far as Manchester and Merseyside to purchase the exotic machines, some with price tags approaching £3,000.

Menter Fachwen and Antur Waunfawr, on the other hand, are quite small organisations.

'We don't always have the time to explore everything; we have to keep a focus on our core business.'

All the organisations we visited were good at promoting themselves, but they were also strikingly honest. All have had to compromise their ideals simply to manage the environ-ment in which they work, and they acknowledged this, while also remaining committed to improvement.

'We have to find a balance between presenting a positive image and recognising our limitations.'

Low earnings

None of the people using the current community businesses was earning over the Income Support disregard levels. However, the business that Co-options had floated off was profitable partly because at least some employees with learning disabilities were productive enough to be thinking about coming off benefits.

The other businesses simply did not generate sufficient income for people to make the switch, though this doesn't necessarily mean they will never be able to pay more than £15. The current benefits system effectively leaves people with the choice of sticking with the disregard or seeking full-time work with sufficient pay to replace benefits.

Jeff

Jeff's contact with the supported employment service began when he left the 'special needs' unit at his local college. Jeff is quite traditional and wanted 'men's' work, which to him meant a factory job. The service contacted a local company making a range of products including devices for defurring kettles. They were keen to help and clear they did not want Jeff singled out.

Initially Jeff produced about 40% of the average output so he worked part-time and continued to receive Income Support. However, his productivity increased, matching (and at times even exceeding) that of other workers. After discussion with his employer and the family, Jeff decided to go full-time and come off benefits completely. He now works four days a week for take-home pay of £140.

Jeff's self-confidence was a key factor. He knew he could do the job and that he fitted in. The company had full order books so he knew his job was secure for the foreseeable future.

Staff in the community businesses were concerned about people's lack of 'real wages', but felt that gains in other areas compensated for this. Most professionals recognised that low earnings were a source of discontent for a few people, but that others were less concerned.

'If anything they tend to be rather grateful. It's a case of "I'm out of the centre".'

People with learning disabilities we talked to were less critical than the professionals. As one man commented,

'[£15] is better than nothing, isn't it? It means I can go to the pub'.

However, it is important to remember that people's aspirations have often been suppressed by those around them.

'Mum says I can't earn any more.'

The minimum wage

At the time of our visits, the national minimum wage had not yet been introduced. While all the organisations supported the idea in principle, they felt it might no longer be possible to negotiate with employers so that productivity levels are built into the 'rate for the job'. Their worries were also echoed by two employers we met.

There was also concern that, if employers paid the minimum wage but it was not justified by productivity, the employee's role would change from that of valued employee contributing to the business to that of someone being subsidised by the employer.

The community businesses also feared it would be difficult to generate the additional income to cover a potentially large increase in their wage bill.

Housing and work

Apart from Antur Waunfawr's rather interesting lateral approach linking housing and work, the messages coming from the community businesses were depressingly familiar. Work is not yet providing a route into a home of one's own for people with learning disabilities, partly because people are generally sticking at the earnings disregard. People earning significantly more (in Co-options) had usually been able to do so because they were living with their families.

The impact on families

Potential loss of income is not a risk just for the individual, but for the family as well. In an area of high unemployment, the loss of benefits to an individual can have an impact on the whole household, particularly where a family may have given up economic opportunities in the past to care for a dependent relative. The loss would be compounded if, as a result of greater independence, the person with learning disabilities left home.

> 'It would be a big loss for some families, and not just in money terms. For some of the more elderly carers it would be the company too.'

Participation

Community businesses have some parallels with worker co-operatives (see **Chapter Nine**), though people with learning disabilities have little formal role in decision-making where the former are concerned. Attempts have been made to include the views of people with learning disabilities, mainly through individual planning or in small worksite meetings. Menter Fachwen had tried including the workers with learning disabilities in the AGM, but felt people had found it intimidating.

Co-options has had people with learning disabilities on the Management Board in the past and workers have been supported to join People First. However, this contrasts with the prominent role played by people with

learning disabilities in SWALLOW (see **Chapter One**).

Strategic change

Although the All Wales Strategy played an important part in developing work opportunities for people with learning disabilities, the problem remained: how to release resources from congregate services for individuals without having a negative effect on those still using day services. In the case of employment services, there was increasing resistance from families and other groups who saw the safety net of 'their' centre being dismantled.

The idea for Popty'r Garn was based on 'saving' the centre – recognising a need for a community resource. However, as people left to take up work opportunities, the centre could not carry on as before. The solution was to bring meaningful work opportunities, along with local people, into the centre.

This had several effects. First, it decreased resistance to further change. Second, it meant that people who had opted to remain at the centre also got a new range of opportunities. Finally, they have continued to build bridges into the community. Some of the Centre's options are a compromise, but Popt'yr Garn represents a very radical departure from the old day centre.

The new developments have occurred broadly within the constraints of the old budget. As people took up options nearer home, it was possible to transfer money from the formerly huge travel budget into more intensive support. People no longer spent two hours a day on the bus. It is also possible to do things that could not have been contemplated with the original staff:user ratios.

Equal opportunities

The Welsh language introduces a distinctive twist to equal opportunities. In North Wales, enabling people to speak in their preferred language was a matter of concern. Language was a central issue at Antur Waunfawr and it had made contact with a CAT whose workers' first language was Breton. Staff mentioned concern about speech therapy assessments in English, which they felt risked under-estimating people's capacities if their first language was Welsh. Furthermore, opportunities to speak Welsh will not necessarily be reflected in the workplace in open employment.

Some things never change though. Community businesses report frequent sexual stereotyping in the way that people are referred to them. For example, in Menter Fachwen it is mainly men who work on the environmental projects and mostly women in the canteens, though they have tried to ensure that people can subsequently switch between the canteens and the other projects.

Chapter Nine

Worker Co-operatives which Include People with Learning Disabilities

Introduction

Worker co-ops are businesses legally owned and controlled by their workforce. They aim to make a profit, which is re-invested in the business or distributed among the worker-members. Worker co-ops are part of the wider co-operative movement, whose shared characteristic is common ownership.

Worker co-ops are more common elsewhere in Europe, and Italy has been a leader in worker co-ops involving people with learning disabilities and those with mental health problems (Samoy, 1992; Grove *et al.*, 1997). Maggi Sikking's guide to co-ops (1986) has a useful discussion of issues associated with involving people with learning and other disabilities. The role of co-ops, especially in Italy, also features in Grove *et al.* (1997).

Gillygate Wholefood Bakery, York

Gillygate, which started in the 1970s, is a mixed community, including people with learning disabilities and others potentially disadvantaged in the workplace. In the late 1970s and early 1980s the co-op ran a bakery, shop and café, and enjoyed commercial success as a wholefood pioneer. By the mid-1980s, however, increased competition and its location (just outside the centre of York) were affecting its viability, and by the early 1990s its financial position had worsened. Of a total workforce of forty, just four had learning disabilities, and all of them were working only a few hours a week.

At the time of our visit, the café had closed and the shop's future was uncertain. The co-op was still making cakes and pastry products, but had had to stop baking bread. Two people with learning disabilities were still working part-time, both within the Income Support earnings disregard. Pat, who had moved into a housing association bungalow, worked three mornings a week and Kim, who lived in a flat, came in about three times a week.

Since our visit the co-op has changed radically. The premises have been sold, and some original members have left. The co-op now provides staff for a wholefood (predominantly organic) shop and coffee bar.

Food and Futures

Food and Futures was set up by a founder member of Gillygate with the aim of creating either co-ops or self-employment for people with 'special needs'. However, 'special needs' has been widely defined, and many of the co-ops have had no remit to provide work for people with learning disabilities.

Employment was likely to be linked to the food industry because it provided a range of jobs for people with different skills. The aim was always to work alongside people, taking on board their ideas and helping them to set up the business. Funding has come from the European Social Fund, charitable trusts, and local authority (though not social services) grants.

Although the co-ops usually started as a local community initiative and people were initially prepared to help each other, they tended to become less inclusive, particularly once they had been floated off. Indeed, some ceased to be co-ops and became ordinary businesses.

The Water Garden was started by Food and Futures with the specific intention that it should remain under their control and be more inclusive. The co-op grew bean sprouts and alfalfa and provided work for some people with learning disabilities from local residential care homes, on a very part-time basis (within the earnings disregard).

> '*When Adrian first started he came with his care assistant… who explained that Adrian was incapable of working. They did not expect him to last long… I showed Adrian the first job, labelling punnet lids… he and the care assistant took on the job together… Then one day, Adrian was dropped off alone. The care assistant was ill… the sprouting chamber had flooded… all of us were mopping up furiously we just left him to get on with it. By the time I stopped to notice… he had disappeared behind a pile of labelled punnet lids.*'
> (Blackburn *et al.*, 1990)

Unfortunately, food scares about salmonella and listeria caused the co-op to go into voluntary liquidation after only 11 months.

Cleansweep: self-employment for people with learning disabilities

Cleansweep is unusual by any standards, being **founded by and made up of people with learning disabilities**. It reflects a growing interest in self-employment for people with learning disabilities and

collective action by disabled people (Neath & Schriner, 1998).

The idea of a co-operative was floated at a conference workshop session on '*What else can we do?*'. Keith Bates, from the local Mencap Pathway, gave a presentation to local day-centre users, which led to his working with a group of those interested in exploring this further. With Keith's help, they considered:

- ideas for working co-operatively
- proposals for different kinds of business opportunities
- what it means to run a business.

The group found itself returning to catering and cleaning, largely because it had no capital – although some groups in Canada have obtained low-cost business start-up loans (Roeher Institute, 1996). These 'food and filth' options often dominate work opportunities for people with learning disabilities, but cleaning has certain advantages, including the fact that it provides steady year-round employment.

The first business opportunity cropped up when a local business centre wanted to change its cleaners. The group wanted to stop talking and start doing, so it put in a tender, including a free three-week trial. The offer was accepted, the trial was a success, it got the contract and has not looked back. Starting with six workers and one contract, three and a half years later it has nine contracts and fifteen workers.

The co-op generally has no problems getting contracts – mainly through word of mouth. Advertising is minimal. A poster describes its services, and it advertises in the annual supplement of a local magazine. Given that the work it does is of sufficiently good quality, many customers *like* the fact it is a 'co-op with a difference'. Like most contract cleaners it has also lost the odd contract, but these have been important learning opportunities.

All Cleansweep members work fewer than 16 hours a week. Some earn above the benefits disregard, although the system effectively ensures that they are no better off for doing so. Benefit options have been explored (including working longer hours and claiming DWA), but because office cleaning is usually at the end of the day, it's quite difficult to build up more than 16 hours a week. While this may limit the opportunity to work full-time, people who want to can work part-time *and* keep a foothold in the day centre.

Although many workers pay themselves relatively low hourly rates because of the benefits system, the contracts bring money into the co-op. This offers some flexibility; with small contracts for only a few hours, members can decide to bring more than one worker, so that people have moral support and company.

Office cleaning is sometimes criticised for providing minimal opportunities for direct contact with other people. Cleansweep specifically avoids situations where offices will be empty, partly because this avoids security worries, but also because it ensures that co-op members spend a significant amount of their time in genuinely integrated settings.

Cleansweep's structure is fairly typical of a small co-operative. Company law requires a board of directors, but the main decision-making forum is the weekly staff meeting, to which all workers can contribute. However, members have not always found it easy to work in a co-op with no 'bosses'. In fact, Cleansweep has 'team leaders' (not supervisors) – people who have the most experience, who know and understand the contracts, and who will liaise and negotiate with clients.

The co-op has generally been supportive of members who need more assistance at work. This additional help is usually provided by other members rather than bringing in people from outside. For example, one man

was always thrown by bank holidays and tended not to get up for work the next day. Now, other members ring the group home the previous Friday to ensure that he does.

Keith describes Cleansweep as a 'supported co-operative'. Members do control the co-operative, but require some assistance in running the company. Keith's role as advisor includes:

- helping members develop systems they can use to sustain the workings of the business

- helping individuals sort out benefits

- ensuring the legal obligations of the company are met, by assisting the company secretary

- being a familiar and reassuring figure members can turn to if there is a problem.

Keith has *not* been a member of the co-op, but now the members would like him to join formally, and share the role of company secretary.

Pathway provides some assistance with recruiting new workers. It runs a check on the people for whom it has completed a vocational profile, identifies those interested in doing cleaning work and passes their details to Cleansweep which interviews potential new workers. This is an interesting example of how supported employment can help sustain a co-op, rather than being an alternative.

An initiative which started within learning disability services has now gained a foothold within the wider co-operative movement in Bristol. The latter has become increasingly involved with, and supportive of the business, and could take over Keith's role in the future.

Keith is now exploring possible similar ventures. Having run courses for local day-services users, he is working with one group to explore whether an outside catering team currently within a day centre could be 'floated off' as a workers' co-op.

Pathway has been part of a successful bid for a European-wide initiative which will establish a number of small 'social enterprises' designed to provide paid work for women with learning disabilities (and other disadvantaged groups) in non-traditional areas of employment.

The case for co-ops

While acknowledging that co-ops are one of a range of options, Maggi Sikking suggests that they are '*especially well-equipped to employ people with different needs and abilities*' because of:

- their inclusive system of decision-making and self-government

- their social commitment

- the dual role of members as both employers and employees so '*they can make sure that each* [member] *is accorded as much respect as a person as is the profit they generate*'

- their view that work provides not only financial reward but also social activity and is '*in the broadest sense spiritual, feeding a common human need to feel useful and self-reliant*'.

However, co-ops also have drawbacks. Most UK co-ops are fragile and small and, like many small businesses, suffer from under-capitalisation and insecure markets. Co-ops are not charities, and as Maggi Sikking points out, they need to be '*successful enough commercially to be able to afford a special needs employment policy*' (Sikking, 1986). Without this, benefits such as inclusion in decision-making can be somewhat hollow. A further drawback is that wages tend to be low and co-ops may have difficulty paying a statutory minimum wage.

Co-ops also appear to have more difficulty attracting charitable or statutory funding. Gillygate's lack of statutory funding to support workers with learning disabilities was in marked contrast with the social services funding for an adjacent craft workshop. However, SHAW (**Chapter Ten**), which is registered as a charity and a company, has successfully attracted funding from a variety of sources.

Perhaps the strongest argument in favour of co-ops is the promise of an equal role in decision-making. Yet we need to consider the extent to which this actually happens, especially when people with learning disabilities are in a small minority. At Gillygate, although they attended the monthly co-op meetings, legal problems meant that they were not full members. This has been challenged by Grove *et al.* (1997), which concluded that:

> '*this over-cautious approach to legal issues is more to do with lack of self-confidence in the organisation than with reality. We know of no reason why an adult, who is not barred by criminality or a compulsory detention order, should be unable to be a company director… we do not think such statements should be allowed to pass unchallenged and untested*'.

Whether a co-operative structure is *necessary* to promote involvement in decision-making is a moot point. It works very well for Cleansweep, but may be less practicable where people with learning disabilities are in a minority and are working part-time. SWALLOW, on the other hand, is a charity, yet manages to include people with learning disabilities in much of its decision-making. Perhaps we need to look beyond the formal structures to what happens in practice.

Chapter Ten

SHAW (Sheltered Housing and Workshops) Projects

SHAW combines a range of housing, employment and training options and in some ways most closely resembles the CATs.

Origins and services

SHAW's provision includes:

- a wholesale plant nursery
- a garden centre and shop
- a contract landscaping and gardening team
- a printing firm
- two supported employment services
- Community Link, which helps people not in work to access community activities
- education and training courses in partnership with local colleges
- residential homes for people resettled from long-stay hospitals
- shared supported housing, in partnership with a housing association.

All the employment projects employ a majority of people with learning (and sometimes other) disabilities. The focus in this report is on the nursery and garden centre and the shared supported housing, as these elements are closest to the CAT model.

In the late 1970s, a group of professionals had the idea of developing a village community on a rural site, providing housing and employment for people with learning disabilities. However, the funding proposal submitted by North (now Home) Housing Association to the Housing Corporation was turned down.

By 1982, SHAW was an incorporated company and registered charity. The original plans had changed to a horticultural nursery and ten four-bedroom cottages. Funding for both was obtained two years later and the shared housing and nursery opened in 1986.

SHAW has since developed a range of services, including a garden centre and a shop. Funding was secured from a number of sources, including European money, health authorities and social services, and the Department of Employment, plus significant fundraising and income from trading activities.

A workshop making garden furniture and conservatories closed in 1996 because it was trading at a deficit. The substantial loss was a financial blow, but SHAW was large and financially secure enough to survive.

The nursery

The nursery raises pot plants, bedding plants and shrubs for sale to retail outlets such as garden centres. Its large glasshouses have sophisticated semi-automatic lighting, watering and spraying, and machines for sowing and potting. Health and safety is an important issue, especially the use of chemicals.

The nursery competes in a very demanding market, so quality control has to be excellent. The marketing leaflet mentions the charity's aim to provide employment for people with a disability, but emphasises that:

'SHAW Nurseries is not a "therapeutic unit" and is managed very much along commercial lines. We offer ourselves to the trade as wholesale growers to be judged on our quality of plants and the service we provide'.

There is a workforce of twenty: sixteen workers with learning and other disabilities, including two chargehands (one driver, one handyman), a nursery manager, two supervisors and an administrative assistant. The role of non-disabled staff is similar to that of the CAT *moniteurs*. All had a background in horti-culture or administration rather than care.

In the early days, most workers lived in the supported housing on site and the rest lived with their parents. When we visited, four were living in the on-site housing, four were renting from housing associations or private landlords, and eight lived with parents.

The manager thought that most of the workers would have difficulty with less sheltered employment, mainly because of their reduced output, which for some people was directly linked to health problems such as epilepsy. Like the CATs, there wasn't much move-on, partly because of local job shortages. There were only two female workers, mainly because few women were referred to SHAW.

The garden centre

A garden centre adjacent to the nursery came on to the market and, after a major fundraising exercise, SHAW seized the opportunity and bought the centre, which operates as a wholly-owned subsidiary and

limited company. There is an extensive retail area, a café-restaurant, and outdoor attractions including a children's wildlife centre and play area.

The nursery is staffed by a manager, a deputy manager, a house-plants manager, a van driver and 16 workers with learning and other disabilities, plus seasonal part-time staff for busy periods. The centre opens seven days a week and everyone works alternate weekends. None of the workers lives in SHAW housing; some live with parents and others are in rented housing. A handful have moved on into ordinary jobs, and some have left for other reasons.

There is plenty of contact with the public, and workers with disabilities do most things. Like the nursery, the garden centre primarily markets its products and facilities, although publicity leaflets mention in passing that SHAW's aim is to provide employment for people with disabilities.

Supported employment

Following increasing interest within the learning disability field, SHAW had also tried developing supported employment.

However, people working in supported employment outside SHAW tended to be earning less. Finding suitable and reasonably paid jobs in a traditionally low-wage area like the North East could be difficult. One employer they had used paid all employees only £80 a week, and anyone paying £4 an hour was described as 'very good'. However, although people could turn down a job offer if they felt the wages were too low, no-one had done so.

Housing and support

SHAW's supported housing comprises 10 shared houses, providing 40 places. The original aim was to provide housing and employment on the same site, but they are now quite separate.

Each house has four bedrooms plus shared living-room and kitchen; some are mixed, others are single-sex. Residents cannot choose housemates, although they are consulted about new people moving in and staff would try to arrange a move if there were problems.

Although residents do not have to work, over half are employed either part- or full-time, some through SHAW's supported employment services. Those not working can use SHAW's support service which helps people access community-based facilities in areas such as leisure or training.

Funding for the supported housing comes from rents, Housing Benefit, Special Needs Management Allowance (through Home Housing Association), and health and social services. All residents are referred by social services departments and have an individual contract (charges depend on how much support is needed, but are lower than residential-care fees). There is quite a high level of support, with 17 (mostly part-time) care staff, and 24-hour on-call staffing.

At the time of our visit, residents held licences, although a switch to assured tenancies was under discussion. Housing was paid for via Housing Benefit, and care and support by social services. Although it was unclear whether people would be better off working than on benefits, what really matters is that housing costs are separated from care and support costs.

Workers' and residents' views

In talking to workers and to people living in the shared housing, the first point which came up was that some people regretted the decision to sever the close link between housing and work. They had come to SHAW wanting work, so were disappointed when it was not always available. As Robert said, for example:

> 'I was meant to be provided with a job along with the house… the job was the main thing… I came here for the independence'.

Flavia, who had lived in 'the street' (the shared houses) and worked at the nursery for ten years, remembered when most people there had worked for SHAW.

> 'I've got to have something to do or it would drive me round the bend… my brothers and sister were at college… or working… and I felt the odd one out, I wasn't going to have Mum and Dad all my life, I want to settle down and work but not for the money, just to have something to do.'

Although she obviously enjoyed her job, Flavia was realistic about it.

> 'It's hard work, not light work like people think… heavy trolleys, 15 wet plants in a tray is heavy… it tires you out sometimes… but I enjoy it. I've made a lot of friends here and at the club in Cramlington.'

Like people in the packaging workshops at CAT Avèze, they were conscious of the commercial pressures on SHAW's trading activities.

> 'People who can do it fast get picked if there's a hurry and a lot of pressure… sometimes it's hard picking out the best plants.'

Some residents were interested in living in less supported housing, but doubted whether they could manage without 24-hour staff cover (sometimes for medical reasons). They would have needed support services (similar to the French models) but that was not available because of funding constraints.

The location of the houses on the edge of a new town is not ideal. Residents used a minibus service to get into town, and buses or trains to go to Newcastle. Going out in the evening was more problematic and expensive as they had to use taxis.

Key issues

SHAW has very successfully accessed a wide range of funding and its businesses do sufficiently well to pay decent wages. Everyone is on the same pay scale and terms and conditions. Workers with disabilities are at the lower end of the pay scale, earning £6,700–£7,000 a year. Those with responsibilities (such as the chargehands in the nursery) earn more, and, like the CATs, there are also small differentials in wages (£5–£6 weekly), according to ability and attitude.

Unlike the co-ops, SHAW has managed to obtain funding from statutory agencies, and unlike the community businesses, it engages in significant fundraising. It also mentions its role in employing people with disabilities in its literature and advertising.

Like the CATs, SHAW has operated flexibly, developing a range of projects to suit changing circumstances and exploit new funding initiatives. It has built up a 'critical mass' and has a positive reputation and staff expertise in both employment and housing and support. Like the CATs, it sees the future in a combination of sheltered workshops and supported employment.

Developing shared supported housing was innovative in its time but now seems rather old-fashioned; its design was dictated by the constraints of the Housing Corporation funding that was then available. In France, people were assisted to rent ordinary housing dispersed throughout the local community, whereas SHAW's support service is linked to the existing 'bricks and mortar'. This has led SHAW to explore the idea of more flexible support services which could assist SHAW workers wherever they chose to live.

Finally, despite its success, SHAW does not have secure long-term funding, something exacerbated by the recent growth of the contract culture.

Chapter Eleven
Lessons and Recommendations

Introduction

This chapter sets out the main lessons from the research and attempts to explore the implications for policy. As before, space precludes anything more than a few brief recommendations. Readers interested in broader policy issues might therefore want to follow up these points in the companion report *Home, Work and Inclusion* (Simons, 1998).

Lessons from the research

As we suggested right at the start of this report, we would not argue for replicating CATs in the UK. They have their strengths (and their weaknesses), but they are an essentially French phenomenon. However, the contrast between the French and the UK systems helps clarify some of the current policy issues, as set out below.

Employment is a feasible option

Meaningful employment is a feasible option for most people with learning disabilities. This emerges clearly from both the French and the UK context. Indeed, it is not only feasible, but also desirable; for many, a foothold in the workplace is likely to bring significant benefits. These include greater self-confidence, and the opportunity to learn new skills which also help with independent living. Most people are not better off financially, because of the constraints imposed by the present benefits system. Despite this, some people felt that their wages were 'better' than money received from benefits because they had earned it. In other words, there were different meanings attributed to the money received which depended on its source. At a more practical level, some people in supported employment were able to take advantage of company facilities such as a canteen. Some of the supported employment workers had access to private or company pension schemes, as did the workers at SHAW. This enabled them to benefit from employers' contributions and save towards their retirement. Thus there is a wide range of potential benefits from working which will impact on people's health and wellbeing.

None of this is to suggest that we should ignore or devalue other options that people may currently access as part of 'day services' (including social and leisure activities, as well as continuing education). However, it does suggest that there is scope in the UK for a much more concerted attempt to increase both the scale and the scope of employment-related options.

This report adds to the considerable body of existing research highlighting the strength of the 'place and train' model of supported employment. Arguably, access to supported employment programmes ought to be a key feature of all comprehensive local services for people with learning disabilities.

We also think there is a case for developing a more plural approach to employment. While supported employment may be a 'core' requirement, we recognise that ideas like community businesses or social firms also have something to offer. Not least, one of the strengths of the framework that Co-options (**Chapter Eight**) had developed was that it combined supported employment and community businesses in ways which promoted both choice and strategic change.

Some have argued that options like community businesses produce 'manufactured jobs', designed simply to keep people occupied. However, we would argue the work *can* have real value if it provides goods or services that local communities want; this in turn can give people a valued role within their local community. This point was most vividly illustrated by a staff member at the Avèze CAT who heard one of the locals greet a worker with learning disabilities with the words '*Bonjour, boulanger*' ('Good day, baker'). In rural France, the boulangerie is a mainstay of the village and bread is a cultural artefact; to be a baker is be someone!

This generally positive conclusion needs to be qualified. First, we need to look critically at all forms of employment support to see whether they are delivering what people want, including meaningful work which reflects choice and strengths, in non-segregated settings, and a decent income with reasonable working conditions. Our experience suggests that achieving these aims is often a struggle, whatever model of employment is adopted. As a result it is important not to make simple assumptions about outcomes based solely on 'form'.

Equally, while there is arguably scope to make much more of employment initiatives in the UK, it is also clear that that there are some significant barriers to further development.

The potential impact of employment in the UK has been minimised

However, despite the positive developments in the UK employment services, access to work has continued to have relatively little impact on the options open to people. Most importantly, far from opening up a range of housing options (as was the case to some degree at least in France), in the UK the converse has remained the case. As we suggested right at the beginning of the report, where people live tends to determine whether it is feasible to take more than a minimal degree of paid work.

The point is reinforced by another international comparison. In the USA, supported employment agencies have been able to support individuals with learning disabilities to work much longer hours with correspondingly higher earnings and less time spent in non-income-generating services. Cost-benefit studies in the US (Beyer *et al.*, 1997) have shown that, despite the support costs involved, investment in supported employment can produce a net gain for the state (particularly with experienced supported-employment agencies). In contrast, the cost-benefit analysis of the UK system carried out by Beyer and colleagues (1997) revealed much lower rates of return.

The constraints imposed by the UK benefit system

These differences may be due in part to different working methods, and/or greater experience on the part of agencies in the USA.

However, the wider policy context has a role to play too. The relative inefficiency of supported employment in the UK, according to Beyer and his colleagues, is in part a function of the disincentives posed by the UK benefit system, which ensures that people opt to:

> '...earn only up to the therapeutic earnings disregard limit, retain their welfare benefits, and pay no tax'.

Our experience confirms that conclusion. If anything, we found that many people were stopping at the Income Support disregard level of £15, and not even earning up to the higher therapeutic earnings limit. This is not surprising, once you take into account the problems people encounter if their income exceeds the £15 disregard (which has remained unchanged for many years, but is expected to increase to £20 from 1 April 2001).

Firstly, if they are only getting a small Income support top-up which will be lost if they earn higher wages, they risk losing the right to an automatic 'passport' for other benefits (including free prescriptions and optical and dental care, which can be very valuable). Even though they may still be able to make a separate claim for these other benefits because of low income, most people do not do so: it takes time, effort, and knowledge of the system.

Secondly, if they are receiving Housing Benefit and their earnings vary, they are likely to have problems over liaison between the Benefits Agency and their local council Housing Benefit office; in extreme cases this can lead to eviction for rent arrears, and at the very least it causes much stress when arrears letters are received.

Thirdly, there are complications over benefits in kind and expenses (such as transport costs), and people can have benefits stopped with no warning. In the past, expenses or benefits in kind were not included in the disregard calculation, but for some years, any benefits in kind (eg bus pass, free lunch) were. This means that someone receiving free lunches and transport valued at £15, or paying taxi fares of £15 per week (not unusual in areas with poor public transport like the Welsh Valleys) is no better off working. Once the 'hidden' costs of working (such as the need for smart clothes) are included, some of the UK organisations we spoke to felt that people could actually be worse off through working.

Fourthly, couples who are both disabled receive only one Income Support disregard per household, rather than per individual.

Finally, some people we spoke to had experienced problems over whether or not what they were doing met the definition of therapeutic work, and this had led to a sudden and unanounced withdrawal of Income Support. Stories like this then dissuade others from trying to work, because they worry people with learning disabilities and their carers and advisors.

The reluctance of people to move off incapacity benefits may be frustrating for those convinced that full-time work is a viable option for many people. However, in the current framework, such decisions may well be perfectly sensible for the individuals involved. Despite the introduction of in-work benefits (the Disability Working Allowance, now the Disabled Person's Tax Credit) the step of moving off incapacity benefits continues to be an uncertain and risky option for many people with learning disabilities.

There are three fundamental characteristics of the UK benefit system that ensure that it does not work well for people with learning disabilities.

1 It is geared around the notion of 'incapacity'

The core problem with the benefit system is that it deems some sections of the population to be physically or mentally 'incapable' of work, and at the same time tries to assist them back into the workplace, with all the inherent contradictions this implies. Indeed, the assumption of 'incapacity' is no mere semantic nicety, but critical to the way the system works. We started from the premise that whether or not someone can do a particular job will inevitably depend on a number of interlocking factors, including his or her motivation, the nature of the work, the work environment and the support available, as well as the individual's impairment. It is true that for some people it may be very difficult to line up all these factors, and work will remain an unlikely aspiration, but it does not seem sensible to start from the assumption that significant proportions of the population cannot work.

It has been argued that the introduction of in-work benefits (particularly Disability Working Allowance/Disabled Person's Tax Credit) implicitly recognises the notion of 'partial capacity'. However, while some features of these in-work benefits may be helpful, they have not been a great success. Not least, their introduction has maintained the arbitrary and artificial divide between 'remunerative work' (more than 16 hours) and 'therapeutic' work' (fewer than 16 hours).

2 It discriminates against people who have never been economically active

As a group, people with learning disabilities are particularly likely to be reliant on Severe Disablement Allowance. This in turn means they are also likely to require Income Support (which is severely means-tested) to top up their income. This effectively leaves them worse off than people who have worked in the past and who now receive Incapacity Benefit (which is not means-tested). The historical distinction between contributory and non-contributory benefits effectively discriminates against people with learning disabilities (Mental Health Foundation, 1996). There are proposals to abolish Severe Disablement Allowance for new people coming into the system (effectively replacing it with Incapacity Benefit without the contributory requirements). However, it appears likely that people will have to claim this benefit before the age of 20 (25 for people in higher education or undergoing vocational training). This appears to concede the principle, but risks having little impact in practice. Larger numbers of people are likely to still be relying on Income Support, including:

- the existing claimants of Severe Disablement Allowance

- those who fail to claim Incapacity Benefit at a sufficiently early age (encouraging people to declare themselves 'incapable' of work while they are still exploring the options involved in the transition into adulthood does not seem a sensible strategy)

- those who have worked in the past but who fail to meet the more demanding contributory requirements for Incapacity Benefit.

So far, welfare reform has failed to address this situation.

3 It is over-complex

Finally, the benefit system is simply too complex, with vast amounts of time, energy and resources wasted administering it and guiding people around it. Insufficient expertise also means that people are losing out (Corden, 1997). Any changes must make the system less, not more, complex. While some degree of complexity may be inevitable, there also needs to be more security for vulnerable people.

The marginalisation of supported employment

An additional constraint has been the relative marginalisation of supported employment initiatives within Employment Services generally. Most agencies have been funded by social services or through the European Social Fund; the contribution from Employment Services has so far been tiny (Beyer *et al.*, 1996). Faced with mounting financial pressures, social services have increasingly focused on people with greater needs, and those with relatively few support needs who could gain a great deal from employment are at risk of exclusion. The marginalisation of supported employment is reflected in the continuing confusion around the use of the term itself. Most references to supported employment outside the learning disability field confuse and conflate 'place and train' approaches with employer subsidies and sheltered workshops.

The potential contribution of the national minimum wage

Although somewhat bureaucratic, the French system, where disabled individuals are able to combine wages and benefits up to the national minimum wage levels, demonstrates the potentially positive effect of introducing a minimum wage. Yet in the UK many of those to whom we talked were concerned about the potential effects on some people with learning disabilities of just such a development. Beyer *et al.* (1996) found that in 1995 the average hourly wage for people using supported employment was £3.50, suggesting that most were likely to be earning at or above the £3.60 per hour rate at which the national minimum wage was eventually established in April 1999. Those earning a little below the prescribed level will probably have found themselves with a welcome pay rise. However, our respondents in this survey had expressed worries about the potential impact on some particular sub-groups. These concerns effectively reflect **three separate factors, all of which continue to be concerns since the implementation of the national minimum wage in the UK**.

1 The lack of proposed adjustments to the Income Support regulations

The upper level of the therapeutic earnings limit was raised to bring it into line with the introduction of the national minimum wage. However, the Income Support disregard of £15 was not changed. Given that Income Support is means-tested (£1 less benefit for every extra £1 earned), many employment agencies had sought a pragmatic adaptation to this situation, effectively negotiating a wage of £15 for individuals regardless of the actual hours worked. The introduction of the national minimum wage at the rate of £3.60 an hour effectively made these arrangements illegal unless people were working no more than a little over four hours. People who were working more hours but getting less benefit were not likely to be affected.

There is another problems with only being able to work about four hours a week: many people with learning disabilities take time to learn new tasks, or find it hard to remember from one week to the next. They may need to work a reasonable number of hours (though not necessarily full-time) to keep up their skills. Because the system makes it so difficult for them to work more hours, their opportunity to grow and learn is compromised.

2 The lack of proposed accommodation for people with very low productivity

Groups seeking to support people with more complex needs into employment were concerned at the failure to allow any accommodation for people who, because of much lower productivity, were unlikely to be able to command a wage at the level of the minimum wage. As it is, people with complex needs remain relatively marginalised within the different forms of supported employment, and there were fears that the national minimum wage could only service to exacerbate this situation. While in theory it might be possible to use continuing support to ensure that the individual remains sufficiently productive, for some this will be an expensive solution that is difficult to deliver.

3 The financial fragility of some community businesses

Finally, some of the community businesses were paying people £15 as a compromise between the benefit system and their limited income. They, as much as any other employer, are required to pay the minimum wage. However, while many would aspire to be commercial entities capable of paying living wages to all employees, in practice some were too financially fragile to pay the full rate, particularly in the early stages of their development. The concern was that the introduction of the national minimum wage would increase the pressures on social firms to be productive at the expense of being inclusive.

The perverse structure of housing services and housing funding systems

The lack of impact of employment on other life choices is partly a function of the kinds of factor identified above. However, it also reflects the continuing perverse structures for funding housing and support options.

The situation is particularly difficult for people currently living in residential care, which is simply geared to the assumption that residents will not be working. Effectively, residential care acts as a charging framework that ensures that people have no incentive to move off incapacity benefits.

The problem is compounded by the continuing widespread assumption that residential care is the only appropriate option for people with learning disabilities, particularly those needing substantial levels of support (Simons & Ward, 1997). This is despite the evidence that supported living options can be a very viable alternative (Emerson *et al.*, 1999). Further, despite a policy aim of promoting independence, there are continuing perverse incentives for commissioners in favour of residential care, including the Residential Allowance component of Income Support, and 'preserved rights' to enhanced social security payments for people who moved into residential care prior to 1993 (Simons, 1998).

Moreover, 'special-needs housing', as currently structured, *cannot* deliver the volume required. More people *must* be supported in general-needs housing. The French system demonstrates that, if people are allowed to combine wages and benefits (including 'housing benefit') and can access appropriate support, then renting private and social housing is possible on a large scale.

Given the advantages of ordinary housing, support services must not be tied to a particular building or employment base. SHAW and CAT Avèze demonstrate how this can limit people's options. If people are gaining more independence by working, it is likely that they will also want to extend that to their home life, but many will need flexible support at home as well as at work.

However, even if more people with learning disabilities are enabled to access mainstream housing options, there are still likely to be significant numbers of people living in residential care for the foreseeable future; by implication, some changes will be required to the charging framework for residential care. Work ought to be an option which is encouraged and facilitated whatever the individual's living arrangements.

Recommendations

All these conclusions add up to an argument for substantial reforms. Normally, we would be hesitant about arguing for wholesale 'reform' of 'the system', not least because there is little evidence that calls for radical change have much effect. We are certainly not the first to recognise many of the problems that exist. However, there are reasons to believe that a debate about these issues would be timely. We have a Government that appears to be committed to welfare reform (although the results so far have not been entirely helpful). Similarly, the recent White Paper on 'modernising' social services argued that the latter have a significant role in promoting '*social and economic participation*' and asserted that employment is one of the best '*pathways to independence*'. Finally, one of the Government's flagship policies has been the introduction of the various 'New Deals', including a version specifically targeted at disabled people.

All this provides a context in which positive change might just emerge. However, the risk is that people with learning disabilities will find that such changes pass them by. The particular set of circumstances in which people with learning disabilities tend to find themselves (reliant to much greater extents than other groups on the uncomfortable combination of means-tested Income Support and residential care, coupled with marginalisation both in the work place and in employment services) is unlikely to have been in the forefront of policy-makers' minds. The recommendations that follow are inevitably tentative. However, by starting with the issues as they face people with learning disabilities, and trying to work out what might work for them, we hoped to stimulate some debate about these issues.

1. Abandon the concept of incapacity, replacing the current incapacity benefits with a guaranteed income that reflects a 'disadvantaged in the job market' status

The notion of 'incapacity' should be abandoned. The real issue is whether people are disadvantaged in the job market because of their needs for support and/or workplace adaptations, or indeed because of discriminatory attitudes or practice. For some people it may be that it is simply not in their interest to seek work. Others may fail to find the kinds of work or support they need. People disadvantaged in the labour markets should therefore be paid a benefit set at a level that allows them to live in acceptable comfort and dignity, and reflects the increased risk of long-term poverty.

2. Allow people to retain the status of 'disadvantaged in the job market' for as long as they meet the criteria, regardless of how long they have been in work

When someone with learning disabilities loses a job, they are still likely to be disadvantaged in the job market and the resources they require to live comfortably will not have diminished. Given that the fear of losing benefits if a job does not work out is commonplace among people with learning disabilities (and families, supporters and advisors), some security is necessary.

The principle established with the Disability Work Allowance should be extended and embedded in the new system. The new minimum guaranteed income should be available to people as long as they still fit the original criteria for inclusion. If someone loses their income from work, or has that income reduced, they should automatically qualify for benefit at the original level, not just for two years, but for as long as they remain at a disadvantage in the job market.

3. Abolish the current arbitrary distinction between incapacity benefits and in-work benefits based on the 16-hour cut-off

We suggest that all current incapacity benefits plus the Disabled Person's Tax Credit should be merged into a single guaranteed income for anyone accepted as disadvantaged in the job market. For anybody working more than a nominal amount this could take the form of a tax credit. Abandoning the 16 hours dividing line would represent an acceptance that all work is valued. It would also be much more flexible (and most important) secure; there would be no risks inherent in working more hours, or complexities for people who need to vary their hours up or down. Such a change would have the effect of ironing out the current gaps and complexities inherent in switching between incapacity and in-work benefits.

Rather than the current (very acute) means-testing of Income Support, the guaranteed income would be tapered (as the Disabled Person's Tax Credit is now) ensuring there is a much more consistent incentive to work longer hours.

There will still probably be a case for a 'disregard' (effectively a point below which there is no adjustment of benefits), since this would reduce the administration costs for people who want to make an initial foray into the world of work.

In some ways this proposal is less outrageous than it might seem. Effectively, it would involve nothing more than extending the current Disabled Person's Tax Credit 'downwards'.

4. Allow people to combine benefits and earnings up to and beyond the minimum wage level

The benefits system should be linked with the minimum wage to provide an incentive for people to work, regardless of the number of hours involved or their level of productivity. Arguably, the current use of employers' subsidies should be redirected as a mechanism for ensuring that people with the most complex needs (who require long-term support) are not excluded from the workplace (for more detailed suggestions see Jackson *et al.*, 1999).

5. Review the funding mechanisms for housing and support

The current perverse incentives and rigidities, which encourage commissioners to rely on residential care as the main form of housing and support for people with learning disabilities, need to be addressed. Since we completed our fieldwork, there have already been a number of government proposals to change funding systems, including the reform of Housing Benefit (Department of Social Security, 1998) and the abolition of Residential Allowance for new people coming into the system (Department of Health, 1998). The full implications of these proposed changes are likely to be complex (see Simons, forthcoming, for more details). However, unless some of the barriers that remain a particular problem for people with learning disabilities (the issue of 'preserved rights' is an obvious example) are addressed, the risk is that their impact will be relatively small. The Government appears unlikely to accept the recommendations of the Royal Commission on the funding of long-term care. As a result, many of the broader issues remain unresolved. For this reason we would argue that there is a case for exploring more flexible approaches to the funding of housing and support options, which could incorporate more consistent financial incentives for commissioners to explore a wider range of housing and support options.

6. Revise the requirements on local authorities to charge for social care services so as to remove the current disincentives to taking paid employment

Current funding and charging rules for residential care are effectively based on the assumption that people in residential care will not be working; once beyond the Income Support disregard, they leave no incentive for the resident to increase his or her income through work. However, this is only the most acute instance of the way charging policies are impacting on all forms of social care. As incomes rise above Income Support levels, then users of social care services are subject to varied and contradictory charging regimes (Audit Commission, 2000). In some cases this interacts with the means-testing of social security benefits (and in some instances Housing Benefit) in ways which ensure that some individuals gain little or nothing from paid work; what Kestenbaum and Carva (1998) have called the '*personal assistance trap*'.

We think people should be able to work for financial gain even if they are in residential care, or are using domiciliary or other services. There would inevitably be financial implications for purchasers, but there is a strong case for rethinking the framework for charging for services in order to avoid the risk that charging undermines the introduction of the wider policy aims of promoting independence through work.

7. Review the regulation of social care services

One of the reasons behind the over-reliance on residential care has been the lack of statutory regulation of the alternatives (Simons & Ward, 1998). Yet again, since the original draft of this report was completed, this is an area in which the Government has proposed reforms, including the development of independent commissioners in care standards and the regulation of domiciliary care agencies. However, as in the other examples of reform already discussed, however helpful these developments may prove to be, in themselves they are unlikely to address all the relevant issues.

Not least, the ambiguities in the boundary between residential care and domiciliary services are likely to remain a problem. We argue that supported living arrangements, where there is clear contractual separation between housing and support providers, and where individuals have security of tenure, should be seen, in regulatory terms, as domiciliary services. Similarly, where adult placements are established as part of an approved scheme overseen by the appropriate regulators, they should not (in regulatory terms) be treated as a residential care home.

More fundamentally, there is little evidence that thinking about regulation has moved on from assumptions geared largely to existing residential care for elderly people. The functions of a regulatory system need not only to include protection against abuse or neglect from incompetent residential care providers, but also to be seen in the wider context of civil rights, discrimination and exclusion. For these reasons, we argue that the implementation of the existing regulatory changes needs to be accompanied by a radical re-think of the role of regulation. To take one very practical example, we suggest that regulation should be extended so as to include commissioners (as well as providers) within its scope. The aim would be to ensure that appropriate systems are in place that ensure both access to, and protection within, all forms of housing and support services.

8. Develop an effective framework for promoting both supported employment and community business/social firms

The lack of a coherent funding and organisation framework for supported employment (and other employment initiatives) risks undermining the impact of the New Deal for Disabled People. Even the most successful and established of the organisations we visited wsere dependent on complex combinations of mainly short term funding (eg spot purchase, European Social Firm grants). Some had been unable to continue, partly because of funding problems. One of the strengths of the French model is the (relatively) secure funding system which underpins not only CATs but other employment and support services. There is a case for a re-think involving a number of government departments, including the Department for Education and Employment, the Department of Health and the Department for Trade and Industry, in order to ensure the development of a more coherent framework. This is likely to include:

- greater recognition of the value of 'place and train' options

- better access to Employment Service resources

- more flexible funding arrangements, particularly in terms of money assigned for vocational training

- further thinking about the role of social services in enabling people with learning disabilities to access the New Deal

- mechanisms for disseminating good practice and yardsticks against which to measure the performance of providers

- development of 'inclusive' regeneration strategies, which recognise the potential of supported employment and community business/social firms, and which provide access to regeneration funding.

9. *Review approaches to strategic change in day services*

There will still be an important role for social services departments in the development of supported employment, even if the contribution from other sources becomes more significant. Yet the evidence is that most resources within 'day services' for people with learning disabilities remain locked up in day centres (Jones & Wright, 1996; Department of Health, 1999). In this context, the management of strategic change in day services will become increasingly important. Without some release of resources it will be hard to develop reliable alternatives to day centres on a sufficient scale to convince both people with learning disabilities and their families. Yet the consequential closure of some day centres will inevitably generate real fears and concerns about the future on the part of those same users and carers. Managing the process of change will be a real challenge. As we have suggested, in some areas, community businesses and social firms have played an important role in addressing these issues. The use of direct payments (Holman & Collins, 1997) may well also have a part to play in freeing up resources. However, arguably, there needs to be a much more concerted attempt to develop structures for the orderly reconfiguration of day services, including attempts to focus 'modernisation' resources in this area.

A final word

What is unusual about this report is the fact that we have attempted to set the issue of work in the context of housing and support options. Whatever reforms come about, unless the link is recognised and policy suitably adjusted substantial numbers of people with learning disabilities will continue to be forced to make the difficult choice between having their own home and having a 'proper job'. This is not a compromise that people should have to make.

References

Audit Commission (2000) *Charging with Care: How councils charge for home care.* London: Audit Commission.

Beckett, S. (1997) Real jobs, real pay. *Values Into Action Newsletter* **87** Winter 96/97.

Beyer, S. (1993) Supported employment, the fragile truth. *LLAIS* **28** Spring 15–17.

Beyer, S. (1995) Real Jobs and Supported Employment. In: T. Philpot & L. Ward (Eds) *Values and Visions: Changing ideas in services for people with learning difficulties.* Oxford: Butterworth Heinemann.

Beyer, S., Goodere, L. & Kilsby, M. (1997) *The Costs and Benefits of Supported Employment.* London: The Stationery Office.

Booth, T., Simons, K. & Booth, W. (1990) *Outward Bound: Relocation and community care for people with learning disabilities.* Milton Keynes: Open University Press.

Corden, A. (1997) *Supported Employment, People and Money.* Social Policy Reports No 7. York: Social Policy Research Unit, University of York.

Davis, A., Murray, J. & Flynn, M. (1993) *Normal Lives? The financial circumstances of people with learning disabilities.* Manchester: National Development Team.

Department of Health (1989) *Caring for People: Community care into the next decade and beyond.* London: HMSO.

Department of Health (1999) *Facing the Facts: Services for people with a learning disability.* A policy impact study of social care and health services. London: DoH.

Department of Health (1998) *Modernising Social Services: Promoting independence, improving protection, raising standards.* Cd 4169. London: The Stationery Office.

Department of Social Security (1996) *Social Security Statistics.* London: The Stationery Office.

Department of Social Security (1998) *Supporting People: A new policy and funding framework for support services.* London: Department of Social Security for the Inter-Departmental Review of Funding for Supported Accommodation.

Emerson, E., Robertson, J., Hatton, C., Gregory, N., Kessissoglou, S., Hallam, S., Knapp, M., Jäbrink, K., Netten, A. & Noonan Walsh, P. (1999) *Quality and Costs in Residential Supports for People with Learning Disabilities: Summary and implications.* Manchester: Hester Adrian Research Centre.

Flynn, M. (1989) *Independent Living for Adults with Mental Handicap: 'A place of my own'.* London: Cassell Educational Ltd.

Griffiths, S. (1997) *Housing Benefit and Supported Housing: The impact of recent changes.* York: York Publishing Services Ltd for the Joseph Rowntree Foundation.

Grove, B., Freudenberg, M., Harding, A. & O'Flynn, D. (1997) *The Social Firms Handbook.* Brighton: Pavilion.

Holman, A. & Collins, J. (1997) *Funding Freedom.* London: Values Into Action.

Insertion et Travail Adapté (1994) **99** June. Cergy Pointoise, France: Editions Dialogues.

Insertion et Travail Adapté (1995) **109** October. Cergy Pointoise, France: Editions Dialogues.

Jackson, T., Everett, G. & Beyer, S. (1999) *Reforming the Supported Placement Scheme to Promote Career Development and Access for People with Greater Support Needs.* Cumbria: Association for Supported Employment.

Jones, C. & Wright, K. (1996) Public expenditure on services for people with intellectual disabilities. *Journal of Applied Research in Intellectual Disabilities* **9** (4).

Kestenbaum, A. & Carva, H. (1998) *Work, Rest and Pay.* York: Joseph Rowntree Foundation.

Kilsby, M., Beyer, S. & Evans, C. (1995) *Supported Employment – Full or part-time services?* Cardiff: Welsh Centre for Learning disabilities.

Labourdette, A., Laforcade, M. & Videla-Haidick, M. (1990) L'évaluation des centres d'aide par le travail: l'exemple de l'Aquitaine. *Revue Français des Affaires Sociales* **44** 133–159.

Lister, T. & Ellis, L. (1992) *A Survey of Supported Employment Services in England, Wales and Scotland.* Manchester: National Development Team.

McGrath, M. (1995) Employment-focused day services in Wales. *LLAIS* **37** Summer 6–9.

Mental Health Foundation (1996) *Building Expectations: Opportunities and services for people with a learning disability.* Report of the Mental Health Foundation Committee of Inquiry. London: Mental Health Foundation.

Neath, J. & Schriner, K. (1998) Power to people with disabilities: empowerment issues in employment programming. *Disability and Society* **13** (2) 217–228.

Pozner, A., Hammond, J. & Tannam, V. (1993) *An Evaluation of Supported Employment Initiatives for Disabled People.* London: Department of Employment Research Services No 17.

Roeher Institute (1996) *Disability, Community and Society: Exploring the links.* North York, Ontario: Roeher Institute.

Samoy, E. with Waterplas, L. (1992) *Sheltered Employment in the European Community: Final report to the Commission of the European Communities.* Brussels: Commission of the European Communities.

Schmitt, M. J. (1995) Employment Policies for People with Disabilities in France. In: K. Leichsenring & C. Strümple (Eds) (1995) *Mandatory Employment or Equal Opportunities? Employment policies for people with disabilities in the UN-European region.* Vienna: European Centre for Social Welfare Policy and Research.

Shanley, A. & Rose, J. (1993) A consumer survey of adults with learning disabilities currently doing work experience: their satisfaction with work and wishes for the future. *Mental Handicap Research* **6** (3) 250–261.

Sikking, M. (1986) *Co-ops with a Difference: Worker co-ops for people with special needs.* London: ICOM Co-Publications.

Simons, K. (1993) *Sticking up for Yourself: Self-advocacy and people with learning disabilities.* York: Joseph Rowntree Foundation.

Simons, K. (1995) *My Home, My Life.* London: Values Into Action.

Simons, K. (1998) *Home, Work and Inclusion: The social policy implications of supported living for people with learning disabilities.* York: Joseph Rowntree Foundation.

Simons, K. (forthcoming) *Pushing Open the Door: The impact of the Housing Options advisory service.* (Brighton: Pavilion.)

Simons, K. & Ward, L. (1998) *A Foot in the Door: The early years of supported living in the UK.* Brighton: Pavilion Publishing/ National Development Team.

Szivos, S. (1990) Attitudes to work and their relationship to self-esteem and aspiration among young adults with a mild mental handicap. *British Journal of Mental Handicap* **36** (2) 108–117.

Thornton, P. & Lunt, N. (1997) *Employment Policies for Disabled People in Eighteen Countries: A review.* York: Social Policy Research Unit, University of York.

Velche, D. & Ravaud J-F. (1995) Progressive Implementation of the Employment Obligation of People with Disabilities in France since 1987. In: S. Bengtsson (Ed) *Employment of Persons with Disabilities: Colloquium in connection with a research project.* Copenhagen: Social Forsknings Instituttet.

Vivre Ensemble (1993) **15** January–February. Paris: UNAPEI.

Vivre Ensemble (1995) **28** June–August. Paris: UNAPEI.

Wertheimer, A. (1992a) *Changing Lives: Supported employment and people with learning disabilities.* Manchester: National Development Team.

Wertheimer, A. (1992b) *The Real Jobs Initiative (1990–92): An evaluation.* Manchester: National Development Team.

Zafiropoulos, M. (1981) *Les Arriérés: de l'asile à l'usine.* Paris: Payot.

Zibri, G. (1995) Les emplois semi-protégés: un levier pour l'insertion professionnelle et sociale (France). *Handicaps et Inadaptations: Les Cahiers du CTNERHI* **65–66** January–June 43–49.

Glossary of French acronyms and terms

AAH
Allocation aux Adultes Handicapés
Disability benefit for adults (similar to UK Disability Living Allowance)

ADAPEI
Association Départementale des Amis et Parents d'Enfants Inadaptés de …(name of département eg Tarn)
Association of the friends and parents of disabled children in … (name of département eg Tarn); similar to local MENCAP branches in UK (see also entries below for UNAPEI and UNAREI)

AGEFIPH
Association pour la Gestion du Fond pour l'Insertion Professionnelle des Personnes Handicapées
Funding organisation for vocational integration of disabled people

Allocation Logement
French housing benefit (available for both social rented and private rented housing)

APAJH
Association pour les Adultes et Jeunes Handicapés
Association for disabled adults and young people (similar to MENCAP in UK, but founded by professionals rather than parents, with local groups in each département and a national organisation)

atelier protégé
sheltered workshop

CAT
Centre d'Aide par le Travail
Centre of help through work

COTOREP
Commission Technique d'Orientation et de Réclassement Professionnel
Commission for occupational guidance and rehabilitation (also carries out assessment for disability benefits: one for each département)

département
administrative unit equivalent to UK county

DDASS
Direction Départementale des Affaires Sanitaires et Sociales
Decentralised central government organisation (responsible to the national Ministry of Health and Social Affairs) for each département; the name is the same in all départements

DDSS	Direction du Développement Social et de la Santé du Gard County Council Social Services and Public Health Department for the Département of Gard (note that the name will vary slightly from département to département; the DDSS is responsible to the Conseil Général du Gard, the equivalent of the county council; not to be confused with the DDASS, which is an organ of national government)
éducateur (spécialisé)	(male or both genders) social worker specialising in working with children, young people or adults in institutions and in resettlement and support services including those linked to CATs; training is three years full-time including placements (*pro rata* longer if part-time), entry requirement equivalent to UK A level (many candidates study at postgraduate level, following their first degree; those already working and with five years experience can also apply)
éducatrice (spécialisée)	female éducateur spécialisé
EPSR	Equipe de Préparation et Suite de Réclassement Team for preparation and continuation of rehabilitation (one model of supported employment organisation in France)
foyer occupationnel	occupational centre, equivalent to UK day centre
HLM	Habitation à Loyer Modéré Housing at Reasonable Rents, ie social rented housing with (relatively) low rents, and the organisations providing this, approximately equivalent to UK council housing or housing associations
IRTS	Institut Régional du Travail Social [de … name of region eg Languedoc-Roussillon] Regional institute for the training of social work professionals [de … name of region eg Languedoc-Roussillon]
moniteur (d'atelier)	(male or both genders) work-based supervisor specialising in working with disabled young people or adults in institutions, including Ateliers Protégés and CATs; specialist training available, but all must already have experience in their trade or profession
moniteur éducateur	(male or both genders) social worker specialising in working with children, young people or adults in institutions, including CATs, and resettlement and support services; training is two years full-time including placements (*pro rata* longer if part-time), entry requirement equivalent to UK A level (those already working can also apply)
monitrice (d'atelier)	female moniteur
monitrice éducatrice	female moniteur-éducateur

région	region (important administrative and organisational entity in France, somewhat similar to Northern Ireland, Scotland and Wales in the UK)
RMI	Revenu Minimum d'Insertion Minimum income for disadvantaged people (similar to UK Income Support)
SMIC	Salaire Minimum Interprofessionnel de Croissance Minimum base salary/wage for all posts (French minimum wage)
Service de Suite/ Service d'Accompagnement	French services providing resettlement and floating support (supporting people in mainstream housing in the community)
UNAPEI	Union National des Associations de Parents d'Enfants Inadaptés National union of ADAPEIs, ie associations of parents of disabled children (similar to national MENCAP in UK)

Contact list

Antur Waunfawr
Menna Jones
Antur Waunfawr
Bryn Pistyll
Waunfawr
Gwynedd LL55 4BJ
Tel 01286 650721
Fax 01286 650059

Cleansweep and Bristol PATHWAY Employment Service
Sean O'Brien
Pathway Employment Service
Barton Hill Settlement
43 Dulcie Road
Barton Hill
Bristol BS5 0AX
Tel 0117 955 9219

Co-options Ltd
Andie Lowe
Co-options Ltd
Co-options Building
Victoria Avenue
Prestatyn
Denbighshire LL19 9DF
Tel 01745 851454
Fax 01745 851458

Menter Fachwen
Christine Jones/Simon Higgins
Menter Fachwen
London House
Cwm-y-Glo
Caernarfon
Gwynedd LL55 4DT
Tel 01286 872014

SHAW Projects
Peter Elliott
Chief Executive
SHAW Projects
Kielder Avenue
Beacon Lane
Cramlington
Northumberland NE23 8JT
Tel 01670 733966
Fax 01670 590115

South East Wales PATHWAY Employment Service
Alan Morgan
South East Wales Pathway
Employment Service
5a Gravel Lane
New Market Square
Blackwood
Gwent NP12 1AG
Tel 01495 222899
Fax 01495 222852

Welsh Initiative for Supported Employment (WISE)
Kaynie McLellan
Welsh Initiative for Supported Employment
17 Mansel Street
Swansea SA1 5SG
Tel 01792 538538
Fax 01792 538539

Acknowledgements

I would like to express my gratitude to the parents who made submissions to the Inquiry and for whom the telling of their stories was painful and distressing. Their participation was fundamental to my understanding of the practices of the past and the need for legislative change for the future. I am also very grateful for the co-operation I received from organisations involved in supporting bereaved families as their expertise and experience in this regard was essential to my recommendations.

I would also like to thank most sincerely the clinicians, pathologists, medical social workers and hospital managers who assisted the work of the Inquiry in any way. Their professionalism and acceptance of the need for change was of great benefit in writing this Report.

I would like to record my appreciation to colleagues in Northern Ireland, England and Scotland whose experience of dealing with similar Inquiries was of immense interest and value to me.

Dr. Deirdre Madden
Chairperson

20th December 2005

Executive Summary

1 General Overview

1.1 This Report aims to set out the general facts in relation to paediatric post-mortem practice in Ireland from 1970 to 2000, the way in which information was communicated to parents of deceased children in relation to post-mortem examinations, and how these practices might be improved upon for the future. It is written in the knowledge that many of the practices related here are historical, and that professional guidelines and hospital policies have changed significantly since 2000. It is acknowledged that some of the recommendations made herein may already have been implemented in many hospitals. However, despite the changes that have been made, it is important for bereaved families and the general public to be made aware of the practices of the past in order that the recommendations for legislative change made in this Report can be understood in context.

1.2 The death of a loved one is probably the most difficult event any of us will experience in our lifetime. When the death is that of a child, the trauma and grief is immeasurably increased, whether or not death was expected. The death of a child is inherently against the natural order of life where the oldest die first, and it can cause lifelong heartbreak for parents, siblings, grandparents and extended families. Parents instinctively seek to protect their child's body from any further perceived invasion and simply want to bury him/her with as much love and dignity as possible.

1.3 In some circumstances a coroner may order a post-mortem examination to be carried out to ascertain the cause of the child's death. This is done in order to comply with the legal requirements of the justice system. It is a compulsory post mortem and the consent of the child's parents is not required or sought. Compulsion is always difficult, and having choices taken from them often angers parents. However, despite their grief and anger, many parents want to know as much as possible about the process of the coroner's post-mortem examination. Although they are not in control of the legal process, they want to be informed as to what the process entails, and as to what choices they have following the conclusion of the post mortem.

1.4 In other cases that do not involve the coroner, hospital clinicians may seek to have a post mortem carried out on a child who has died in the hospital. This is to ensure that all appropriate clinical procedures were carried out to the child's best possible advantage, and that as much information as possible may be given to the family as to why the child died.

1.5 Removal of organs during a post mortem is a necessary element of the examination. Standard practice in this respect remains the same today as it was in 1970. Organs are removed, weighed, examined and sampled in an effort to establish in detail the cause of the patient's death. In the past, organs were retained for further examination and sometimes subsequently used for educational and research purposes. Retention is particularly required for examination of the brain as it is an extremely soft tissue which requires fixation for a period of time prior to examination. In the case of other organs such as the heart, retention facilitates more detailed and specialist examination, often in consultation with surgeons and other clinicians involved in the patient's treatment. This is done in order to provide a more accurate and detailed diagnosis of the cause of death and is not confined to paediatric post mortems.

1.6 Although this Report frequently refers to 'clinicians' or 'medical professionals' or 'doctors', other healthcare professionals were, and are, also very much involved in caring for bereaved families. These expressions are intended to encompass all those involved in the team caring for the child and its parents. 'Autopsy' and 'post mortem' are used interchangeably throughout the Report. 'Parent(s)' is intended to include the child's legal guardian(s).

2 Communication

2.1 It is important to stress at the outset the distinction between coroner and hospital post mortems in relation to the communication and consent process. In a coroner's case, a hospital pathologist acting on behalf of the coroner will usually carry out the post-mortem examination. It has not always been explained to parents that the pathologist in such cases is not entitled to discuss the post mortem with the family, as this is a matter for the coroner. Communication in such cases has usually been very limited and this has often caused distress and anxiety to families. Information has not always been disclosed to families in relation to the legal process undertaken by the coroner and any rights the parents may have on conclusion of the investigation by the coroner. Consent is neither required nor sought from parents in such cases.

2.2 In hospital post mortems, the evidence submitted to the Inquiry shows that in the past the policy in all hospitals was to seek a form of consent from parents for the examination. However, it was not hospital or professional policy to inform parents that in the course of a post mortem to be carried out on their child, organs may be retained, stored, and subsequently disposed of. The shock, anger and betrayal felt by families at the revelation of these long-standing practices highlight the existence of a significant communication gap between the medical establishment and the general public that has been at the root of this controversy.

2.3 In the past, communication regarding post-mortem practice was not always what it should have been when judged by today's standards. The standards of disclosure of information and the legal norms upon which those standards were based would undoubtedly be judged inadequate today. The discomfort that may have accompanied discussions around the issue of hospital post mortems in the past may sometimes have been interpreted as clinical arrogance or insensitivity, but there is no evidence to suggest that it was malevolent or ill-intentioned. It may well be described as professional paternalism, typified by the attitude that 'doctor knows best'.

2.4 In the context of disclosure of information to patients relating to retention and ultimate disposal of organs, doctors argue that their reluctance to inform families of the details surrounding the post-mortem examination and retention of organs was to protect rather than insult, that they had a different professional perspective of the body, that the information was likely to cause more grief and pain than it alleviated, and that therefore they were behaving ethically. This argument has a clear and reasonable humanitarian appeal but rests on a paternalistic basis that patients, parents, and the general public now interpret as unnecessarily secretive and disrespectful. Medical paternalism is unacceptable by modern standards whereby doctor and patient now stand in a different relationship to each other, one that is based on mutual trust and shared understanding.

2.5 For the future, communication and authorisation are vital and must be enshrined in legislation. Language, timing, and venue are all-important aspects of this process. It is not intended to prescribe how the information is imparted to parents, as each family will react differently to the situation. Disclosure of information should evolve in a discussion between clinician and family, assisted by the expertise of a pathologist if required by the family, and/or an information booklet that the parents can read, have explained to them if necessary, and take home with them if they so wish. Given the importance of commencing an autopsy within a certain time after death, it may not always be possible for parents to have as much time as they would like to reflect on the choice they are presented with. However, this does not detract from the obligation to impart as much information as necessary in the circumstances and to answer any questions the family may have regarding the process.

3 Consent

3.1 Although pathologists have been denounced for the practices of the past, they generally had no involvement in obtaining consent for hospital post-mortem examinations. This was seen as the responsibility of the clinical team looking after the patient and the pathologist rarely had any direct contact with the child's parents. The treating clinician was deemed best placed to discuss the child's death and post mortem with the family as he/she already had a relationship with them in many cases. Also it was not deemed appropriate or desirable that the parents should meet the pathologist who would perform this procedure on their child, as such an encounter might be too distressing for parents. This situation remains unchanged, though pathologists now receive a copy of the consent form signed by parents prior to performance of the post-mortem examination. Exceptionally, in one hospital the pathologist routinely meets the parents prior to the post-mortem examination and explains the performance of the examination to them. Some pathologists in other hospitals also facilitate such meetings on request.

3.2 Although it was and is hospital policy to obtain consent from parents for a hospital post-mortem examination to be carried out on their child, up to 1999 this was generally not informed by an explanation of what the examination entailed or the possibility of organ retention. In the context of post-mortem examinations, consent was and is not required or sought to an autopsy ordered by a coroner in the exercise of his/her legal functions on behalf of the State.

3.3 A balance must be struck between ensuring that the appropriate amount of information is given which facilitates a genuine choice, and causing further distress and anguish to grieving parents. This is a balance that may only be struck on an individualised basis as people differ widely in their informational needs and comprehension levels. The clinician who is engaged in discussion with the parents must take on the responsibility of ensuring that parents are given the information they require to put themselves in the position whereby they are equipped to ask pertinent questions and to make a genuine decision. Details as to what the autopsy involves must always be offered but should not be forced on unwilling and grieving parents against their will. To do so would be a denial of choice and respect for their autonomy, as well as being harsh and cruel.

4 Why were Parents not Told about Organ Retention?

4.1 This Report concludes that, up to 1999, parents were generally not told that organs might be retained at a post-mortem examination carried out on their child. There are differing perspectives on the reasons why parents were not told of organ-retention practices. This Report cannot reconcile these views in individual cases.

4.2 Doctors argue that they did not tell parents about organ retention for the parents' own good; parents were upset enough already and did not need the information. The giving of such disturbing and distasteful details to distressed and vulnerable parents could be a complex, lengthy and upsetting process, not easily or speedily undertaken. It was thought to be unnecessarily cruel to discuss incisions and organ retention with newly bereaved parents. This approach contrasts sharply with the views of some parents that, for them, the worst had already happened – the death of their child – and that further information could not have added to their upset. Parents are angry and distressed that this practice took place without their knowledge, that their child's organs were retained for various periods of time, and then disposed of in a manner and place unknown to them.

4.3 Another reason given for the non-disclosure is that doctors had a different perspective in relation to organs and did not equate organs with the body as a whole. Doctors generally did not see the organs as having any emotional significance once the child was dead – ensuring that the body be released for burial within the timeframe sought by the family was more significant, in their view, than all the organs being replaced in the body for burial. Doctors were trained to pay less attention to the emotional and symbolic aspects of organs, and to concentrate on the functional or medical aspects. Doctors looked at organs to determine how well they were working or whether a particular intervention had been successful. They generally did not consider that relatives might have looked at organs in a different way. Pathologists also held this functional view of organs. They felt that organs, though clearly deserving of respect, could be considered separately from the body and were not essential for the purposes of viewing and burying the body. Clearly, many parents did not and do not share this view, and regard the heart or brain as symbolic of their child's spirit and personality. For these parents, the burial of the body without the organs is an affront to their grief and the child's dignity.

4.4. Some parents perceive that doctors did not tell them because the doctors believed that parents would not consent if they were told the truth of what was involved in the post mortem, or that parents would not understand, or that doctors did not have the inclination to spend the necessary time explaining the process to the parents. Some parents are of the view that the actions of pathologists in performing a post mortem and retaining organs showed disrespect for the child's body.

5 Medical Culture

5.1 The truth as to why parents were not told about organ retention is probably a mixture of the motivations outlined above, depending on the individual clinician and the time and culture when the child died. There is no doubt that in recent years paternalism has dissipated to a large degree in Irish medical practice, with greater recognition of the autonomy of the patient and the therapeutic alliance formed by trust and communication between doctor and patient. However, during the earlier years which are the subject of this Report, paternalism was very much part of the culture and ethos of the profession, with the result that many clinicians who may be the subject of complaint by parents in their submissions to the Inquiry may have been behaving no differently from their peers in other branches of medicine. Their attitude was not one of disrespect, but rather a pragmatism borne from medical education and training. This is not to seek to justify the practices of the past, but rather to put them in the context of the time.

5.2 Although the stories recounted by the parents are traumatic and shocking by today's standards, fairness demands that the conduct of doctors be judged by the standards of the time, not by the ethical principles that are now expected as standard practice. However, as the culture of the medical relationship changed over the years, particularly since the early 1990s, anyone in the medical profession who reflected on the practice of retaining organs without consent should have recognised that it was contrary to changing expectations of openness and transparency. That this reflection, and corresponding change in practice, did not take place within the medical profession sooner than it did, must be recognised as a serious weakness in the system.

5.3 Every profession must review its practices on a regular basis to ensure that the highest standards are being maintained and that practices comply with changing societal and ethical expectations. Although the technical performance of post mortems in Ireland was in keeping with best international practices, this does not entirely excuse the profession of its responsibilities. Medical education and training in the 1990s began to emphasise the importance of keeping patients informed and obtaining consent in relation to surgical and other medical treatment. Although there was a general policy to obtain consent to hospital post-mortem examinations, this did not commonly include disclosure of the details of the examination and the possibility of organ retention. The need to apply the same standards of disclosure to post-mortem practice does not appear to have been considered by the profession.

5.4 Hospital management also have a role to play here. Although it is not their role to interfere in clinical autonomy and decision-making in the treatment of individual cases, they nevertheless owe a duty to patients and next-of-kin to ensure that all treatments and services provided by the hospital are of the highest clinical and ethical standard. Hospital managers were unaware of pathology practices and post-mortem retention of organs, in the same way as they would have been unaware of the details of clinical procedures or pharmacological treatments. Their remit was confined to resource and budgetary issues, quality control management, and other administrative matters. This position would have been common to all hospitals through the 1970s and 1980s. In the 1990s more emphasis began to be placed on medico-legal considerations as litigation became more commonplace in the healthcare sector. Consent forms began to be more carefully drafted, protocols became more tightly controlled and so-called 'defensive' practices began to creep in. However, none of this appears to have impacted upon hospital post mortems, save that written consent forms became more common in hospitals and, in some cases, more detailed. Consideration does not appear to have been given to the disclosure of organ retention as part of that process, or whether in the absence of such disclosure consent could be 'informed'.

6 Post-1999

6.1 When organ retention practices became public knowledge in late 1999 parents were confused, distressed, hurt and angry. They felt betrayed by the hospitals and doctors who had cared for their children in life, and were distrustful of the information they now received about the care of their children after death. For the parents, the whole controversy shows a failure to empathise with those who have faced the devastation of losing a child, and the failure to recognise the parent's need to protect the child after death. The fact that for many parents the essence of the child is contained in organs such as the heart or the brain engendered feelings that the child had been violated, and that the parent had not been able to protect him/her. The way in which some elements of the media highlighted this sensitive and emotive area did not help to ease the renewed grief of these parents.

6.2 The function and responsibility of hospital managers became crucial when revelations about organ retention began to be published in 1999. At that point, their role was to set clear protocols for the accurate dissemination of information to parents. In some cases managers and boards quickly realised the scale of the controversy and set about putting in place structures to ensure that information was disseminated as accurately and quickly as possible in the circumstances. In other cases, the reaction of management was not as well coordinated as it should have been. Inaccurate information, delays, and insensitivity exacerbated the grief and anger of the parents in many cases. Though the hospitals defend their responses on the basis that they were unprepared, that the controversy was unprecedented, that information was not readily available, and that records were sometimes poorly maintained, the effect on the parents was an additional trauma that perhaps could have been avoided or minimised by a more centralised leadership from the health boards and the Department of Health and Children. As occurred in other countries, a moratorium could have been imposed on the dissemination of information until audits had been carried out and accurate and complete details collated. Though this would inevitably have led to a further delay for the parents, it may have proved to be a better option.

6.3 The Department of Health and Children did not see itself as having any role or function in relation to the regulation of post-mortem practices until this controversy arose in 1999. There appears to have been no discussion at policy level, and no issues were raised or questions asked by officials within the Department regarding hospital post mortems, other than in relation to the safe and hygienic disposal of clinical waste in accordance with European Directives. Until the issue of organ retention arose in the course of the Bristol Inquiry in England, no one in the Department appears to have considered the issue, or the likely effect of the subsequent revelations on bereaved parents and families. When the controversy became public in late 1999, the Department should have made more strenuous efforts to reassure the public that although there were issues to be addressed regarding consent and communication, the practice of organ retention was a standard and necessary part of post-mortem examinations, and that post mortems were carried out in Ireland to the highest international standards. This might have allayed some of the fears and concerns of parents at that time.

6.4 It is clear from evidence submitted to the Inquiry that significant changes have been made in recent years in hospital policies, though the changes are not necessarily consistent across all hospitals. Since 2000 the Faculty of Pathology and the National Working Group on Organ Retention have issued guidelines in relation to post-mortem practices. Both sets of guidelines stress the importance of communication and consent. Guidance is also given on the storage of organs, choices to be given to families regarding the disposal of organs and record keeping. It was not the function of this Inquiry to carry out an audit of conformity by the hospitals with the national guidelines.

7 Conclusion

7.1 On the evidence submitted to the Inquiry, this Report concludes that post-mortem examinations were carried out in Ireland according to best professional and international standards and that no intentional disrespect was shown to the child's body. The root causes of this controversy have been a lack of communication with parents as to why organs were retained, the difference in perspective as to their symbolic significance, and the legislative vacuum on the role of consent in post-mortem practice.

7.2 There are lessons to be learned from this controversy. There has been a breakdown in communication, and consequently in trust and confidence, between parents and medical professionals. This will not be resolved by blame. The practices of the past were not due to personal or individual misconduct, but rather to a system and culture that failed to take into account the views and feelings of parents. It may be some explanation for organ-retention practices to say that there was no legislation governing post mortems in Ireland, and that, in the legal vacuum that existed, doctors followed the custom and practice of their profession. The practice of retaining organs without the knowledge and authorisation of parents, which would now be unacceptable, was the product of the paternalistic culture of the time and a lack of consideration of the rights and interests of parents. That was how things were, not only in Ireland but also in other countries.

7.3 This Report concludes that the best resolution of this issue for bereaved parents is to enact clear and unambiguous legislation to ensure that such practices cannot happen again in the future without their knowledge and authorisation.

Recommendations

The terms of reference of this Report deal with paediatric post mortems and the recommendations are based on findings made in that regard. However, the principles that underpin these recommendations, in particular, respect for the dignity of the deceased, and the importance of communication and authorisation are equally applicable to all post mortems.

Consideration should be given to the implementation of the recommendations made in this Report to other post mortems, namely those carried out on babies who have died before or during birth, minors and adults. Although this Report does not specifically address post mortems in those groups, many of the recommendations may apply generically to all post-mortem practice. However, it should be acknowledged that these post mortems also raise distinct legal and ethical issues that were not within the Terms of Reference of this Report. If the recommendations in this Report are adopted, a Working Group should be established to ensure that appropriate adaptation in relation to those issues takes place. It must include membership from relevant stakeholders and family representative organisations.

It is acknowledged that some of the recommendations made in this Report have already been implemented at a policy level in many hospitals since 1999/2000, and particularly since national protocols were adopted in 2002. However, to ensure clarity and consistency across all hospitals, these recommendations must form the basis of new legislation, which would serve to restore public trust and confidence in post-mortem practice in Ireland.

1 Need for legislation

1.1 Legislation must be introduced as a matter of urgency to ensure that no post-mortem examination will be carried out on the body of a deceased child and no organ will be retained from a post-mortem examination for any purpose whatsoever without the authorisation of the child's parent/guardian, or the authorisation of the coroner in an appropriate case.

1.2 The removal of organs from the body of a deceased child at post mortem is carried out as a necessary part of the examination of the body and diagnosis of the cause of death. It must be made clear in legislation that a post-mortem examination includes the necessary removal of organs for this purpose. Subject to recommendation 2.3, parents must be clearly informed of this prior to their authorisation of the hospital post-mortem examination.

1.3 The retention of organs at post mortem may be necessary in certain circumstances in order to make an accurate diagnosis of the detailed cause of death. Subject to recommendation 2.3, parents should be clearly informed of this prior to their authorisation of the hospital post-mortem examination. As part of this process parents must be informed as to the reasons for retention, the likely retention period, and must be offered such further information as they require.

1.4 Subject to recommendation 2.3, parents must be informed of the benefit of retained organs for audit, education and research, and given the option to authorise retention for such purposes. Parents must also be given choices in relation to subsequent return, burial or cremation of the organs.

1.5 It is recommended that legislation should provide that where both parents are legal guardians of a deceased child either parent should be able to give authorisation for a hospital post-mortem examination, though ideally both should participate in the decision. Situations may exceptionally arise in which the parents of the child disagree as to whether or not to authorise a hospital post mortem on their child. In such situations or where only one parent is the legal guardian, the hospital would be legally entitled to proceed with the post mortem on the authorisation of one parent. However, best practice should ordinarily be not to proceed with a hospital post mortem in the face of objection from either parent irrespective of their marital or living arrangements.

1.6 The health and safety aspects of the storage, use and disposal of human organs derived from post-mortem examinations must be regulated by legislation.

1.7 Legislation must prohibit the removal of human organs from a deceased child at post mortem examination for supply by hospitals to any pharmaceutical company or other third party without the knowledge and authorisation of the parents. Where such organs are supplied, such arrangements must be clearly approved by hospital management and documented, and all information supplied to the parents on request.

1.8 An appropriate legislative framework must be put in place to govern hospital post mortems. A regulatory model that facilitates guidelines to be updated when necessary to keep pace with medical and scientific developments is recommended. Legislation must clearly set out the purposes for which a post-mortem examination may be performed. In order to restore and maintain public confidence in the system, the legislation must set out clear safeguards for patients and their families, and encourage medical education and research. Penalties must be imposed for non-compliance with these safeguards.

1.9 Although not specifically addressed within the terms of reference of this Report, it is clear that human tissue legislation is urgently required to deal with issues relating to removal, storage and uses of human biological material from the living and the deceased. Provision should be made in such legislation to facilitate and encourage medical education and training, and approved medical research, while maintaining the principle of respect for the donor, the deceased person and the bereaved.

2 Information for parents and the authorisation process

2.1 The grief and anguish suffered by parents who discovered that their children's organs had been retained and in some cases later disposed of by hospitals, was caused by a failure by medical professionals to communicate openly and honestly with parents at the time of death. The main aim of this Report is to place parents/guardians at the centre of decision-making and control in respect of hospital post-mortem examinations to be carried out on their children. However, the doctrine and language of informed consent is considered to be inappropriate in this context and is not recommended.

2.2 It is recommended that the alternative concept of authorisation be adopted. This is a stronger and more powerful recognition of the active role and choice of parents in decision-making in relation to post mortems. It is recommended that systems and policies be put in place to ensure that all parents are offered such information as they require to make the decision as to whether or not to authorise a post mortem examination to be performed on their child. This must be viewed as a process and not a once-off event.

2.3 Parents must be given the option of authorising a post-mortem examination to be carried out on their child on the understanding that this is being performed to provide further information as to the cause of death and the possible effects of treatment. Some parents may wish to authorise a post mortem without wanting to receive any further information or consultation. Their right not to receive this information must be respected. It must be made clear to them that they can come back with a future request for more information at any time. For those parents who choose this option, it must be stated on the authorisation forms that this includes authorisation of all actions necessary as part of that examination. The accompanying information booklet to be given to parents to read if they so choose must explain that this will include removal and sampling of organs, and may include retention of organs for diagnostic purposes. It must be made clear that organs retained at post-mortem examinations will not be used for any purpose other than diagnosis without the authorisation of the parents/guardian.

2.4 If they require further information prior to authorisation, parents must be told that the performance of a post-mortem examination involves the examination of the body of the deceased child. It includes the dissection of the body and the removal of organs, tissue samples and blood/bodily fluids. It is carried out to provide information about or confirm the cause of death, to investigate the effect and efficacy of a medical or surgical intervention, to obtain information regarding the health of another person/future person, and for audit, education, training or research purposes. Parents must be made aware that in certain circumstances it may be necessary to retain organs in order to complete the examination.

2.5 Parents should also be informed of the potential benefits of retention in terms of education, training and research. If the retention period is short, they must be made aware that it may be possible to delay the funeral in order that the organs may be reunited with the body. In other cases, they must be made aware of their options in relation to disposal of the organs at a later date.

2.6 Parents must be given the option to authorise a limited post mortem. They may choose to limit the examination to particular organs but, in making that choice, must be informed that this will mean that samples will be taken from the organs being examined, and that information will not be available on other organs which may have contributed to the child's death.

2.7 It is recommended that the means by which and the place in which parents are informed about the post mortem process be as sensitive and respectful as possible in the circumstances. If possible, a dedicated bereavement room should be available and adequate time should be given to parents to consider the issue. Information must be offered to parents/guardians and an open dialogue entered into prior to the authorisation of the hospital post mortem. The information must be presented in a clear and comprehensible but sensitive manner. A bereavement liaison officer should assist the parents in getting the information they need prior to their decision.

2.8 It is not intended to make specific recommendations as to the most appropriate person to discuss post mortems with the family, as this is deemed unnecessarily prescriptive. It will usually be a senior clinician who has a relationship with the parents, though a team approach may be preferable in some cases, involving nursing and midwifery staff in particular. Where possible, consultation with the hospital pathologist should take place prior to discussion with the parents so as to concentrate that discussion on issues of most relevance to the particular child. If the parents so request it, a pathologist must be available to answer specific queries or explain the post mortem in more detail.

2.9 The confidentiality of the post mortem report raises issues regarding its disclosure to other persons. Hospital post-mortem reports must be made available to the consultant clinician who treated the child, if there was one, and the child's general practitioner. It is recommended that the post-mortem report must also be offered to parents of deceased children with advice to seek any necessary explanations from their general practitioners, consultants or the relevant pathologists. Where possible, a follow-up meeting between parents and clinicians must be arranged to discuss the post-mortem findings in as much detail as the parents require. If necessary or desirable in the circumstances, the pathologist may also be requested to attend such meetings. This facility must be made known to parents at the time of authorisation of the hospital post-mortem examination. Protocols must be put in place to provide a structure whereby parents receive a timely and appropriate response to their request for information.

2.10 Standardised authorisation forms and clearly written information booklets must be drafted and used on a national basis to ensure consistency and transparency.

3 Coroners Post Mortems

3.1 The recommendations of the Report of the Working Group on the Coroners Service must be implemented without further delay. A new Coroners Act must be enacted to clarify the legal duties and rights of coroners, and the procedures to be followed from the reporting of a death through to the holding of inquests. Clear structures must be established to deal with information to be provided to families, the appointment of a coroner's officer to liase with parents following a post mortem, and the provision of support to families through the inquest process.

3.2 The role and responsibility of the coroner's office in relation to communicating with families must be clearly outlined in coroner's rules. Although it is common for the coroner's post mortem to take place within a hospital, hospital staff are obliged not to discuss the post mortem with the family as this is a matter for the Coroner. This can create difficulty and tension between the hospital and the family and must be avoided by clear mechanisms being put in place to inform families of the process and their rights. Disclosure arrangements with relatives must be reviewed so as to ensure that relatives are kept informed as far as possible, subject to the proviso that there may be circumstances in which the coroner cannot provide full information because of the nature of his inquiry and any accompanying criminal investigation. Coroners post mortem reports must state when organs have been retained and the reasons for retention.

3.3 Where a coroner's post mortem is required, parents must be so informed clearly and without delay. They must be told that their consent is not required. An information booklet setting out the powers and functions of the coroner, and the procedural aspects of the coronial jurisdiction, must be made available to the family. They must also be told that organs may only be retained as part of this process for as long as is necessary to establish the cause of death and other relevant matters relating to the child's death. Parents must be told that they have the opportunity to decide on disposal of the organs once the coroner's purposes have been satisfied. Good effective communication in all aspects of this discussion is of paramount importance.

3.4 Coroners are entitled and obliged at law to direct retention of organs to assist in the investigation of the cause of death. Retention for any other purpose such as teaching or research is outside of the remit of the coroner and, if it is to take place, must be clearly authorised by the child's parent/guardian.

3.5 The legal position pertaining to the status of organs lawfully retained as part of a coroners post-mortem examination must be clarified by legislation. Pathologists performing post-mortem examinations at the request of a coroner must have clear protocols agreed with the coroner for the retention of organs.

3.6 In some cases there may be cultural or religious objections by the family of the deceased to the holding of a post mortem examination and/or the retention of organs. Insofar as it is possible to do so, these objections should be respected. However, such objections cannot interfere with the lawful exercise of the coroners' jurisdiction and obligation to investigate the cause of death.

3.7 All instructions from the coroner to the pathologist must be documented in writing. The responsibilities and rights of pathologists carrying out coroner post mortems must be clearly established by legislation.

3.8 It is recommended that the new Coroners Act provide for options to be made available to families of deceased persons in relation to disposition of the organs when the death investigation has concluded. These options would include return of the organs to the family for burial, donation of the organs to an appropriate hospital for teaching or research, burial in a hospital plot, or cremation. The cost implications of these options should also be dealt with by the legislation.

3.9 In the case of a coroner's post-mortem, parents must be given the post mortem report on request, though the timing of its release may depend on whether or not an inquest is required in the circumstances. This must be made clear to parents in information provided to them from the outset of the process.

4 Hospital post-mortem policy

4.1 All post mortem examinations must be carried out by a qualified pathologist in accordance with the professional guidelines of relevant training bodies. This does not necessarily mean that a specialist paediatric pathologist will perform all paediatric post mortems as this may be impossible from a resource and personnel perspective.

4.2 Standardised authorisation forms must be drafted in consultation with interested parties, and used in all hospitals in conjunction with standard information booklets. A copy of the authorisation form must be kept on the patient's medical record as well as sent to the pathology department where the post mortem is carried out. The pathologist must ensure that authorisation has been given prior to proceeding with the examination. Parents must also be given a copy of the authorisation form.

4.3 Measures must be adopted by all health service providers to ensure that all patient care staff receive mandatory training in responding to grief and bereavement.

4.4 Each hospital must have a bereavement liaison officer available to offer practical help and support to bereaved families and staff caring for those families. This officer must liase with the relevant pathology department and should have a good understanding of pathology practices so as to provide assistance to the family if required. Although it is the clinician's responsibility to discuss the post mortem with the parents, this may be done as part of a team approach with the bereavement liaison officer, who may provide appropriate follow-up support.

4.5 Post mortems must be viewed as a continuation of patient care and therefore part of clinical governance within the hospital. Although professional autonomy dictates the technical detail of the performance of the post mortem, responsibility for the administrative aspects of the process rests with hospital management who must make certain that protocols are in place to ensure all legal requirements as to authorisation and record keeping are satisfactorily complied with. This also requires that an effective audit of post mortem practice be regularly undertaken to reassure the public that past practices cannot recur and that the hospital's policies and practices conform to current legal requirements.

4.6 Healthcare providers must ensure that health service employees are instructed in post-mortem policy and relevant procedures for giving information to parents. This must be included as part of the induction process for new entrants to the healthcare service.

4.7 An independent audit must be carried out of currently retained organs in all hospitals in the State. The Department of Health and Children and the Health Service Executive should engage in a public information campaign informing relatives that they may reclaim any currently retained organs within a 12-month period from the date of this Report. This should be organised and managed via a central enquiry line rather than by individual hospitals. Families who do not contact hospitals in this regard should not be approached with this information. Their right not to know must be respected, provided reasonable efforts have been made to disseminate information publicly.

4.8 If, after this 12-month period, organs remain unclaimed, they must be disposed of respectfully by the hospital in line with written policies. This must be done in accordance with health and safety regulations and will entail either burial in an approved hospital plot, or cremation. Conformity with national policies and regulations must be demonstrated in accurate record keeping and monitored by periodic audit.

4.9 Accurate and detailed record keeping of retention and disposal of organs at post mortem must be maintained in all pathology departments in accordance with best practice guidelines. Physical disposal or return of organs to families must be carried out by technical services staff or the bereavement liaison officer respectively, in accordance with hospital policy and the wishes of the parent/guardian.

4.10　It is recommended that guidance be given by the hospital to families regarding burial or cremation of the organs and that they be advised to use an undertaker for this process. An information sheet setting out the necessary information must be given to families to whom organs are being returned.

4.11　Where organs are to be disposed of by the hospital in accordance with the wishes of the family, this must be done in accordance with health and safety guidelines established by the Department of Health and Children. These guidelines must ensure that the organs are treated with dignity and respect insofar as this can be facilitated by the safe and hygienic disposal method chosen.

4.12　Clear national protocols must be put in place by the Department of Health and Children and Health Services Executive to deal with queries from families in respect of post mortem practices as well as the provision of standardised forms to be used on a national basis. The language to be used in such forms must be clear and comprehensible, and must avoid medical or legal terminology as much as possible. Existing guidelines produced by the National Working Group on Organ Retention in 2002, and adopted by National Chief Officers in 2003 may be used as the basis on which to make any adaptations recommended in this Report. This should be done in consultation with relevant stakeholders.

5 Public awareness

5.1 Measures should be taken to inform the public that post mortem examinations are carried out to safeguard and promote health and well being. The welfare and best interests of the families of the deceased, as well as that of society in general, requires steps to be taken to promote the importance of the autopsy in our health care system.

5.2 The public should be made aware of the process of a post mortem examination, the fact that organs are removed for examination and small specimens kept as part of their medical records for further tests, in their interests. They should also be made aware that, in certain circumstances, it may be necessary to retain whole organs for examination and that the body may not always be returned intact for burial.

5.3 The Department of Health and Children should engage in a public education and information programme to ensure that members of the public are informed as much as possible as to the post-mortem procedure, the value of retention of organs and tissue, the importance of pathology practices in our healthcare system, the value of post mortems in the education of medical professionals and in the carrying out of significant research, and the rights of families in this regard. Restoration of public confidence in medical practice, and specifically pathology practices, is vitally important to encourage a higher rate of post mortems in our hospitals.

6 Medical education and training

6.1 It is recommended that medical and nursing students be permitted and encouraged to attend post-mortem examinations. Legislation should provide for authorisation for such educational viewing to be sought from the parent/guardian of the deceased child or the coroner as appropriate. Guidelines should be drawn up to ensure that such attendance will be carried out in a controlled and respectful manner.

6.2 As part of the education and training of medical professionals, increased attention must be paid to communication skills and the legal and ethical issues involved in the removal and use of human organs and tissue. All relevant hospital staff must be trained in relation to the authorisation process.

6.3 It is recommended that anonymised organs currently retained in pathology museums for teaching purposes should be maintained as a valuable educational resource. Any proposed inclusion of an organ in such a museum in the future must be specifically authorised and documented.

7 Medical Research

7.1 In any discussion about organ retention, parents must be given information about potential uses and benefits of retention for purposes of education and research, unless they indicate that they do not wish to receive such information. Sometimes comfort may be afforded to parents who feel that something positive may come from their child's death. It is recommended that organs may be removed and retained from the body of a deceased child at a hospital post mortem for purposes of education and research, only where the removal and retention for such purpose has been authorised by the child's parent/guardian.

7.2 It is recommended that authorisation of retention for research purposes may be general or specific. Choice must be given to parents as to what form of authorisation they wish to give. A general authorisation will facilitate the use of the retained organs for research purposes that are not presently foreseeable. A specific authorisation may limit the research use of the organs by prohibiting certain types of research being carried out with the organs. The authorisation form must enable full account to be taken of parents' views in this regard.

7.3 Where the purpose of the organ retention following a post-mortem examination is research, it is recommended that in addition to the requirement that the retention be authorised, the research must be also subject to ethical review by an approved Research Ethics Committee.

7.4 Parents may not wish to be told the details of a post-mortem examination and may nonetheless choose to authorise such examination to take place. In these circumstances, authorisation of organ removal and retention for any purpose other than diagnosis of the cause of death cannot be presumed and must therefore be specifically obtained for education, training and research.

Chapter One

Background to the Inquiry and Terms of Reference

1 Introduction

1.1 The background to the establishment of the Post Mortem Inquiry in Ireland is inextricably linked to events that took place in the United Kingdom in June 1998 when the Secretary of State for Health established a Public Inquiry. The terms of reference of that Inquiry, known as the *Bristol Inquiry*,[1] were to inquire into the management of the care of children receiving complex cardiac surgical services at the Bristol Royal Infirmary and relevant related issues. It was conducted between October 1998 and July 2001. The Inquiry heard evidence in relation to the treatment of the child's body after death and the information given to the child's parents in that regard. There was an outcry that, without the parents' knowledge or consent, hearts had been systematically taken from the bodies of children undergoing post-mortem examinations at Bristol and used for a variety of purposes such as audit, medical education or research, or had simply been stored. The *Alder Hey Inquiry*[2] confirmed that these practices were not confined to the Bristol Royal Infirmary but were in fact common practice in other hospitals also.

1.2 As a consequence of the media and public attention focused on this issue in the United Kingdom, questions began to be asked in Ireland as to whether similar practices could have taken place in Irish hospitals. A parent of a child who had died at Our Lady's Hospital for Sick Children at Crumlin in Dublin (Crumlin Hospital) telephoned the hospital on 12 February 1999 to ascertain whether her child's organs had been retained. This was not, in fact, the first such enquiry to the hospital relating to organ retention as the hospital had dealt with one other such enquiry prior to this time.

1.3 On 12 September 1999 a national Sunday newspaper, *Ireland on Sunday*, published an article about the retention of children's organs at Crumlin Hospital. It was followed on 7 December 1999 by a detailing of the issue on the main RTÉ news bulletin and was raised in Dáil Éireann on 9 December. On that date the Minister of State for Health informed the Dáil that Crumlin Hospital had retained the organs of 98 children on whom post-mortem examinations had been carried out. On 10 December there was a detailed discussion on the television programme *The Late Late Show* about the retention of children's organs and a number of parents recounted their own personal stories on that programme. As a consequence there was further publicity in the media about the issue and hospitals quickly began to receive telephone calls from worried and distressed parents anxious to discover whether organs from their deceased children and relatives had been retained.

---

[1] *Learning from Bristol: the Report of the Public Inquiry into Children's Heart Surgery at the Bristol Royal Infirmary 1984-1995*, CMND 5207
[2] *The Report of the Royal Liverpool Children's Inquiry*, 2001

1.4 On 19 December 1999 a group of over 200 parents met to formally establish the Parents for Justice group in order to establish the facts about what happened to the organs of their deceased children. The group advocated strongly for an Inquiry to be established in order to ascertain the facts in relation to organ retention at post-mortem examinations.

1.5 On 9 February 2000 the Minister for Health, Mr Micheál Martin, announced that he was to establish an Inquiry relating to all post-mortem examinations, organ removal, retention and disposal at Crumlin Hospital and that it might also be extended to other hospitals.

1.6 The Post Mortem Inquiry was established by decision of the Government on 4 April 2000. Ms Anne Dunne SC was appointed Chairman of the Inquiry on 6 April 2000. This Inquiry ceased to exist on 31 March 2005 following a Government decision to that effect. On that date Ms Dunne delivered to the Tánaiste and Minister for Health, Ms Mary Harney, a report dealing with the three Dublin paediatric hospitals. This report comprised 3,500 pages and was accompanied by 51 boxes of appendices in the form of submissions from parents/next-of-kin, hospitals, health boards and professional bodies. On the advice of the Attorney General it was decided not to publish this report. On 3 May 2005 the Government appointed Dr Deirdre Madden to complete a final report on post-mortem practice and organ retention by 21 December 2005.

2 Terms of Reference

Terms of reference for Dr Madden's work were published on 14 July 2005 as follows:

1   To inquire into policies and practices relating to the removal, retention and disposal of organs from children who have undergone post-mortem examination in the State since 1970

2   To inquire into allegations that pituitary glands were removed from children undergoing post-mortem examination for sale to pharmaceutical companies within and outside the State

3   To examine professional practice in relation to the information given to children's parents in respect of the removal, retention and disposal of tissue and organs and the appropriateness of practices of obtaining consent

4   To review the manner in which hospitals responded to concerns raised by bereaved families relating to post-mortem practices carried out on children

5   To make recommendations for any legislative and/or policy change as deemed appropriate.

Note: Organs removed with consent for transplantation purposes are excluded from the inquiry.

For the purposes of this report:

'Organ' is to be interpreted as a part of the body composed of more than one tissue that forms a structural unit responsible for a particular function(s), for example, the brain, heart, lungs and liver.

'Post mortem' refers to any post-mortem examination of a body after death, including those directed by the coroner.

'Child' or 'children' refers to those born alive and less than twelve years of age at the date of death.

3 Approach to the Report

3.1 The time frame for this Inquiry was from 3 May to 21 December 2005. During that period it was necessary to read as much relevant information as possible within a reasonably short period of time before commencing the drafting of this Report. The volume of documentation collated by the Dunne Inquiry over the period of its existence was considerable, including many thousands of documents, files, reports, research papers, transcripts and statements.

3.2 All submissions from parents of children within the terms of reference were read carefully and analysed to ascertain the principal concerns and grievances of parents. All relevant transcripts of evidence given to the Dunne Inquiry were also taken into account in this regard. Individual cases have not been selected or identified in this Report so as to protect the privacy of the families who made submissions. Their experiences are set out, using their own words, in Chapter Four.

3.3 All submissions from hospitals and health boards (as they then were) within the terms of reference were read carefully and analysed to ascertain the principal facts of post-mortem practice in Irish hospitals since 1970. The length and complexity of the submissions varied between hospitals, with some producing vast amounts of documents, minutes of meetings, clinical audit reports, and other correspondence over the time period covered by the Inquiry. Other hospitals produced little documentary evidence and relied on detailed answers to a set of scheduled questions put to each hospital at an early stage of the Dunne Inquiry. Some hospitals were hampered by lack of post-mortem reports or log books, and in some cases relied on the memory of personnel working at the hospital over the relevant period. In the absence of an independent audit of the pathology department of each individual hospital, the absolute accuracy of the details of post mortems carried out and organs retained, as submitted by the hospitals, cannot be objectively verified.

3.4 In the course of her work Dr Madden read the report prepared by Ms Dunne, together with the appendices submitted with the report. She met with Parents for Justice, the Infant Stillbirth and Neonatal Death Society (ISANDS), Heart Children Ireland, the Faculty of Pathology, perinatal and paediatric pathologists, and professors of pathology from the medical schools of Irish Universities. She visited the Pathology Departments of Crumlin Hospital and St James's Hospital. Dr Madden travelled to Manchester, Belfast, Edinburgh and Glasgow to meet with members of inquiry teams in the UK, Northern Ireland and Scotland who had carried out similar work in those jurisdictions. She also attended two conferences at the Royal College of Pathology in London in relation to the implementation of the UK Human Tissue Act, 2004.

3.5 It had originally been envisaged that some aspects of Dr. Madden's work might be carried out in public and initial attempts were made to organise a public meeting during July. However, having discussed the possibility of a public meeting with the various interested parties, Dr Madden concluded that such a meeting would not be productive at the present time.

3.6 Following publication of the Terms of Reference on 14 July, Parents for Justice called on their members to boycott the work of the Inquiry. Following this decision, no further meetings took place between Dr Madden and Parents for Justice.

4 Conclusion

4.1 The purpose of this Inquiry is to be a fact-finding exercise, not a method of apportioning guilt or blame for what happened in the past. It does not address disputes or conflicts arising in individual cases.

4.2 Parents and families are entitled to have the facts of this controversy set out publicly and acknowledged. They are equally entitled to have their pain, distress and anger recognised and addressed. Parents are justifiably anxious to ensure that the practices of the past never happen again and that the system within which such practices existed changes for the better. These issues were the driving force behind the establishment of the Inquiry. The facts of organ-retention practices must be established so that we can begin to move ahead with recommendations for the future. Public confidence has been damaged by the controversy that led to this Inquiry and must be re-established so that the public can be assured that deceased patients and their families are treated with the utmost sensitivity and respect, and that the importance of medical education and legitimate research is not foregone.

4.3 This Inquiry has examined both coroner and hospital post mortems. It is clear from the submissions of parents that their fundamental concerns relate to the issue of consent to hospital post-mortem examinations, the lack of information given in relation to coroner post mortems, and concerns relating to the storage, use and disposal of retained organs.

4.4 While the terms of reference of this Report focus on the retention of organs from children, the recommendations contained herein may be broadly applied to post-mortem practice in all age groups. Consideration should be given to the application of these recommendations, with adaptations where necessary and appropriate, to post mortems carried out on miscarried foetuses, stillbirths, minors and adults.

4.5 In conclusion, this Report aims:

- To summarise past and current practice in relation to the retention of organs from children

- To set out the main issues and concerns that have arisen from these practices

- To recommend changes to these practices, at both a hospital policy and legislative level, which will ensure:

  - respect for the deceased child and its parents
  - compassionate treatment of bereaved families
  - provision of clear information and explanations by clinicians on the purposes of organ removal and retention
  - effective participation by families in taking key decisions
  - that, with the support of the public, the benefits of greater understanding of disease through research, audit and teaching, using retained organs after death, will help future generations of patients.

Chapter Two

What Happens at a Post-Mortem Examination?

1 Introduction

1.1 There are two categories of post-mortem examination: the coroner's post mortem (also called medico-legal or forensic post mortem) and the hospital post mortem (also called clinical, diagnostic or 'house' post mortem). The post-mortem examination is sometimes referred to as an autopsy (or necropsy). This is argued to be a more accurate description of the examination as including an internal examination of the body. 'Post mortem' and 'autopsy' are used interchangeably in this Report. There is no difference in the technical performance of the different types of post-mortem examination, though the hospital case may be directed to particular problems. The coroner's case is perhaps more extensive in some circumstances, particularly in suspicious deaths, and will include a full external examination, likely time of death, nature of any injuries, toxicological analysis, as well as the usual histology and other investigations carried out in any post-mortem examination.

1.2 Post-mortem examinations are unfamiliar to most people outside of the medical profession. On the rare occasions when those without medical training or education reflect upon such procedures, the details are likely to be inherently unpleasant. One of the reasons why controversy arose in relation to post-mortem practices in this country was the lack of information given to parents or next-of-kin of the deceased person. The public did not and probably still do not have any deep understanding of what a post-mortem examination entails and why it may be necessary or advisable in particular circumstances. This chapter attempts to de-mystify the post-mortem examination and place it in the context of medical practice in general. Emphasis is placed here on paediatric post-mortem examinations, as this is in keeping with the Terms of Reference under which this Report has been written.

1.3 Some readers may find the detailed description of post-mortem examinations in this chapter distressing.

2 Paediatric Post-Mortem Examinations[3]

2.1 This is a short description of the paediatric post-mortem examination. Although the post-mortem examination is often regarded as that part of the examination taking place in the post-mortem room, it should be emphasised that the process begins with an assessment of the clinical history of the deceased and continues until the history and pathology observations have been integrated.

In principle, the technical aspects of paediatric autopsies are no different to adult autopsies, although there are certain points that tend to be more critical. Further, not all examinations are exactly the same, as the procedure will vary depending on the

---

[3] This description was provided by Dr Steve Gould, Consultant Paediatric Pathologist at the Department of Paediatric Pathology, John Radcliffe Hospital, Oxford.

underlying problem and, of course, the conditions of consent. Despite the events of recent years, the examination itself has not changed.

This description will focus on the internal examination, describing it in sufficient detail to ensure an overall understanding of the examination, but not covering every technical detail. Major technical variation will be covered and important ancillary investigations will be included, as the results of many of these studies may influence the conclusions. This does not describe the additional detailed dissection procedures required in forensic paediatric autopsies where suspicion of non-accidental injury is overt.

2.2 History

The examination starts with the pathologist having a full clinical history of the deceased. An incomplete history may lead to an inappropriate lack of focus in some areas of the examination. More importantly, the conclusions drawn are likely to be inaccurate. Pathology diagnoses do not exist in a vacuum.

2.3 External Examination

The body is examined with the same sort of care that any physician or surgeon would make of a living baby or child. This will include a description of structural abnormalities, features of dysmorphism (facial characteristics that make the baby or child look abnormal), the presence or otherwise of jaundice, rashes or other features of disease. In cases of sudden unexpected death, a record of any bruise or sign of trauma will need to be made.

In all cases, a series of measurements will be recorded including bodyweight, height, head circumference and, usually in small babies, foot length and sitting height. Sometimes the abdominal circumference will be recorded. This can be used to assess whether the baby or child has been well nourished and has been growing normally.

2.4 Photography

No amount of description can replace a photograph, so this is routine in many situations. Photographs form part of the medical record and, for instance, may:

- in dysmorphism allow referral to a clinical geneticist for specialist opinion
- provide a record of any pathological feature
- record evidence of trauma for use in medico-legal proceedings
- be used as a teaching aid.

2.5 Radiology

This is a routine requirement in some types of baby or childhood death. In particular:

- in the context of structural or congenital abnormality, radiology may identify bony abnormality not apparent by external examination. This may affect diagnosis which in turn will influence genetic counselling

- in some hospital deaths, radiology will help to demonstrate the position of cannulas and other tubes to ensure inappropriate placement has not contributed to death

- X-rays can help to show calcium deposits which may occur in different pathological conditions

- all unexpected death (cot death) will require complete skeletal examination to demonstrate or exclude old or recent traumatic injury.

2.6 Internal Examination

(a) Incisions

There are a number of initial incisions which may be used, and their use will depend partly on the personal preference of the pathologist but also on the nature of the case. All will include a long incision from the top of the sternum (breastbone), down the midline to pubis. If possible, the incision will be made along previous surgical incisions.

Many pathologists prefer to make a further shallow U-shaped incision at the top, roughly between the shoulders. This has advantages in that these incisions allow access to neck structures, but are kept low so that afterwards these incisions can be easily hidden by the appropriate clothes.

(b) Organ Removal

The next step involves reflecting back the skin to expose the ribcage and the abdominal contents. An anterior, shield-shaped section of the ribcage is then removed to expose the thoracic content. At this stage, most organs can be inspected to identify any major pathology and assess whether any variation in approach to the next stage is required.

There are two major variations in the following step of the examination. Perhaps the more common involves completely eviscerating the body, removing all organs in continuity, from the top of the neck to the lower abdomen including the bladder. The alternative is to remove the organs in particular 'blocks' in sequence. Depending on circumstance, both have advantages. The latter approach will be described.

(c) Thorax

Immediately below the thoracic shield lying in front of the heart is the thymus. This is removed before the major dissection of the chest takes place. The first major block to be removed includes the heart and lungs, together with the neck structures which will include the oesophagus and tongue.

(d) Cardiovascular System

After removal, because numerous vessels connect the heart and lungs, they are dissected in continuity to demonstrate normal or abnormal communication. The heart itself is then examined and this includes opening the chambers to assess their normality or otherwise, the four main sets of valves, the blood supply to the heart itself (i.e. the coronary arteries) and the heart muscle, this latter process requiring section of the myocardium (heart muscle).

Such an approach may be inadequate when the heart shows a major complex structural abnormality. In this circumstance, it may be preferable to keep the heart and lungs (or at least part of each lung) and fix in formalin solution. The heart then becomes more rigid and can be examined, usually within 24–48 hours, often with clinical colleagues, and a fuller appreciation of the abnormality acquired.

After the heart has been examined, the other major arterial branches are explored and this will include the aorta and the main arterial branches to the neck.

(e) Respiratory System

The larynx and trachea is part of the thoracic block and, after inspection, it is opened along its length. The examination of the lung connections with the heart have been described above. The lungs are then removed from the 'block' and examined separately.

The arterial supply and the main bronchi within the lung itself are opened along their length. The lung tissue is then sliced to look for other focal lesions or processes such as infection.

(f) Abdomen

The small and large bowel are inspected and then removed in entirety. The next organ block removed includes the liver, stomach, pancreas and spleen.

(g) Gastro-Intestinal System

The oesophagus is opened along its length as part of the thoracic block. The stomach is opened and the content and lining inspected. The small and large bowel, having been removed, as described above, may be opened depending on the background of the case. The connection between the liver and first part of the small bowel, the bile duct, is checked. The liver is inspected and then sliced.

(h) Genito-Urinary System

The kidneys are removed and examined in continuity with the ureters and bladder. After slicing the kidney, the ureters and bladder are opened.

Male genitalia are examined by pulling the testes back into the abdomen and inspecting and slicing. The female genitalia are examined in the same block of tissues as the urinary bladder and require opening.

(i) Endocrines

The endocrine organs, although usually described together, are examined individually as part of their respective organ block with which they are removed. The pituitary, which sits in the base of the skull, is examined after the brain has been removed (see below), and may require the small plate of bone lying just to the back of it to be removed first.

The thyroid is examined as part of the thoracic and neck organ block. It can be dissected away from the front of the trachea and inspected. The pancreas is inspected and sliced as part of the liver and stomach block (see above). The adrenals, sitting just above the kidney, may be removed and inspected separately.

(j) Reticulo-Endothelial System

The thymus gland which lies at the front of the chest, as described above, has already been examined. The spleen is removed from near the tail of the pancreas, inspected and sliced. Lymph nodes, distributed around the body, are examined and a general note of the lymph node size is recorded, to ascertain whether or not they are increased in size.

(k) Central Nervous System
Although described last, the brain is often the first organ examined.

The incision in the head is made behind one ear and this passes upward over the crown of the head to the rear of the other ear. An attempt is made to make this incision as far back as possible and thus make it invisible when a small cap or bonnet is used later to cover the incision.

The scalp anterior to the incisions is reflected forward, and the scalp posterior to the incision is reflected backward to expose the skull. The skull may be opened in one of two ways, depending on the age of the baby or child. In the older age group the top part of the skull is removed by a largely horizontal cut through the skull, normally by use of a mechanical saw.

In young babies, sometimes the skull can be opened by incising along the yet unfused or loosely fused suture lines; scissors are commonly adequate for this procedure. The resulting incisions allow the individual bones of the skull to be opened outward in a 'butterfly' fashion to expose the brain.

When the brain has been removed, if there is any question of pathology, it needs to be fixed in formalin. In recent years by using a variety of techniques and stronger formalin, the period felt necessary to fix, or preserve, the brain has reduced considerably. This period may be anything between 3–4 days up to about 7–10 days. There will still be some circumstances when even longer fixation is to be preferred. Fixation makes the brain more firm and allows accurate inspection of the fixed slices and of sampling (see below).

After fixation, examination of the brain involves external inspection and then slicing into 0.5–1 cm slices. Where there is likely to be complex structural abnormality or an underlying neurological condition, it is far preferable for the brain to be examined by a specialist neuropathologist, if possible.

The spinal cord is not examined as a routine. Usually the spinal cord is removed only in the presence of a suspected significant neuromuscular disease or perhaps suspected trauma (e.g. shaken baby syndrome). The usual route by which the spinal cord is approached is from the front, after all the other organs have been removed. The bony vertebral column that sits in front of the cord is removed, allowing access to the cord. This approach means no further incisions other than those described above need to be made.

The eyes are usually examined only in the context of possible shaken baby syndrome.

(l) Musculo-Skeletal System
As indicated above, the initial part of the examination of the skeletal system is an X-ray. Often, little more is needed as direct examination of a bone may reveal relatively little additional information. A sample growing point between the cartilage and bone

in the rib may be removed. Histologically, it may show abnormal growth when the baby or child has been ill in previous weeks.

Specific muscle examination is not routine. However, in the presence of a suspected neuromuscular disorder a small biopsy may be removed from exposed muscle such as that on the front of the chest. Occasionally, a biopsy from the muscle on the front of the thigh is preferred.

2.7 Organ Weighing and Tissue Sampling

As part of the examination of every organ, it is separated and weighed. A small sample is then taken for histology. Organ weights are a critical measurement and, in each case, the organ weight is compared to normal charts so that any variation from the expected weight may be determined. Significant variation from normal may provide objective evidence of a disease process. In some situations, it is the ratio between various organ weights that is as critical as the absolute values.

All organs need sampling for histological examination.[4] Especially in paediatric autopsy, abnormality may be hidden to the naked eye; normality also needs to be confirmed if present. Further, tissue sampling after processing to paraffin wax block allows the block to be stored and for there to be a permanent record of the pathology. This can be revisited at any time in the future and diagnoses reconsidered.

2.8 Microbiological and Other Sampling

Sampling of tissues for bacteriological and/or virological study is a part of most paediatric autopsies. The most common samples taken during the course of the procedure include: blood, cerebro-spinal fluid, samples of lung, spleen and any other potentially infected organ.

Some samples may be valuable for metabolic or genetic studies and should be taken depending on the case history. This may include: skin and spleen samples for genetic or DNA studies; bile or urine for metabolic studies; vitreous humour for biochemical studies.

2.9 Reconstruction

At the end of the autopsy the body should be reconstructed carefully. Organs that are replaced in the body are not returned to the site from which they were removed but are placed in the abdomen. In some hospitals in the United Kingdom the brain is returned to the cranium, but this is not usual practice in Ireland.

While the major lines of incision cannot be completely hidden, they should be sufficiently discreet that with appropriate clothing it is possible for viewing to occur after the autopsy.

2.10 Conclusion

The autopsy may be considered finished when the post-mortem findings, the histology and the results of all the various ancillary investigation are collated and interpreted in the light of the history.

---

[4] Histology is concerned with the study of the structure, composition and function of tissues.

3 Distinctions between Adult and Paediatric Pathology[5]

3.1 Paediatric pathologists confine their work to the foetus, infant and child. The scope of their work is defined by the age of the patient rather than the disease or organ affected. This speciality involves clinical services including surgical and post-mortem pathology, teaching, research, and audit. Although this Report concentrates on paediatric post-mortem examinations, the principles of post-mortem practice outlined here are generally applicable to all post mortems irrespective of age. However, there are a number of distinctions between paediatric and adult pathology:

- The spectrum of disease in the child is different from that in adults, particularly in relation to inherited and congenital disorders, and malignant tumours.

- Understanding abnormalities in children requires a detailed knowledge of normal developmental changes and processes.

- Preparation of samples from a child requires a more labour-intensive and individualised approach.

- Access to a dedicated paediatric pathologist is regarded as essential in a paediatric hospital to which children with complex or serious disorders are referred.

- There are distinct dedicated textbooks, journals, and international meetings covering paediatric pathology.

- Neonatologists treat and care for small, immature and often sick infants, some of whom do not survive. A post mortem carried out on a newborn baby will usually examine both the infant and placenta. It will provide feedback to the bereaved parents, with information that may be important in understanding why their baby died and for making future plans. It may help the neonatologist in auditing the effectiveness and appropriateness of treatment. It may also be beneficial to obstetricians in providing information about infant and placenta, which will be useful in managing future pregnancies.

- An Inquiry in the UK into stillbirths and deaths in infancy concluded that there was an association between unsatisfactory post-mortem reports and examinations carried out by non-specialist pathologists. 'This supports the strong argument for all perinatal autopsies to be performed by specialist perinatal pathologists.' (2003 Confidential Enquiry into Stillbirths and Deaths in Infancy, Project 27/28, www.cemach.org.uk).

- Deaths following paediatric surgery require specialist investigation in order to enable the bereaved families and the clinicians to understand why the surgery went wrong, and whether there were previously undiagnosed anomalies.

- In the treatment of paediatric cancer, accuracy of diagnosis and disease classification is essential, as survival depends on targeting treatment to the

---

[5] Royal College of Paediatrics and Child Health: *The Future of Paediatric Pathology Services* (March 2002)

specific type, grade and stage of tumour. Many tumours are unique to children; specialist knowledge and experience are required to interpret samples sent for testing.

4 Removal and Retention of Organs

4.1 It has always been common practice in pathology to remove and retain specimens derived from post-mortem examination for a period of time, primarily in order to be able to answer further questions in relation to the post-mortem report or diagnosis. This is common to all post-mortem examinations, irrespective of the age of the deceased person. Organ retention may also be necessary for the following reasons:

- Retention facilitates further examination if necessary, in the light of the development of a possibly related condition by a family member.

- In circumstances where the post-mortem examination is incomplete at the time at which the funeral has been arranged, pathologists retain organs for later examination rather than delay the funeral.

- In some circumstances the organ removed at post mortem cannot readily be examined or dissected while fresh and it is necessary to fix it for a period of time in order to enable examination to be made at a later date.

- Retention of organs for teaching in medical schools has long been advocated as the best means of instruction of medical students. The organs are stored in transparent containers and coded so as to preserve anonymity.

- Organs may also be retained for research purposes so as to enable review and comparison between healthy and diseased organs in order to investigate the cause of death. This is illustrated in the case of research carried out into the causes of Sudden Infant Death Syndrome (SIDS) in which organs from children diagnosed as having died from this syndrome would be compared with organs of children who had died from other causes in order to try to discover what organs were affected by SIDS and why this might have occurred.

- For safety reasons, in cases of known or suspected infectious disease where the health of the pathologist or post-mortem technician is at risk, organs may be retained and fixed for later examination. This applies, for example, in the cases of Hepatitis B, HIV, Tuberculosis and variant CJD.

- In cases where death may have been caused by disease of the central nervous system, examination of the brain and/or spinal cord is necessary. Although it is possible in some cases to examine the fresh brain, this examination is not possible in infants or young children where dissection is prevented by the fluidity or soft structure of the brain. Fixation is necessary in order to enable the pathologist to carry out a thorough examination of the brain and is recommended as best practice

- by guidelines from professional organisations. In some cases the brain may be sent for specialist neuropathological examination to Cork University Hospital, Beaumont Hospital or St James's Hospital. The Department of Health and Children has established guidelines for the referral of brains from patients with suspected CJD to Beaumont for examination.[6]

- In examination of the lung, inflation by infusion of formalin into the air spaces facilitates thorough histological examination. Sometimes the pathologist will examine one lung at the time of post mortem and retain the other for inflation-perfusion. This is particularly relevant in paediatric post mortems where assessment of pulmonary maturity is greatly aided by this procedure.

- The heart is usually examined fresh at the time of autopsy. However, previous cardiac surgery or congenital heart disease may make this impossible. In these cases the quality of the dissection is improved by fixation and sometimes perfusion of the heart. Children's hearts may be referred to Our Lady's Hospital for Sick Children in Crumlin for examination by paediatric pathologists there. The examination will be carried out in consultation with paediatric cardiologists and cardio-thoracic surgeons in the hospital who have special expertise in this area.

- Sometimes it is necessary to retain other organs for detailed examination, for example retention of the eye in cases of suspected non-accidental injury in children such as shaken baby syndrome. In such cases the globe of the eye is removed and fixed for examination.

- In the case of foetal or perinatal death, the clinician may seek specialised examination by paediatric or perinatal pathologists. This may involve referral of the whole body or of certain organs to another hospital for examination.

5 Storage of Organs

5.1 In the past, organs retained for the reasons set out above were usually stored on shelves in or beside the autopsy room and, if not retained for teaching purposes, later disposed of. Records of retention were rarely maintained other than perhaps in the case of brains kept for examination by a neuropathologist. Organs were usually disposed of within months, but in some cases the disposal was delayed by the necessity of having to carry out a further review or examination for a specific diagnostic purpose, or for teaching/research. In some cases organs were not disposed of due to human error in filing or dating the organs incorrectly, or due to difficulties in arranging for disposal facilities to be made available. In some cases organs were retained for longer than five years and became dried out or desiccated.

5.2 Policies and practices of hospitals in relation to storage, record keeping and disposal of organs have changed significantly in recent years. This is elaborated further in later chapters of this Report.

---

[6] *Creutzfeldt-Jakob Disease Surveillance Associated Costs of Transportation for Post Mortems.* Department of Health and Children Memorandum. Staunton N., Secondary Care Division

6 Disposal of Organs

6.1 Best pathology practice advocates the retention of tissue, and in some cases whole organs, for further investigation and histological examination. Having derived the necessary information from the tissue, and created wax blocks and slides for permanent storage as part of the medical record of the deceased, the surplus material is then commonly disposed of. In some cases where storage capacity is problematic, blocks and slides have also had to be destroyed.

6.2 Until recent years hospitals did not commonly differentiate between tissue removed at post mortem and that removed during surgical intervention on a live patient. All surplus tissue, including organs, was destroyed according to hospital policy and guidelines issued by the Department of Health and Children.[7] Safety in handling and disposal of clinical waste was the primary consideration rather than the need for respectful disposal or consultation with next-of-kin. European Directives also cover safe disposal of human organs and tissues as waste but are silent about the wishes and intentions of relatives of the deceased person.

6.3 Many hospitals had an incinerator to which this material was sent for disposal. In the late 1990s waste material was exported abroad for appropriate disposal in keeping with environmental protection standards and protection from hazardous risk.[8] According to a circular from the Department of Health and Children in 1999, to which all hospital laboratories had to subscribe, identifiable anatomical waste was to be placed in a rigid box with a black lid for export. In the case of large amputations, disposal was to be carried out in accordance with the patient's wishes, but no mention was made of consultation with the patient or next-of-kin in relation to disposal of organs or other waste.

6.4 Disposal of retained organs is now carried out in consultation with the family of the deceased. Families are given the option of having organs returned to them for burial or disposed of by the hospital. This is discussed later in the Report.

7 Conclusion

7.1 It is not the function of this Report to second-guess the expertise of pathologists whose training and experience determine the technical performance of the post-mortem examination. It is presumed that a qualified pathologist carries out post-mortem examinations to the highest professional standards and subject to any limitations imposed by request of the family. Anything less than that would clearly be unacceptable.

---

[7] *Civil Service Laboratories Advisory Committee Guidelines for the Disposal of Laboratory Waste 1993.* Circular BMC.PH10.TB. Circulated to all laboratories operating under the remit of the Department of Health and Children. 'In general, samples of materials such as bodily fluids, tissues, organs and faeces etc. should be destroyed by incineration.'

[8] Department of Health and Children Circular, 'Segregation, packaging and storage guidelines for healthcare risk waste' 29/10/99 (as amended).

8 Recommendations

1   The public should be made aware of the process of a post-mortem examination, the fact that organs are removed for examination and small specimens kept as part of their medical records for further tests, in their interests. They should also be made aware that, in certain circumstances, it may be necessary to retain whole organs for examination and that the body may not always be returned intact for burial.

2   All post-mortem examinations must be carried out by a qualified pathologist in accordance with professional guidelines of the relevant training bodies. This does not necessarily mean that all paediatric post mortems will be carried out by a paediatric pathologist as this may be impossible from a resource and personnel perspective.

Chapter Three

Conduct of Post Mortems in Ireland

1 Coroner Post Mortems

1.1 The history of the coroner in Ireland probably begins sometime in the late twelfth or early thirteenth centuries, though the exact date is impossible to ascertain with certainty.[9] The office of coroner was exercised by city sheriffs until 1617 when a court of the King's Bench decided that the office should be exercised by two elected aldermen with terms of office ranging between one and three years. The coroner swore to perform the duties of the office in the interests of the Crown. Violent deaths would often bring revenue to the Crown and, thus, the coroner had a duty to inquire into unnatural or suspicious deaths. The identity of the deceased was always a fundamental priority and the coroner usually viewed the body at the place of death if possible. Inquests were held with juries in the presence of the body. The coroner's inquest had an important role in criminal investigation and law enforcement at this time and although there were no specific legislative enactments dealing with the office of coroner, provisions relating to coroners sometimes came within enactments dealing with the administration of justice.

> As the financial connotations of sudden death gradually relaxed, or were diverted to other offices, the position of coroner declined until it was revived in the middle ages. At that time the coroner's attention was specifically directed to the establishment or exclusion of criminality, a principle that persisted until the nineteenth century. Gradually, with changing conditions, the importance of the coroner's fiscal duties declined and the holding of inquests on unnatural deaths became for all practical purposes his only function.[10]

1.2 Between 1829 and 1908 there were nine acts specifically dealing with the office of coroner, and sections on coroners were also contained in other pieces of legislation. The modern office of coroner was established by the Coroners (Ireland) Act, 1846 which provided for the division of each county into districts, the election and appointment of coroners, and their remuneration. The Coroners Act, 1881 had required a coroner to be qualified as a medical practitioner, a barrister or a solicitor. The executive functions of the coroner and his duties to safeguard the financial interests of the Crown changed over time with increased importance being placed instead on investigation of the cause of death and judicial functions. In the newly independent Ireland, Coroners Acts were introduced in the 1920s, based in large part on similar provisions in England at that time. However, the principal legislation dealing with coroners in Ireland is the Coroners Act, 1962, which remains the primary Act at the present day.

---

[9] Farrell B., *Coroners: Practice and Procedure* (2000), Ch. 1
[10] *Review of the Coroner Service*, Report of the Working Group, p.24

1.3 A Working Group was established in 1998 to examine the role of the coronial service and how it might be developed. This Group reported in 2000 with over 100 recommendations, including the necessity for a new Coroners Act.[11] It also recommended that the concept of regulation-based Coroners Rules should be an essential element of a new legislative environment for the new Coroner Service. These rules 'should be established by statutory regulation and be capable of being amended. They should cover the various options and procedures available to coroners throughout the cycle of their functions from death reporting right through to the carrying out of formal inquests.' The report recommended the establishment of a Rules Committee to devise these rules. A Rules Committee was subsequently established, and Coroners Rules published in 2003 following discussion between appointed experts and consultation with interested parties and the public. It is anticipated that a new Coroners Bill is to be published shortly.

2 Current Arrangements

2.1 Responsibility for the coroner service lies across a number of government departments at the present time. The Department of Justice, Equality and Law Reform deals with legislation and policy relating to the office of coroner. The Department of the Environment, Heritage and Local Government has responsibility, through the local authorities, for the appointment and remuneration of coroners and in some areas the maintenance of mortuary facilities. The Department of Health and Children has responsibility to fund pathology services and post-mortem facilities used by coroners.

2.2 There are 48 coronial districts in the State with a coroner and deputy coroner in each district. Approximately half of the coroners currently in office are doctors, and the remainder are solicitors or barristers. They are paid a basic set fee depending on the size of the district and additional fees for various duties they perform. There are approximately 32,000 deaths annually in Ireland of which approximately 7,250 are reported to coroners.[12] Coroners do not generally have dedicated office premises or staff and tend to work out of their own professional offices, though this is not the case in Dublin or Cork City.

2.3 The Coroner is indemnified by the State in respect of an award of damages made against him, and/or costs, in relation to performance of his duties. He is traditionally given immunity and absolute privilege in the same way as a judge, while performing the duties of the office. The High Court is empowered to judicially review the acts of coroners.

3 Duties of the Coroner

3.1 A coroner is an independent office holder with legal responsibility for the investigation of sudden, unexplained, violent and unnatural deaths within his district. This may require a post-mortem examination followed by an inquest if the death was

---

[11] *Review of the Coroner Service*, Report of the Working Group (2000)
[12] *Review of Coroner Service*, p. 25

due to unnatural causes. The inquest is inquisitorial by nature, as opposed to adversarial. The focus is on a finding of fact, not on apportionment of blame.

3.2 The principal relevant duties of the coroner include the following:[13]

- **To be available at all times to receive notification of deaths, to make preliminary inquiries, and to direct post-mortem examinations to be undertaken**. Under the 1962 Act, section 18 (5), particular persons are obliged to notify the coroner of a death. This duty is discharged if notification is made to a member of the Garda Síochána, not below the rank of sergeant. A medical practitioner in the hospital or place where the body is located pronounces death before the body is removed to the mortuary. The Garda notifies the coroner under s.18(3), usually by telephone or fax to the coroner's office or home. This is recorded on a telephone report form. A C.71 form is sent to the coroner with demographic information, a description of the circumstances of the death, confirmation of the identity of the deceased, and the identity of the doctor who pronounced the death.

- **To direct the performance of a post-mortem examination**. Where a coroner is informed that a body is lying within his district and that the circumstances of death require investigation, he must make a preliminary inquiry as to whether the death had occurred with no apparent unnatural cause and whether a medical practitioner is in a position to sign a medical certificate as to the cause of death. This may be the deceased's general practitioner or a hospital doctor. A doctor signing the medical certificate of the cause of death must have seen and treated the patient within one calendar month before death. The doctor must know the cause of death, and death must be due to natural causes. If this is not the case, he must report the death to the coroner who will arrange for a post-mortem examination to be carried out on the body. If, having discussed the circumstances of the death with the doctor, the coroner is satisfied that despite not having seen the deceased for more than one month prior to death, the cause of death is clear, he may direct the doctor to certify the death (known as the Pink Form). This may occur, for example, where a person has been chronically ill for some time and was expected to die. Where a person is dead on arrival at hospital or dies shortly after admission (usually within 24 hours), the hospital doctor will not usually be in a position to give a medical certificate as to cause of death and will notify the coroner.

- **To inform certain persons**. The coroner or his officer (usually a member of the Garda Síochána) will inform family or next-of-kin of the deceased of the time and place of the post-mortem examination. A family member will usually be asked to formally identify the deceased to the Garda, who in turn will identify the body to the pathologist prior to commencing the post-mortem examination.

- **To release the body**. The coroner will authorise the release of the body following the post-mortem examination. In cases of suspicious deaths, this will be done in consultation with the state pathologist who will usually have performed the

---

[13] Farrell, Ch. 2

autopsy and may take a number of days. The body is released to the family for burial only after the coroner is satisfied that no further examination is necessary.

- **To hold an inquest**. Section 17 of the 1962 Act provides: 'Subject to the provisions of this Act, where a coroner is informed that the body of a deceased person is lying within his district, it shall be the duty of the coroner to hold an inquest in relation to the death of that person if he is of opinion that the death may have occurred in a violent of unnatural manner, or suddenly and from unknown causes or in a place or in circumstances which, under provisions in that behalf contained in any other enactment, require that an inquest should be held.' This means that if the coroner has reasonable cause to believe that death occurred within the criteria set out in the Act, he must hold an inquest.

- **To send a certificate to the Registrar of Births and Deaths**. When the coroner has completed his inquiry or inquest he must furnish a certificate as to the cause of death to the Registrar, to enable the death to be registered.

Certain deaths must be reported to the coroner, either under legal rules or rules of practice that have evolved in the coronial system.[14] These include the following:

- Sudden, unexpected or unexplained deaths
- Where a medical certificate as to cause of death cannot be obtained because the deceased had not seen a doctor within the previous month
- Where the deceased's doctor is not satisfied as to the cause of death even where the deceased was treated within one month prior to death
- Sudden infant death syndrome (SIDS), also known as cot death
- Where a death was directly or indirectly due to unnatural causes such as a road traffic accident or any other accident, any physical injury, drug abuse, burns, starvation, neglect, exposure, poisoning, drowning, hanging, firearms
- Where the death resulted from an industrial disease or accident
- Where the death may be attributable to any surgical or medical procedure regardless of the lapse of time between the procedure and death
- Where there is any allegation of medical negligence or misconduct
- Septicaemia which may be caused by an injury
- Death occurring during a surgical procedure or anaesthesia
- Abortions and certain stillbirths
- Acute alcoholism/alcohol poisoning
- Deaths connected with suspected criminal activity
- Where death may be due to homicide or suspicious circumstances
- Death of a person in custody
- Death of a person connected with a pensionable disability
- Death of a patient in a mental hospital
- Death of a child in care
- Where a person is found dead
- Where the cause of death is unknown
- Where the body is to be removed outside of Ireland

Deaths reportable under rules of practice include the following:

---

[14] Farrell , Ch 7

- Where a person is brought in dead to hospital
- Where a person dies in casualty department of hospital
- Where death occurs within 24 hours of admission to hospital
- Where death occurs after the administration of an anaesthetic, surgical or other procedure
- Certain deaths which occur in a hospital department such as radiology, or out-patients
- Where a person dies in hospital having recently been transferred from a nursing home or other residential institution including a prison
- Where there is any doubt as to the cause of death.

4 Powers of the Coroner

4.1 A coroner has legal possession of the body of the deceased from the moment his jurisdiction arises. This occurs on notification that the body of a deceased person lies within his district. The coroner then commences his inquiry into the cause of death. The right of the coroner to possession of the body pending investigation of the cause of death means that no other person has prior rights in respect of the body. This may be difficult for family members or next-of-kin to understand at the time of bereavement, particularly if they are unhappy at the concept of a post-mortem examination being carried out. However, the coroner is obliged by law to investigate the cause of death and to do so must have prior rights in relation to possession of the body for examination.

4.2 Subject to the coroner's powers in relation to possession of the body in order to carry out his functions under the Act, the personal representatives of the deceased (as opposed to family members) have the right to possession of the body, once the coroner has released it for burial purposes. The personal representatives of the deceased are either the executor of the deceased's estate, as identified in the deceased's will, or the administrator of the estate in cases where the deceased dies intestate or without having made a will. The personal representatives are entitled to act in relation to the affairs of the deceased from the moment of death.

5 Objectives of Coroner Post-Mortem Examinations

5.1 The objectives of a post-mortem examination differ as between a coroner's case and a hospital case. Some may not apply at all in the context of the death of an infant or child but are stated here for the sake of completeness. In a coroner's case the general objectives may be stated as follows:

- To positively identify the deceased. The spouse, next-of-kin or friend of the deceased identifies the deceased to a member of the Garda Síochána acting as coroner's officer. The Garda will in turn identify the deceased to the pathologist carrying out the examination

- To ascertain the time of death. This information is of particular relevance in criminal cases but may also be sought by relatives of the deceased. It is not always possible to pinpoint the time of death with strict accuracy but an external examination of the body together with evidence of witnesses may be of some assistance

- To determine the cause of death.

- To determine and describe all external and internal abnormalities, diseases and other findings. The latter may be of relevance to relatives, medical practitioners, and others

- To retain appropriate samples for toxicological analysis, histology, microbiology, virology and serology as appropriate

- To retain any specimens found on the deceased which may provide evidence in a criminal investigation

- To provide a full written report of the findings, with photographs or drawings

- To take account of the implications of toxicological reports

- To give an account of the cause of death and any contributing diseases

- To describe the cause of death from the anatomical findings.

6 Conduct of a Coroner's Post Mortem

6.1 If a coroner reasonably believes that it is necessary to conduct an investigation into a death, he requests a histopathologist to carry out a post-mortem examination. The pathologist is given access to the clinical history and circumstances surrounding the death so as to enable special focus to be given to particular areas during the autopsy if appropriate.

6.2 Though the examination will usually take place in hospital premises, when performing a coroner's post mortem, the pathologist is acting independently of the hospital as an officer of the coroner. The pathologist should therefore not discuss the findings of the autopsy with any person other than the coroner, unless authorised to do so. On completion of the examination the post-mortem report will be sent to the coroner. Though the post mortem may have been carried out at a hospital facility, the family should be made aware that the hospital is not at liberty to make any post-mortem findings known to them as this is a matter for the coroner's office.

6.3 If the death is due to natural causes the Coroner's Certificate will be issued to the Registrar of Births and Deaths who will proceed to register the death. The Registrar will then issue the Death Certificate. If the death is due to unnatural causes an inquest must be held. The death will be registered when the inquest is concluded.

6.4 Where an inquest is not required by the coroner, the post-mortem report is generally made available to families, often through their general practitioners, on request to the coroner's office. Where an inquest is required, the report is not available until after the legal process has ended and the verdict recorded.

6.5 Consent from the family or next-of-kin of the deceased for a coroner's autopsy is not required by law, and is therefore not sought by the coroner. Authorisation of retention of tissue samples for further investigation as to the cause of death is encompassed in the authorisation to perform the autopsy. However, this does not include authorisation to retain organs or tissue for any other purposes such as teaching or research as this is outside the remit of the coroner. The Working Group on the Review of the Coroner Service stated that the coroner has the right, through the pathologist who acts as his/her agent, in performing the post mortem, to authorise the removal and retention of organs, body parts and ante-mortem samples. 'This right applies solely in the context of establishing the cause of death.' This was subsequently reiterated in paragraph 3.4 of the Coroners Rules.

6.6 Once the investigation is complete, the status of the organs or tissue retained as part of the investigation into the cause of death is unclear. On the one hand it might be argued that once the coroner's function has ended, the tissue is regarded as the property of the pathologist who has worked on it, on the basis of the exception to the 'no property in the human body' rule.[15] Based on this argument, the pathologist could legitimately use the tissue for research or teaching purposes without seeking consent from relatives.

6.7 On the other hand, it could be counter-argued that since the coroner's jurisdiction displaces the right of next-of-kin to possession of the body for burial, once the coroner's function ends, the right to possession reverts to the next-of-kin for burial purposes. If the next-of-kin choose not to exercise this right, the pathologist may dispose of the material. The *Bristol Report* accepted the latter view as the more accurate representation of the law in the UK at that time. The legal position in Ireland is unclear.

6.8 The Coroners Rules state that the bereaved family has the right to make a choice in relation to the context and timing of information about organs and body parts. This should be discussed with a designated bereavement liaison officer. The Rules Committee recommends that there should be legislation enshrining these rights for the bereaved families and a corresponding duty on coroners. However, it also recognises the impracticability of imposing a personal duty on coroners to ensure that the rights of the bereaved have been respected in each case, and states that coroners should be able to ensure that appropriate arrangements are in place. It also recommends the provision of an information leaflet for relatives, setting out the relevant information and the choices they have the right to make.

6.9 The Review of the Coroner Service recognised that 'one of the weaknesses in the existing service lies in the lack of administrative support required to deliver optimal services to relatives.' The Review acknowledged the critical importance of continuing support of, and provision of information to, relatives during the coroner's investigation, but pointed out that the lack of administrative support often puts impossible strain on the coroner's resources in this regard. It recommended that a new

---

[15] Discussed further at Ch. 8, para.12.3

post of coroner's officer should be introduced at a regional level to support the services provided by the coroner.[16] The duties of this officer would include, insofar as is relevant to this Report, liaison with pathology services and families, ensuring that families are kept as informed as possible about the current progress of the investigation and ensuring that appropriate support is provided for relatives through voluntary and statutory agencies. This Report strongly endorses that recommendation.

7 Hospital Post Mortems

7.1 The purpose of the hospital post mortem, or 'house case' as it is sometimes called, is to confirm or clarify the nature and extent of disease, the patient's response to treatment, and the detailed cause of death. Hospital autopsies are currently carried out at the request of a clinician with the consent of the next-of-kin of the deceased. In many hospital autopsies the principal cause of death is already known, the identity of the deceased is clear, and the time of death is also certain.

7.2 Whereas the coroner's post mortem falls within the legal jurisdiction bestowed by the Coroners Act, 1962, the hospital post mortem does not have a statutory framework within which to operate.

8 Benefits of Hospital Post Mortems

8.1 In relation to hospital post mortems, some of the foregoing objectives also apply. However, there are also other benefits of post mortems that may be seen as particular to this category.

- In up to approximately 20 per cent of cases, post-mortem examinations yield new information about the deceased's condition which doctors did not know when treating the patient. The rate is higher in perinatal post-mortem examinations as the infant may not have been treated for a lengthy period of time prior to death and very little may have been known about his/her condition. This enables doctors to discover more information that might be of benefit to future patients with the same condition. Such has been the case, for example, in relation to congenital heart disease in children. Examination of paediatric hearts has enabled significant advances to be made in the diagnosis and treatment of such abnormalities.

- In relation to post mortems carried out on babies or young children, the information obtained from the examination may be of assistance in advising the child's parents in regard to existing siblings or any future pregnancies.

- Material and information obtained at post mortems provide an invaluable and essential source of education and training to medical students. Pathology and anatomy form an essential part of the education of future doctors and enable them to understand how disease changes organs and tissue. Training in diagnosis and treatment pathways cannot be accomplished to the high standards expected by society without access to such material. It also helps to inform attitudes to death

---

[16] *Review of the Coroner Service*, Report of the Working Group (2000) para. 3.4.2

amongst future practitioners and helps to instil in them respect for the dignity of the human body after death.

- Post mortems provide a means of auditing the performance of the medical teams and the hospital by establishing the cause of death. It can help to clarify whether the patient's diagnosis was accurate and whether treatment was administered appropriately. Given continued discrepancies between perceived clinical diagnoses and post-mortem results, quality assurance demands that treatment outcomes be benchmarked to ensure the highest possible standards of care. The general level of medical care within an institution such as a general hospital is lowered in the absence of routine autopsy work.

- Post mortems help doctors to identify and understand new diseases or variants of existing conditions previously unknown, for example AIDS and variant CJD, by the maintenance of archived tissue.

- The information derived from the post mortem may provide assistance to the family in their bereavement by answering questions relating to the death. This may help alleviate any guilt they might feel as to whether their intervention or actions might have contributed to the death. It may be of comfort to them to know that no action on their part could have prevented the death.

- Provision of accurate information relating to the cause of death is important for the compilation of national mortality statistics and the identification of health hazards. Although some statistical data can be gleaned from medical certificates of death, these are not necessarily reliable sources of information as to the exact cause of death. Studies have shown a large disparity between causes of death when an autopsy has or has not been carried out. In the absence of autopsies, the precision of the death certificate may be inadequate, which in turn is damaging for the development of surgery and for hospital practice in general. Accurate data are necessary in the development of national healthcare policy and in decisions as to the allocation of healthcare resources. The importance of accurate data can also be seen in relation to epidemiological studies such as in the monitoring of infectious diseases.

- Post mortems help in the validation of the effectiveness of new therapies or surgical techniques. Although new imaging techniques have been introduced in the past two decades to the benefit of patients, autopsies may disclose findings missed or misinterpreted by these techniques. The correlation between images in life such as CAT scanning, or MRI, and the post mortem have been of immense value in learning about these new techniques.

- Benefits to the community may be seen in relation to changes in the labelling and packaging of medicinal products following information derived from post-mortem examinations. For example, Reye's Syndrome was discovered by a paediatric pathologist who compared tissue from children who had died unexpectedly after a febrile illness. The syndrome was later linked to use of aspirin in children following chicken pox, influenza and viral fevers. As a result of the identification of this link, aspirin packaging carries a warning against use for children with these conditions. Consequently, the incidence of this syndrome dropped dramatically from 555 deaths in the US in 1980, to 7 cases annually in the late 1990s.

- Post mortems contribute to advancement of medical research. Some of the research using organs and tissue obtained post mortem are of major significance for the health of people in this country and elsewhere. These benefits include, for example:

  - the analysis of organs following death to understand better the long-term effects of drug therapy, both to develop improved treatments and identify side-effects that might have gone unrecognised in life
  - the study of cells taken from organs after death to explore the way in which cancers progress or might be stopped from developing
  - the examination of tissue from people with Parkinson's disease to understand the cause of this disease and potential cures, treatment and prevention
  - the study and monitoring of the levels of chemicals and radioactive elements absorbed from the environment.

8.2 There are also many examples where researchers have been able to go back to tissue collected many years previously and held in archives, to establish important links in the causation of disease. For example, the study of brains of people who have died from dementia can be to investigate whether they had Alzheimer's disease or whether they were undiagnosed cases of variant Creutzfeldt-Jakob disease (vCJD).

8.3 Large-scale storage of human biological materials occurs in other countries. The 1999 report of the National Bioethics Advisory Commission (NBAC) in the USA estimates that over 282 million specimens had been stored and were accumulating at around 20 million specimens per year. This comprised all types of human biological material including blood, tissue samples taken during diagnosis or treatment as well as material taken after death. Individual collections of human biological materials ranged from fewer than 200 to more than 92 million individual quantities of material. They ranged from large tissue banks, repositories and organ banks to unique tissue collections covering specialist areas. The NBAC report does not identify the size of pathology holdings of organs or tissue specifically gathered after post-mortem examination but these are likely to be very substantial. The National Disease Research Institute provides 140 different types of human tissues obtained from post-mortem examination and delivers them to researchers across the US for research into over 100 different types of disease. Other repositories in the US loan pathological material for patient treatment or research, whilst banks of organs, for example brain banks, are also seen as a valuable resource for biomedical research or educational purposes.

8.4 Despite these benefits, the use of tissue and organs after death other than for transplantation has become a source of serious public concern. It is noteworthy that the taking and use of tissue during life has not raised the same level of controversy.

9 Role of Clinicians in Relation to Post Mortems

9.1 In Ireland there is no statutory obligation to obtain consent prior to the carrying out of a hospital post-mortem examination. However, it is clear from the evidence submitted to the Inquiry that since 1970 it has been general hospital policy to have consent obtained for a hospital post-mortem examination.

9.2 The role of the clinician in relation to a post-mortem examination insofar as the family is concerned is primarily to discuss a hospital post mortem with the relatives of the deceased and provide follow-up information when the post-mortem report has been completed. It has been the tradition and culture in Irish hospitals, as elsewhere, that the clinician who treated the deceased in life is the most appropriate person to broach the subject of a post-mortem examination with the deceased's family, though in some cases families have been approached by nurses, midwives or other hospital personnel. The subject matter is a difficult and emotional one and sometimes clinicians do not feel it appropriate in particular circumstances to raise the issue. This is particularly the case since the controversy surrounding organ retention began, as some clinicians have expressed the view that they are now even more uncomfortable than in the past in bringing up the subject with the bereaved family.

9.3 In treating patients in hospital, a close relationship often develops between clinicians and nurses and the patient's family. Ideally, information is mutually exchanged and the clinical team is usually trusted and appreciated for its hard work and dedication in caring for the patient. In those circumstances the clinician knows best the family member who may be able to take in the important information regarding a post-mortem examination, and is able to gauge the timing of that conversation.

9.4 In some cases, however, perhaps where no pre-existing relationship exists between the clinical team and the next-of-kin, or where the deceased has died suddenly, this element of trust may be absent. Sometimes the bereaved family are in deep shock and may not be in a position to engage in a conversation regarding post-mortem examination at all. In these cases it is very difficult for a treating clinician to approach a family to discuss an autopsy, and very difficult for a family to cope with the necessary information about a post-mortem examination.

9.5 In the past, clinicians approached families for verbal consent and recorded this on the patient's medical chart or asked families to sign a basic consent form to indicate permission for a post mortem. They were motivated by conflicting aims, to impart relevant information to families by which they might be able to make a decision in relation to a post-mortem examination (which the clinician felt to be in their best interests), and to protect them from further grief (which the clinician also felt to be in their best interests). Sometimes in these conversations clinicians undoubtedly struck the wrong balance and underestimated the family's wish and need for information, and their right to the appropriate information on which to base their decision. This is discussed further later in the Report.

10 Public Attitudes to Post Mortems

10.1 In a recent study commissioned by the Department of Health and Children[17] and conducted by a team of researchers based at the Royal College of Surgeons in Ireland

---

[17] *Public Perceptions of Biomedical Research*, a survey of the general population in Ireland, June 2005

(RCSI), of those involved in the decision to allow a hospital post mortem, 64 per cent considered that the explanation given to them about what a post mortem involves was good or very good. Satisfaction with the explanation given in relation to a coroner's post mortem was lower at 44 per cent. Similar ratings (60 per cent and 46 per cent respectively) were found in relation to satisfaction with how post-mortem findings are reported. The authors suggest that the lack of engagement with the coroner's post-mortem process, the lack of contact with a hospital bereavement co-ordinator, and the higher level of uncertainty where a coroner's post-mortem examination is ordered within a short time of a sudden death, may account for the differences in the rates of satisfaction between the two.

10.2 Another relevant finding in this study points to the difference in satisfaction levels amongst those on whose relatives post mortems had been carried out in recent years. Seventy-five per cent of those who reported on a post mortem carried out in the last 5 years considered the explanation they received to be good or very good, as opposed to 63 per cent in the last 6-10 years, and 62 per cent in the last 10-25 years. This indicates that satisfaction with the information given to relatives prior to consenting to a post-mortem examination has changed over time or that, at least, contact with a bereavement co-ordinator has yielded higher levels of satisfaction with the process.

10.3 The authors conclude that: 'these findings suggest that satisfaction with post-mortems have not been significantly negatively influenced by the recent organ retention controversy in the last five years. Furthermore, the majority of participants (68 per cent) who reported that a post mortem had never been conducted on a deceased family member, indicated that they would consent to a hospital request to conduct a post mortem on a family member. Nine per cent indicated that they would not agree and 23 per cent were unsure. This indicates a relatively high level of public support for post mortems. However, willingness to allow the use of organs or tissue of a deceased family member for medical research was lower than consent to conduct a post mortem, with just over half (51 per cent) supporting the use of such tissue. Twenty-two per cent stated that they would not agree and a further 27 per cent were unsure what they would do if asked.'[18]

10.4 In relation to the reasons why relatives were not told about organ retention, 24 per cent believed it was because doctors did not want to cause further upset to the family. Fifty-one per cent believed it was because doctors did not want the added trouble of having to ask the family. Twenty-five per cent were unsure. Eighty-one per cent identified the lack of hospital policies as a major problem and 78 per cent felt that the way in which the hospitals dealt with the families concerned was unsatisfactory. Eighty-three per cent considered it a major problem that organs were disposed of without asking the family's wishes, and the same number considered it a major problem that most cases involved young children and babies. Seventy per cent considered the response of the Department of Health and Children to be unsatisfactory.

---

[18] para. 3.4

11 Role of Department of Health and Children

11.1 There was no official national policy on post mortems in Ireland from 1970 to 2002. No guidance was issued by the Department of Health and Children relating to the benefits of post mortems, the information to be provided to relatives, the distinction to be drawn between coroner and hospital post mortems, the retention of organs, the dissemination of post-mortem results to families, or the need to respect the wishes of bereaved parents in this regard.

11.2 The only area in which the Department seems to have taken a role in this context is in relation to the disposal of healthcare risk waste. As a result of the closing down of some hospital incinerators by 1993, the Department prepared a Health Services Waste Policy in 1994. The purpose of this policy was to minimise the impact of waste on the environment and to ensure the safety of those handling waste. A strategy was developed for the shredding and decontamination of healthcare risk waste on three sites within the country. Incineration was not favoured due to high costs and technical difficulties, as well as localised public opposition to incineration facilities. By 1995 all hospital incinerators had been forced by the Environmental Protection Agency to close, and risk waste was exported to England for incineration. This was subsequently discontinued by a prohibition in the UK on importation of waste for incineration, and was replaced by export to Belgium and Holland.

11.3 The Department of Health and Children does not seem to have been aware of the issues surrounding organ retention until 1999 when the first complaint was made by a bereaved parent against Crumlin Hospital. There does not appear to have been any discussion at a policy level within the Department before that time relating to pathology practice. In late 1999 the Chief Medical Officer wrote to the Chief Executives of all the voluntary hospitals and health boards asking them to ensure that a policy of informed consent by next-of-kin to the carrying out of post mortems and organ retention was operational in their agency. This letter instructed them to put mechanisms in place to dispose sensitively of any remaining organs retained by the hospitals, and to deal sympathetically with families.

11.4 In relation to the extraction of pituitary glands at post mortems, the National Drugs Advisory Board at the Department of Health and Children was aware of the distribution of growth hormone to Irish patients since the license for the product was issued in 1976. No concern appears to have been raised by the Department regarding the issue of consent for the extraction and supply of the pituitary glands used in the manufacture of this product until 2000. The supply of pituitary glands by Irish hospitals is dealt with further in Chapter Six.

11.5 The Faculty of Pathology of the Royal College of Physicians of Ireland raised concerns with the Department in August 1999 regarding the retention of tissue for diagnoses, training and research. It recommended that specific consent be obtained for retention of tissue for all post-mortem examinations and informed the Department that export of tissue for incineration was unacceptable in the view of the Faculty. It forwarded to the Department a consultation document emanating from the Royal

College of Pathologists in England which had been drafted following the Bristol Inquiry. The issue was raised in Dáil Éireann on 30 September 1999 when the then Minister for Health and Children, Mr Brian Cowen, referred to the review of consent arrangements undertaken by the Faculty.

11.6 Guidelines published by the Faculty of Pathology in 2000 were circulated by the Department to all hospitals where post mortems were undertaken. The Eastern Regional Health Authority also produced guidelines for hospitals in responding to families in relation to post-mortem practices.[19] Following the establishment of a National Working Group in 2000 and consultation with relevant stakeholders, these guidelines/protocols were adopted by the National Chief Officers in March 2003 as the national protocols in relation to post-mortem practice and responding to families' requests for information. An implementation plan was subsequently endorsed in January 2004.

12 Conclusion

12.1 Post-mortem examinations take place in Ireland either under the legal direction of the coroner, or by consent of the family of the deceased. The jurisdiction of the coroner is crucially important to our justice system and must be maintained and protected. The Coroners Act 1962 must be updated as a matter of urgency. In order for the coronial system to continue to develop in tandem with modern advances in medicine and corresponding changes in legal principles, a regulation-based system of rules would best accommodate the necessity for amendment.

12.2 Hospital post-mortem examinations are carried out to confirm or clarify the patient's response to treatment and the detailed cause of death. They are carried out at the request of a clinician with the consent of the next-of-kin of the deceased. The hospital post mortem does not take place under any legislative framework at the present time. This is clearly highly unsatisfactory as it places families, clinicians, pathologists and hospitals in an ambiguous position regarding their rights and duties in relation to the post-mortem procedure.

12.3 The lack of a national policy on post-mortem practice until 2002 is not unique to Ireland. However, when the organ retention controversy arose, more could have been done by the Department of Health and Children to reassure the public that although families were rightly concerned about the lack of consent for retention, the practices themselves were in line with best international standards.

---

[19] Eastern Regional Health Authority, *Protocol/Guideline for Hospitals and other relevant agencies in providing a quality response to families in relation to queries from past post mortem practices* (2001); *Protocol/Guideline for Hospitals and other relevant agencies in providing a quality response to families in relation to Coroners post mortem practices* (2002); *Protocol/Guideline for Hospitals and other relevant agencies in providing a quality response to families in relation to non coroners post mortem practices* (2002)

13 Recommendations

13.1 The recommendations of the Report of the Working Group on the Coroners Service must be implemented without further delay. A new Coroners Act must be enacted to clarify the legal duties and rights of coroners, and the procedures to be followed from the reporting of a death through to the holding of inquests. Clear structures must be established to deal with information to be provided to families, the appointment of a coroner's officer to liase with parents following a post mortem, and the provision of support to families through the inquest process.

13.2 The role and responsibility of the coroner's office in relation to communicating with families must be clearly outlined in coroner's rules. Although it is common for the coroner's post mortem to take place within a hospital, hospital staff are obliged not to discuss the post mortem with the family as this is a matter for the Coroner. This can create difficulty and tension between the hospital and the family and must be avoided by clear mechanisms being put in place to inform families of the process and their rights. Disclosure arrangements with relatives must be reviewed so as to ensure that relatives are kept informed as far as possible, subject to the proviso that there may be circumstances in which the coroner cannot provide full information because of the nature of his inquiry and any accompanying criminal investigation. Coroners post mortem reports must state when organs have been retained and the reasons for retention.

13.3 Where a coroner's post mortem is required, parents must be so informed clearly and without delay. They must be told that their consent is not required. An information booklet setting out the powers and functions of the coroner, and the procedural aspects of the coronial jurisdiction, must be made available to the family. They must also be told that organs may only be retained as part of this process for as long as is necessary to establish the cause of death and other relevant matters relating to the child's death. Parents must be told that they have the opportunity to decide on disposal of the organs once the coroner's purposes have been satisfied. Good effective communication in all aspects of this discussion is of paramount importance.

13.4 Coroners are entitled and obliged by law to direct retention of organs in order to assist in the investigation of the cause of death. Retention for any other purpose such as teaching or research is outside of the remit of the coroner and, if it is to take place, must be clearly authorised by the child's parent/guardian.

13.5 The legal position pertaining to the status of organs lawfully retained as part of a coroner's post-mortem examination must be clarified by legislation. Pathologists performing post-mortem examinations at the request of a coroner must have clear protocols agreed with the coroner for the retention of organs.

13.6 In some cases there may be cultural or religious objections by the family of the deceased to the holding of a post mortem examination and/or the retention of organs. Insofar as it is possible to do so, these objections should be respected. However, such objections cannot interfere with the lawful exercise of the coroners' jurisdiction and obligation to investigate the cause of death.

13.7 All instructions from the coroner to the pathologist must be documented in writing. The responsibilities and rights of pathologists carrying out coroner post mortems must be clearly established by legislation.

13.8 It is recommended that the new Coroners Act provide for options to be made available to families of deceased persons in relation to disposition of the organs when the death investigation has concluded. These options would include return of the organs to the family for burial, donation of the organs to an appropriate hospital for teaching or research, burial in a hospital plot, or cremation. The cost implications of these options should also be dealt with by the legislation.

13.9 In the case of a coroner's post-mortem, parents must be given the post mortem report on request, though the timing of its release may depend on whether or not an inquest is required in the circumstances. This must be made clear to parents in information provided to them from the outset of the process.

13.10 Hospital post-mortem reports must be made available to the consultant clinician who treated the child, if there was one, and the child's general practitioner. It is recommended that the post-mortem report must also be offered to parents of deceased children with advice to seek any necessary explanations from their general practitioners, consultants or the relevant pathologists. Where possible, a follow-up meeting between parents and clinicians must be arranged to discuss the post-mortem findings in as much detail as the parents require. If necessary or desirable in the circumstances, the pathologist may also be requested to attend such meetings. This facility must be made known to parents at the time of authorisation of the hospital post-mortem examination. Protocols must be put in place to provide a structure whereby parents receive a timely and appropriate response to their request for information.

13.11 An appropriate legislative framework must be put in place to govern hospital post mortems. A regulatory model that facilitates guidelines that can be updated when necessary in order to keep pace with medical and scientific developments best achieves this. Further legislative recommendations are provided through other chapters in this Report.

13.12 Measures should be devised to inform the public through appropriate means of the benefits of hospital post-mortem examinations.

13.13 The Department of Health and Children and the Health Service Executive should ensure that a national policy and appropriate protocols in relation to post-mortem practice are adopted and implemented in all Irish hospitals as a matter of urgency. The existing policy presented by the National Working Group on Organ Retention in 2002, and adopted by National Chief Officers in 2003, provides a useful template and could be adapted where necessary to take into account the recommendations in this Report.

Chapter Four

Submissions from Parents

1 Introduction

1.1 This chapter concentrates on accounts submitted to the Inquiry by parents of deceased children as to their experiences of post-mortem practices and how the organ-retention controversy has affected them. It was not taken as the function of this Inquiry to investigate individual cases in order to ascertain the precise facts of each case. Instead an overall picture of post-mortem practice from the parents' perspective has been presented. While names of parents and children are not used, in order to protect their privacy, parts of their stories are used along with quotations from their submissions/transcripts of evidence. Direct quotations are italicised. The parents can recount their experiences and perceptions much better than anyone else could ever hope to do.

1.2 It is clear from reading the stories of parents who have been affected by the organ-retention controversy that the grief and heartbreak of losing a child is not temporary or transient; it is a lifelong bereavement process that is replete with emotion, distress, anger, guilt and loneliness. Irrespective of the age of the child or whether the death was anticipated, the natural order of life is disrupted and may never be righted in the minds of the parents. Over time, parents may come to some level of acceptance of their child's death, though the evidence submitted to the Inquiry demonstrates that parents whose children died twenty or thirty years ago often still feel the grief and distress of bereavement as keenly as if the death was much more recent.

1.3 Added to the pain of the child's death has been the discovery that during a post-mortem examination carried out on their child, organs were retained without their knowledge. This has caused anger and renewed hurt for many parents who perceive their child's body to have been '*desecrated*' or '*mutilated*'. One parent said, '*I was devastated to think that they'd do that without even telling one of us ... And for them to go and cut her right down, it was just devastating.*' Parents see themselves as protectors of their children, even after death, and sometimes feel that they have let their child down by not preventing this invasion of the child's body. When they learned that not only were organs removed from their children, but also retained and sometimes disposed of in a manner and time unknown to them, many parents were plunged back into grief and a cycle of serial loss: loss of the child, loss of their belief in the wholeness of their child's body, loss of any emotional stability they had achieved since the death, and loss of trust in the medical profession and hospital where their child had been treated.

1.4 As demonstrated by their submissions to the Inquiry, the main grievance that parents have is in relation to the lack of information and participation in decision-making given to them by doctors about what a post mortem involves and what happens to parts of the body that have been removed and retained. As is the case in other jurisdictions that have had similar controversies, there is no real factual dispute on this issue. Hospitals and clinicians accept that until relatively recently, they generally did not tell parents what happened at a post mortem or subsequent to it.

1.5 Parents therefore did not know that their child's brain could be removed and fixed for a period of time prior to examination or that other organs, principally hearts and lungs, were commonly removed and retained for examination. They did not know that blocks of tissue were inevitably retained on a permanent basis as part of the medical record, nor did they know that after examination the organs would be incinerated with other hospital waste. They did not know any of these things because they were not told, and did not know to ask.[20]

1.6 The parents' submissions have been analysed according to a set of themes or questions designed to elucidate the main facts around post-mortem and organ-retention practices. In many submissions the parents did not clarify whether the post mortem was a coroner's case or a hospital case and it has been necessary, where possible, to draw conclusions from surrounding circumstances evidenced in their communication to the Inquiry. In relation to some of the issues and concerns discussed below, the distinction between coroner and hospital post mortems is not relevant. Where parents raise the issue of consent, this refers to hospital post mortems only, as consent is not necessary in a coroner's case. The communication of information relating to the post-mortem examination was undoubtedly shaped by whether or not the post mortem was a coroner's case, as hospital staff are constrained in the information they provide in such cases, though the experiences related by parents indicate that they were not always aware of the relevance of the distinction.

2 When was the Post Mortem Discussed with Parents?

2.1 The timing of the approach to parents about the post-mortem process varied, with most parents being approached in the hours after the death of the child or, if the child died during the night, the following morning. Some parents recall discussions taking place 10–15 minutes after the death, and some recall the request for consent being made during the same telephone call in which they were informed of their child's death. Discussion about hospital post mortems also took place in a small number of cases before the child died, where death was anticipated and it might be necessary to perform the post mortem within a short period following the death.

3 Where were They Told?

3.1 Most commonly the discussion about a post-mortem examination took place in a hospital corridor close to the unit or ward where the child had been cared for. In particular instances, parents recalled being brought to a room adjacent to the ward or theatre where the child had died, or the discussion may have taken place in the ward where the mother may have been treated. One set of parents recall the discussion taking place in a room full of relatives, a priest and a Garda.

---

[20] *Human Organs Inquiry Report*, Northern Ireland, June 2002, para.4.3

4 Who told Them?

4.1 There is no consistency in the cases submitted to the Inquiry on this point. Different personnel mentioned include senior consultants, junior doctors, nurses, nuns, social workers, Gardaí, and a hospital chaplain. Some parents remember the individual by name, whereas others had never met the person before, despite the child having been in hospital for a period of time prior to death. Some parents did not know to which hospital department the individual was attached.

4.2 In some instances, parents were asked by more than one person to consent. In cases where they were unwilling to consent, parents recall the extent to which different people spoke to them about the post mortem. One mother remembers two different nurses asking her for consent and, having refused, a doctor then spoke to her and again tried to obtain consent.

5 What was Their State of Mind at This Time?

5.1 At the time when the issue of a post-mortem examination was raised with the parents, they were in a state of shock and grief. All parents who made submissions to the Inquiry related the fact that the discussion took place in circumstances of extreme stress. One parent recalls that she was '*too shocked with grief to do anything else but say yes*' to the request to give her consent. Some parents recall how they found it difficult to comprehend what was being asked of them during the discussions, with one parent saying that she felt she '*could have signed anything*'.

5.2 In some instances parents recall the discussion taking place while they were holding their deceased child in their arms. Some mentioned that they themselves were ill at the time of the request, or on medication, or were hospitalised. One mother said she was '*in an awful state*' because she was on painkillers and other medication in the hospital.

6 How Much Time were They Given to Consider the Request?

6.1 The decision about a post mortem was made during the discussion. In most cases parents say they were not given an opportunity to discuss the matter alone between themselves, though some did report having been given some time to think about it. None reported having been given time to get advice on the matter.

7 Location of Post Mortem

7.1 The location for the post mortem was assumed by parents rather than explained by the person seeking consent. A few parents were taken by surprise when they later discovered that the post mortem had occurred in a different hospital. They had not been so informed at the time.

8 Reasons for Post Mortem

8.1 Generally speaking, consent for a hospital post mortem was sought in three sets of circumstances as outlined to the parents. Firstly, to establish the cause of death. Sometimes this was linked to the need to establish if a genetic or other disorder was involved that might affect present or future siblings of the child. Secondly, to help the doctors understand the disease the child suffered from, or the medication/treatment the child had been given. Thirdly, to help others.

8.2 Parents recall the discussion being very brief, though this was not always due to a lack of explanation by the clinicians. In many cases the parents themselves wanted a post mortem to take place because they wanted to know the exact cause of death or because they were worried about having further children with the same condition. Some parents were also highly altruistic, with one parent saying that although a post mortem '*horrified*' her, she thought it was important because it could help in the treatment of others.

8.3 In cases where parents were reluctant to consent to a post mortem, this was often because they were already aware of the child's illness and did not see the need for a post mortem. A number of parents said they did not want a post mortem because their child had already been '*through enough*'. One set of parents referred to their religious beliefs as the reason for their refusal. Most parents were prepared to consent when it was explained to them that it might help other children with similar conditions.

9 What were They Told?

9.1 Parents say they were generally informed of the possibility or necessity of a post mortem occurring, although the word 'post mortem' or 'autopsy' was not always used. In a small number of cases submitted to the Inquiry, parents assert that they never knew that a post mortem had been carried out on their child, or had refused consent for a post mortem, and only discovered that one had been performed from subsequent enquiries made by them. The period of time during which parents remained unaware varied from seven months to 26 years. In the latter case the parents reported that the only information they received was that '*we were told our daughter was dead. Told to go home and come back with the christening robe as they were going to put it on her in the coffin.*' Another set of parents said they were told that a '*blood test*' would be performed and were asked to return to the hospital later. It transpired that a post mortem had been carried out.

9.2 None of the parents recall being given written information about the post-mortem process. Discussions tended to be brief and lacked in-depth detail. The majority of parents submitted that they were provided with little or no information about the process when consent was requested.

9.3 The parents did not generally seek details from the clinicians. Parents explain this by reference to the level of trust they had in the personnel involved. One parent recalls that they trusted the hospital and '*would have done anything they suggested*'. Many were therefore content to agree to what the doctors asked of them because they trusted them with their child. One parent stated that the parents had given permission '*in good faith that the post mortem would be carried out with the greatest of respect shown'* to the child's body.

9.4 Where parents did ask questions or seek further information, explanations were generally given to allay fears of reluctant parents. One set of parents was told that the doctors would *'re-open the incisions and look at the heart, that would be all'*. Another was told that the doctors intended to *'have a look at the baby's head'*. Parents were also given assurances that the child would be treated as if he/she was *'having an operation ... he will be treated with the same respect.'* One parent asked if it was like a biopsy and was assured that it was, while another was told it was like an exam.

9.5 Where parents had worries about the incisions that would be made, they recall being told that they were just going to take a *'tissue sample'*, or that cuts would be made to *'just take swabs and little tissue samples'*, and that *'little incisions'* would be made. In one case the parent recalls being informed that any organs removed would be *'all put back in place'*. Where parents sought assurances that only existing incisions would be re-opened, they were assured that this was the case. Parents accepted the assurances given to them.

10 What was Their Understanding of a Post Mortem?

10.1 There was wide variation in what parents understood was entailed in a post-mortem examination. Some said that they did not know what was involved, though the majority understood it to be an examination to establish the cause of death. Opinions varied as to what parents thought happened at a post mortem. One described it as follows: *'I literally thought they were going to be looking at her heart because the child died of a heart complaint. There was no way I thought when I got her back she was going to be opened everywhere.'*

10.2 Some parents understood that tissue samples would be taken during a post mortem, though they differed on what a tissue sample might be. Some thought that *'microscopic parts'* would be taken, while others envisaged that it entailed the taking of a sample from an organ. Some parents knew that organs would be removed but thought that they would be replaced in the body before it was released for burial. One said they believed that *'they would remove her main organs, examine them in microscopic detail and somehow replace them ... I never for a second thought that we buried our baby without them.'*

10.3 Irrespective of what they understood about the procedure itself, one parent summed up the generally expressed expectations of parents by saying that he thought there *'would not be any desecration of the body'*.

11 Objection to Post Mortem

11.1 Parents were generally not told that they could object to a hospital post mortem. Many recounted that they thought the post mortem was a *'formality'* and that they were informed out of courtesy. On the other hand, some parents stated that they knew they could object to a post mortem from discussions they had about it.

11.2 Where parents did object, they report that staff tried to persuade them to change their minds, with some parents reporting that staff were insistent about it. Numerous attempts to obtain consent were sometimes made by different personnel. In a small number of cases where one parent refused consent, an approach was subsequently made to the other parent. Some parents felt pressurised, with one parent feeling that the doctor was aggressive in his approach. One parent reports that the doctor said he *'would not take no for an answer'*, and another recalls being told that, having refused consent twice to two different nurses, *'it will have to be done anyway'*. Some parents gave permission because they felt it would otherwise be done without their permission, and they received assurances about the procedure to persuade them to consent.

12 Limited Post Mortem

12.1 Parents recall that they were not advised about the possibility of consenting to a limited post mortem. In particular cases parents requested that the post mortem should take place on specified organs only. This request does not always appear to have been observed. In one case the medical records showed that a limited post mortem was carried out on a child, though the parents do not recall limiting their consent in this way.

13 Form of Consent Given

13.1 The predominant mode of consent to a hospital post mortem was verbal, though there are instances where parents recall giving written consent in 1980. The form of consent depended on the hospital and personnel involved. No definitive practice existed across the hospitals.

13.2 In some cases parents are adamant that no consent was given for a post mortem even though one was performed on their child. In some cases where the parents do not recall giving consent, a written record of consent is in existence.

14 Organ Removal

14.1 No information about the removal of organs from the body was provided to parents in the cases submitted to the Inquiry. Most parents did not understand that this would occur during the post-mortem examination. One parent whose child died in 1999 was told that the post mortem was akin to a liver biopsy. She recalls that *'no one told me that organs would be removed from the body. I didn't think anything would happened (sic) to the organs as I never thought that they would be touched.'*

14.2 However, a small number of parents stated that they were aware through their own knowledge and understanding that organs would be removed during autopsy. For example, one set of parents acknowledged that they knew a post-mortem examination would involve *'the removal and examination of organs'*. In addition, some parents submitted that they would have expected that organs would be removed during the post-mortem examination and '*replaced in the body for burial*'.

15 Length of Time for Examination of Organs

15.1 Information was not generally provided to parents about the length of time required to carry out the necessary tests to establish the cause of death. Parents submit that they were not told that some tests could not be done between the time of death and the funeral or at the time of the post mortem itself. One parent explains, '*Nobody told me that samples would be taken for the purpose of a detailed examination under a microscope and I didn't understand what happened during the course of a post-mortem examination.*'

15.2 Some parents say that they were told about the results of the hospital post mortem a few days after the death. But a few parents did realise that samples would be taken for detailed examination under a microscope. In those cases, parents were not given such information and relied on their own understanding that samples would be taken for more detailed examination.

16 Retention and Disposal of Organs

16.1 The singular observation by parents about the retention and disposal of organs was that they were unaware that it would occur during a post mortem. One parent said, '*it never crossed our minds that any organ would be retained for any reason.*' They were not provided with any information nor were they asked for consent to retention. They assumed that they were burying the entire body of their deceased child. '*At no stage did I think that organs would be taken without my consent.*'

16.2 A small number of parents thought that any organs removed during post mortem would be replaced in the body before the child was returned to them for burial. Parents who thought that organs were removed and replaced were resolute in stating that they did not foresee any possibility of organs being retained by the hospital. Where parents were given a post-mortem report they did not realise that the report might have indicated that organs were retained for some time for tests. Parents describe the report as full of medical terminology and '*gobbledeygook*'. In one case where a post-mortem report stated that the brain would be fixed the parent said, '*if we saw that the brain will be fixed, we would have assumed that it would have been removed from the body and had been replaced.*'

16.3 On the other hand, one parent whose child died in 1996 related her attempts to query, in a meeting with a hospital representative, the contents of the post-mortem report where it stated, 'brain retained, photographs taken'. At the meeting she was informed that '*tissues*' would have been taken for examination and the references in the report were explained in that way. The parent was only informed about organ retention in the aftermath of the controversy.

16.4 Some parents offered their child's organs for donation to others, but in several cases the organs were unsuitable for transplantation. Parents were aggrieved that, having made this suggestion, the organs were retained by the hospital for other purposes. One parent said that she thought organ donation was the only circumstance in which organs were retained. Another said, '*we had already ... offered to sign anything for the use of her organs. Now, if we had been informed at that stage that they were going to retain her brain for research, we would gladly have done so.*'

17 Returning the Child for Burial

17.1 Some parents related their anxiety in relation to the delay in carrying out a post mortem. Observations by parents in relation to the appearance of their child after the post mortem varied. In most cases the parents did not examine the child for any signs of surgical procedures. Some did not see their child again once the child was taken from them after death. Many parents were very distressed when hospital staff refused to let them dress their child after the post mortem.

17.2 Where parents recalled the appearance of their child after post mortem, they remembered different things. In a few instances, parents noticed marks on the head and/or stitching on the body when they received the child back from the hospital. One set of parents recalled holding the child and questioning how light the body was. When this was queried with the staff, the parent was told she was mistaken and that '*babies lose fluid*'. Another parent recalled that her child '*just wasn't the baby that I held the week before*' and said that she '*knew something had happened*'.

17.3 Another source of distress and anger is the mode that parents took when leaving the hospital with their child. Parents recall receiving the casket after the post mortem and being asked to leave the hospital by a side door. Others recall prayer services at the hospital before they left.

18 Coroner Post Mortems

18.1 Where coroner post mortems were involved, many parents were informed that a '*post mortem had to be carried out*'. Hospital staff generally imparted the information about a post mortem, with two instances encountered where parents recalled that a Garda provided information. The discussion took place close to the time of death and/or when the baby arrived at the hospital. Where children died from sudden infant death syndrome, parents were informed about a post mortem either upon removal from the family home or upon arrival at the hospital concerned.

18.2 No rationale was provided to most parents to explain the requirement for a coroner's post mortem, nor could they recall any discussion explaining the circumstances leading to a coroner's post mortem and the rules applying to it. In the majority of submissions relating to coroner post mortems, parents said they received no information about a coroner's post mortem and/or that they were not informed that there was a distinction between a hospital post mortem and a coroner's post mortem. Indeed, the term 'coroner's post mortem' was not something parents recollected being informed of. The distinction between hospital post mortems and coroner post mortems was not mentioned in conversations with hospital staff on the matter.

18.3 In one case, however, the parents submitted that they were informed that a post mortem was required by law and that the coroner would direct that a post mortem be carried out. The parents recalled that they were informed that '*blood and tissue samples*' would be taken during it. Some parents recalled that they knew at the time that a post mortem was obligatory, but they remembered being unable to say why they knew so. In one case confusion was engendered in a parent's mind when she was presented with a form to sign but was told that she could not object in any case to the post mortem.

18.4 Parents recalled that there were no arrangements made for obtaining the post-mortem results. One set of parents received them through their general practitioner after the disclosures in 1999. Some parents discovered that a coroner's post mortem took place when they sought the post-mortem records from the hospital. Few mentioned any interaction with the coroner's office, save where they had investigated organ retention after the media disclosures about the issue.

19 Communication of Post-Mortem Results

19.1 Results of post mortems were communicated to parents in a variety of ways, both formal and informal. A large number of parents were never provided with a copy of the post-mortem report. Some parents recalled being told in the day(s) after the death in hospital corridors of the cause of death. In other cases, parents received information through their own general practitioner or through a phone call to the hospital involved. Parents criticised the informality with which results were communicated to them in a number of instances. In some cases parents may have already known the cause of the illness from which their child died and, therefore, were not disturbed when they did not receive any formal post-mortem report. In other cases, parents were dissatisfied that they had received no post-mortem report about their child's death until the organ retention controversy arose.

19.2 Where parents had requested post-mortem reports at the time of the death itself, some found difficulty in receiving the written report. In one case, a parent received a report from the hospital by contacting a clinician working in another hospital to get it for her. Some parents received such post-mortem reports upon making enquiries about organ retention in the last few years. In many cases, a meeting occurred between the treating clinician and the parents a few weeks after the death. Parents were told the cause of death. Some praised the staff for explaining everything in detail so that they could understand the circumstances of their child's death. In contrast, others found that the information was conveyed in technical language that they did not understand. The failure to explain to parents at such meetings that organs were retained for further examination or tests caused them anger and resentment when the controversy arose in 1999–2000.

19.3 In a few instances, parents were not informed of the full post-mortem results in subsequent communications with the hospital. One parent who queried the references to 'retention' in an autopsy report was informed at a meeting that '*tissues*' had been retained for examination.

20 Pituitary Glands

20.1 In a few cases parents were informed that pituitary glands were removed. However, most parents who made submissions to the Inquiry did not address the issue. This is dealt with separately in Chapter Six.

21 Trauma of Controversy

21.1 The overriding emotion of many parents was that their assumption that they had buried their child with all of their organs intact was now incorrect. One set of parents described how they felt cheated that their child had been violated once he died. Others described difficulties in coping with the matter because they felt that '*something was missing*' and that they '*did not bury our child the way God gave it to us*'. One parent commented that '*no family should have to bury [their child] twice.*' Another stated: '*Every time I now go to the grave I don't feel that I have the same kind of sense of contact or belonging.*'

21.2 Parents expressed their anger that their child's body had been treated like a '*piece of meat*' or a '*piece of rubbish and unwanted flesh*', while another parent described the practices uncovered as '*an immoral, degrading mutilation*' of the body. All parents were upset and hurt by the entire matter. One parent stated: '*These were not just body parts and tissues, these were the physical parts of our dearly loved children.*' Others felt guilty for not '*protecting*' their children, with one submitting that, '*I feel I let her down when she most needed me.*'

21.3 Parents relived the trauma of the death itself and described the emotional difficulties involved in having a second burial in some cases. One parent described her feelings as follows: '*I was depressed and felt all the feelings when she died all over again.*' Parents recounted that they had nightmares after receiving the information about retention. One parent stated that she had suffered a nervous breakdown, while another said that she suffered panic attacks and depression in the aftermath of the revelations to her. One parent recorded her feelings as follows: '*... I feel very angry and at the same time powerless. I did not know what was being done to my baby boy and I could not protect him.*'

21.4 In one instance, the parents decided to have the burial of returned organs after Christmas so as not to upset the child's grandparents because they would visit the grave at Christmas. In other cases, parents expressed their anxiety at being unable to bury the organs because they had now been incinerated or otherwise disposed of. One parent stated that she felt '*hard done by*' because organs had not been returned to her but had been returned to other families that she knew. Parents were upset by the news that organs had been disposed of. One parent expressed it in the following terms: '*I thought entire organs to be incinerated in that fashion ... was very insensitive and I was very hurt over that. I would have liked if they had the [organ] and if they wanted to incinerate it and they looked for my permission to incinerate it.*'

22 Attribution of Blame and Loss of Trust in Medical Professionals

22.1 The medical professionals were criticised by most parents for the practices operated by them. Some parents cited the arrogance of doctors as a cause of the controversy, with parents describing the attitude of doctors as one where they could do as they liked. One parent described his perception of the medical professionals' attitude: '*I found that the general attitude and demeanour of the medical profession in general ... was condescending, bordering on arrogance and that "We know best and you don't have to know anything about this".*'

22.2 Some parents expressed their shock and amazement that there were no written procedures for organ retention and disposal, and highlighted this in criticising the medical professionals. A significant factor in the responses of parents was the loss of trust engendered by the disclosures about post-mortem practices. As recounted above, many parents had placed enormous trust in the medical personnel involved in caring for their child. Parents stated that their trust in medical professionals was now damaged. As one parent remarked: '*The deception is what gets to me. It's not being told exactly what is going to be done before it's done, and then not being told for 18 years afterwards that it was done.*'

22.3 Another stated: '*One feels that the medical profession have failed our innocent children.*' In this regard, parents who recalled their misgivings about having a post mortem and/or their questions about the procedure were critical that the responses they received to assure them about it turned out to be inaccurate and misleading. This level of mistrust also extends to the information now furnished by the hospitals. Some parents expressed doubts about whether all of their child's organs were returned and/or whether they had received comprehensive information from the hospitals about the practices employed in them.

23 Parents' Views on Retention of Organs

23.1 Differing views on whether parents would consent to retention of organs were articulated. Parents do not understand why retention was necessary in many cases. This is exacerbated in those cases where the cause of death was known at or close to the time of death itself. Some parents were adamant that they would never have consented to the post mortem, given the details of the procedure which they now know. Parents with this viewpoint wanted to bury their child intact. One parent submitted: '*If it was explained to me what they were going to do I would have told them "No. He is to be left alone".*'

23.2 Other parents focused more on the fact that they were not given an opportunity to consider the matter at the time. One parent stated they would have wished that at the time of death doctors would '*let us make a decision whether we want to do something with her brain or whether we want to bury the brain with her*'.

23.3 Some parents stated that they might have been prepared to consent to organ retention if it would assist research into illnesses or if told that the organs were needed for further examinations. One parent remarked that he '*would donate the organs for research*', another parent stated that he would consent on the basis that '*if I thought that something good was going to come out of it ... I would have done that*', while another remarked that had he been asked to consent to retention for research purposes he '*would have readily agreed to that*'. One parent gave the retained organs back for research purposes when informed that they had been retained without her consent.

23.4 In their submissions, all parents were agreed that the issue should not be allowed to recur, with one stating that '*this cannot ever happen to anyone again*'. Parents wanted the truth of the practices employed to be uncovered. Some parents wanted an apology from the hospitals, whereas others felt that any apologies would be worthless.

24 Conclusion

24.1 This chapter has relayed the accounts given by parents of the circumstances in which a post mortem was carried out on their child, and how the retention of organs has affected them. As stated in the introduction to the chapter, parents' stories are presented as their own recollections and opinions about what happened to their family. It was not taken as the function of this Inquiry to investigate individual cases in order to ascertain the precise facts of each case. Instead an overall picture of post-mortem practice from the parents' perspective has been presented. Much of their accounts are uncontroverted by the hospitals' submissions.

24.2 Parents were generally not told about the retention of their child's organs. If a consent form for post mortem was signed at all, there was little or no information on the removal or retention of organs. Where the word 'tissue' was used on such forms, it was not defined, and was not understood by parents as possibly including whole organs. They commonly understood it to mean small amounts of tissue for microscopic examination.

24.3 Families were not always given time to deal with their grief. They were not always provided with support and clear, unbiased information. They feel that they were not always treated with dignity and respect.

24.4 Parents were sometimes given inaccurate information about what was and was not being retained, and some initial information proved misleading. When organs were returned, this was sometimes done in an inconsistent or insensitive manner. Some parents had to endure multiple funerals as organs were returned on separate occasions.

24.5 No choices were given on methods of disposal of retained tissue or organs. It was taken for granted that human tissue, removed at post-mortem and no longer required, would be disposed of as clinical waste. This came as a huge shock to parents, some of whom feel revulsion at the categorisation of parts of their children as 'clinical waste', and strongly object to the idea of incineration as opposed to burial or cremation.

24.6 In coroner post mortems, little information was given to families on the procedures to be followed. Families were not always given feedback on the results of the post mortem.

24.7 The submissions from the parents outlined in this chapter clearly articulate the anger and grief they sustained as a result of the lack of communication about post-mortem practices and organ retention. Their stories recount distress, guilt and disbelief that this happened to their child. Many now distrust the medical profession and healthcare system and feel let down by their experiences in dealing with hospital authorities.

25 Recommendations

It is acknowledged that some of the following recommendations have already been implemented in a number of hospitals, but for consistency the recommendations are stated here without reference to the practice in individual hospitals.

1   Legislation must be introduced as a matter of urgency to ensure that no post-mortem examination will be carried out on the body of a deceased child and no organ will be retained from a post-mortem examination for any purpose whatsoever without the authorisation of the child's parent/guardian, or the authorisation of the coroner in an appropriate case.

2   The grief and anguish suffered by parents who discovered that their children's organs had been retained and in some cases later disposed of by hospitals, was caused by a failure by medical professionals to communicate openly and honestly with parents at the time of death. The main aim of this Report is to place parents/guardians at the centre of decision-making and control in respect of hospital post-mortem examinations to be carried out on their children. However, the doctrine and language of informed consent is considered to be inappropriate in this context and is not recommended.

3   It is recommended that the alternative concept of authorisation be adopted. This is a stronger and more powerful recognition of the active role and choice of parents in decision-making in relation to post mortems. It is recommended that systems and policies be put in place to ensure that all parents are offered such information as they require to make the decision as to whether or not to authorise a post mortem examination to be performed on their child. This must be viewed as a process and not a once-off event.

4   Parents must be given the option of authorising a post-mortem examination to be carried out on their child on the understanding that this is being performed to provide further information as to the cause of death and the possible effects of treatment. Some parents may wish to authorise a post mortem without wanting to receive any further information or consultation. Their right not to receive this information must be respected. It must be made clear to them that they can come back with a future request for more information at any time. For those parents who choose this option, it must be stated on the authorisation forms that this includes authorisation of all actions necessary as part of that examination. The accompanying information booklet to be given to parents to read if they so choose must explain that this will include removal and sampling of organs, and may include retention of organs for diagnostic purposes. It must be made clear that

organs retained at post-mortem examinations will not be used for any purpose other than diagnosis without the authorisation of the parents/guardian.

5   If they require further information prior to authorisation, parents must be told that the performance of a post-mortem examination involves the examination of the body of the deceased child. It includes the dissection of the body and the removal of organs, tissue samples and blood/bodily fluids. It is carried out to provide information about or confirm the cause of death, to investigate the effect and efficacy of a medical or surgical intervention, to obtain information regarding the health of another person/future person, and for audit, education, training or research purposes. Parents must be made aware that in certain circumstances it may be necessary to retain organs in order to complete the examination.

6   Parents should also be informed of the potential benefits of retention in terms of education, training and research. If the retention period is short, they should be made aware that it may be possible to delay the funeral in order that the organs may be reunited with the body. In other cases, they should be made aware of their options in relation to disposal of the organs at a later date.

7   Parents must be given the option to authorise a limited post mortem. They may choose to limit the examination to particular organs but, in making that choice, must be informed that this will mean that samples will be taken from the organs being examined, and that information will not be available on other organs which may have contributed to the child's death.

8   It is recommended that the means by which and the place in which parents are informed about the post mortem process be as sensitive and respectful as possible in the circumstances. If possible, a dedicated bereavement room should be available and adequate time should be given to parents to consider the issue. Information must be offered to parents/guardians and an open dialogue entered into prior to the authorisation of the hospital post mortem. The information must be presented in a clear and comprehensible but sensitive manner. A bereavement liaison officer should assist the parents in getting the information they need prior to their decision.

9   It is not intended to make specific recommendations as to the most appropriate person to discuss post mortems with the family, as this is deemed unnecessarily prescriptive. It will usually be a senior clinician who has a relationship with the parents, though a team approach may be preferable in some cases, involving nursing and midwifery staff in particular. Where possible, consultation with the hospital pathologist should take place prior to discussion with the parents so as to concentrate that discussion on issues of most relevance to the particular child. If the parents so request it, a pathologist must be available to answer specific queries or explain the post mortem in more detail.

10   The confidentiality of the post mortem report raises issues regarding its disclosure to other persons. Hospital post-mortem reports must be made available to the consultant clinician who treated the child, if there was one, and the child's general practitioner. It is recommended that the post-mortem report must also be offered to parents of deceased children with advice to seek any necessary

explanations from their general practitioners, consultants or the relevant pathologists. Where possible, a follow-up meeting between parents and clinicians must be arranged to discuss the post-mortem findings in as much detail as the parents require. If necessary or desirable in the circumstances, the pathologist may also be requested to attend such meetings. This facility must be made known to parents at the time of authorisation of the hospital post-mortem examination. Protocols must be put in place to provide a structure whereby parents receive a timely and appropriate response to their request for information.

11 It is recommended that parents be told in clear language when a coroner's post mortem is necessary and that, consequently, their consent is not required. They must also be told that organs may only be retained as part of this process for as long as is necessary to establish the cause of death and other relevant matters relating to the child's death. Parents must be given information and options in relation to disposal of the organs. Good, effective communication in all aspects of this discussion is of paramount importance.

12 In the case of a coroner's post-mortem, parents must be given the post mortem report on request, though the timing of its release may depend on whether or not an inquest is required in the circumstances. This should be made clear to parents in information provided to them from the outset of the process.

13 Where both parents are legal guardians of the child, it is recommended that either parent should be able to give authorisation for a hospital post-mortem examination. In the situation where only one parent is the legal guardian, the hospital would be legally entitled to proceed with the post mortem on the authorisation of that parent. Situations may exceptionally arise in which the parents of the child disagree as to whether or not to authorise a hospital post mortem on their child. Although the hospital would be entitled to proceed with a post mortem on the authorisation of one parent, irrespective of the marital or living arrangements of the child's parents, best practice should be not to proceed with a hospital post mortem in the face of objection from either parent.

14 It is recommended that the Department of Health and Children develop a public education and information programme about post mortems so that the public will have a better understanding of what is involved. This will serve to restore and improve public confidence in pathology and, it is hoped, improve post-mortem rates in Irish hospitals.

15 As part of the education and training of medical professionals, increased attention must be paid to communication skills and the legal and ethical issues involved in the removal and use of human organs and tissue. All relevant hospital staff must be trained in relation to the authorisation process.

16 Standardised authorisation forms must be drafted in consultation with interested parties, and used in all hospitals in conjunction with standard information booklets. A copy of the authorisation form must be kept on the patient's medical record as well as sent to the pathology department where the post mortem is carried out. The pathologist must ensure that authorisation has been given prior to

proceeding with the examination. Parents must also be given a copy of the authorisation form.

17 Measures must be adopted by all hospitals to ensure that all patient care staff receive mandatory training in responding to grief and bereavement.

18 Each hospital must have a bereavement liaison officer available to offer practical help and support to bereaved families and staff caring for those families. This officer must liase with the relevant pathology department and must have a good understanding of pathology practices so as to provide assistance to the family if required. Although it is the clinician's responsibility to discuss the post mortem with the parents, this may be done as part of a team approach with the bereavement liaison officer, who may provide appropriate follow-up support.

19 Post mortems should be viewed as a continuation of patient care and therefore part of clinical governance within the hospital. Although professional autonomy dictates the technical detail of the performance of the post mortem, responsibility for the administrative aspects of the process rests with hospital management who must make certain that protocols are in place to ensure that all legal requirements as to authorisation and record keeping are satisfactorily complied with. This also requires that an effective audit of post-mortem practice be regularly undertaken to reassure the public that past practices cannot recur and that the hospital's policies and practices conform to current legal requirements.

Chapter Five

Submissions from Hospitals

1 Introduction

1.1 This chapter analyses the practices that existed in Irish hospitals from 1970 to 2000 in relation to post mortems and organ retention, and the policies, if any, that existed in relation to the obtaining of consent. It also reflects changes in policies and practices that have taken place since 2000. As part of the Dunne Inquiry process, hospitals were invited to answer a set of detailed questions in order to elicit the relevant information on these issues. The information submitted by the hospitals varied enormously in length and complexity, with some hospitals additionally submitting clinical reports, minutes of meetings, any relevant correspondence, consent forms used since 1970, research publications and so on.

1.2 Rather than analyse each hospital in turn, the terms of reference for this report support an examination of general post-mortem practice across the various hospitals surveyed. The evidence presented to the Inquiry demonstrates a high level of consistency between the hospitals in relation to post-mortem practices. For that reason it would be unnecessarily repetitive to detail each hospital in turn. Therefore, an overview of post-mortem practice is presented here rather than an investigation of each individual hospital.

1.3 As in other countries, it has not been usual practice in Irish hospitals to provide information about organ retention to relatives of a deceased person. For many years consent was obtained, either verbally or on a very basic written form, following disclosure of minimal information. Parents of deceased children were usually not told about the incisions that would be made as part of the post-mortem process, or the extent and nature of the procedure, or how the body would be reconstructed following the examination. It was generally felt that disclosure of such disturbing details would be cruel in the circumstances. Retention of organs was felt to be one of the details that the family did not need to know.

1.4 Consent to post mortem was widely acknowledged as a necessary pre-requisite to performance of the procedure in hospital cases. This is clearly evident from documents dating back to the 1970s. However, the validity of such consent and the form in which it was obtained was very much a sign of the times, and has changed significantly over the period considered by this Inquiry. Some hospitals took the view that verbal consent was sufficient, which was then recorded on the patient's medical chart. Others produced a very simple consent form for relatives to sign, indicating their permission for the procedure to take place. By their own admission, clinicians commonly did not disclose details of the post-mortem procedure prior to asking relatives to sign these consent forms. As times changed over the 30-year time span covered by this Report, the concept of informed consent became more widely accepted in medical decision-making and consent forms became more informative. However, retention of organs was not explicitly stated on the consent forms in the description of the post-mortem process up to 1999.

1.5 The retention of *tissue* for diagnosis, education and research was included in the forms used by some hospitals, particularly in later years, but the word 'tissue' was not explained or described either on the form itself or verbally by the clinician. It may have been understood by the medical professionals to include organs, but those to whom the form was presented for signature did not share this understanding.

1.6 Tissue blocks and slides are an important part of the patient record and can provide important information for future reproductive and healthcare decisions. However, as this Report deals only with the retention of whole organs, the status of blocks and slides are not considered herein.

2 Post Mortems on Children Between 1970 and 2000

2.1 The statistics on post mortems provided by hospitals varied. Some hospitals gave a breakdown of figures for coroner and hospital post mortems. However, most hospitals or health boards did not generally provide individual statistics for post mortems performed on children, as this information had not been requested of them in the original set of scheduled questions put to the hospitals by the Dunne Inquiry. It was therefore assumed for the purposes of this Report that hospitals performing a large number of post mortems and/or those with large catchment areas performed post mortems on children at some point during the 30-year time period. In addition, the presence or otherwise of a maternity unit, paediatric unit, gynaecological service or obstetrics service was used in deciding whether to assess a hospital's statement as being within the remit of this Report. It is accepted that this assumption may be mistaken because there is no guarantee that hospitals carrying out large numbers of post mortems necessarily performed examinations on children. However, it was decided that in cases where the issue was unclear, inclusion rather than exclusion was the better approach.

2.2 Submissions were received from some health boards, as they then were, on behalf of hospitals in their area. Following the re-organisation of the health service administration, these health boards have been reconfigured and the hospitals are now under the responsibility of network managers within the National Hospitals Office of the Health Service Executive. Therefore, the following list, though accurate at the time of submission, may not be strictly accurate now. The following acute and private hospitals were included in this part of the survey for the reasons outlined in the preceding paragraph:

- Tralee General Hospital
- Our Lady's Hospital, Drogheda
- Portiuncula Hospital
- Cavan General Hospital
- Monaghan Hospital
- Roscommon County Hospital
- Bantry Hospital
- St James's Hospital, Dublin
- St Vincent's University Hospital, Dublin
- Beaumont, including St Laurence's Hospital and Jervis Street Hospital, Dublin

- Mallow General Hospital
- Mater Private Hospital, Dublin
- St Finbarr's Hospital, Cork
- St Columcille's Hospital, Loughlinstown
- Blackrock Clinic, Dublin
- National Rehabilitation Hospital, Dublin
- St Luke's Hospital, Rathgar, Dublin
- Our Lady's Hospital, Navan
- Letterkenny Hospital
- St Mary's Orthopaedic Hospital, Cork
- Erinville Hospital, Cork
- Our Lady's Hospital for Sick Children, Crumlin, Dublin
- Children's University Hospital, Temple Street, Dublin
- AMNCH (Adelaide and Meath Hospital incorporating the National Children's Hospital), Dublin
- The Coombe Women's Hospital, Dublin
- National Maternity Hospital, Holles Street, Dublin
- Rotunda Hospital, Dublin
- Cork University Hospital
- St Michael's Hospital Dún Laoghaire
- Naas General Hospital
- Mount Carmel Hospital, Dublin
- Mayo General Hospital
- Galway Regional Hospital
- Mercy Hospital, Cork
- South Infirmary/Victoria Hospital, Cork
- Sligo General Hospital
- St John's Hospital, Limerick
- Barrington's Hospital, Limerick (closed 31 March 1988)
- South Eastern Health Board, encompassing Waterford Regional; St Luke's Hospital, Kilkenny, St Josephs Hospital, Clonmel; and Wexford General Hospital
- Mid-Western Health Board encompassing Mid-Western Regional Hospital, Limerick; Ennis General Hospital; and the Hospital of the Assumption, Thurles
- Midland Health Board including Midland Regional Hospital at Portlaoise; Midland Regional Hospital at Tullamore; Midland Regional Hospital at Mullingar; and St Joseph's Hospital, Longford.

3 Policies Regarding Post Mortems

3.1 The majority of hospitals reported that they had not developed any written policies on post mortems during the period under investigation. The lack of a post-mortem policy was explained by stating that 'professional judgement' was used and that 'standard custom and practice applies'. The lack of discussion of post-mortem policy, practice and procedure by medical committees or boards was widespread. Most hospitals stated that they had no record of the matter being discussed until the organ retention controversy broke in 1999–2000.

3.2 Most hospitals have now drafted post-mortem policies in line with Faculty of Pathology Guidelines, Coroner and Non-Coroner Protocols and Procedure documents, and the Quality Response to Families drafted by the National Liaison Group on Organ Retention. An implementation plan for these protocols was agreed by the National Chief Officers in 2003.

4 Policies Regarding Consent

4.1 References to consent in this section, and in other sections of this chapter, necessarily refer to hospital post mortems and not coroner cases as consent was not, and is not, required for the latter.

4.2 Most hospitals had no *written* policy regarding consent, though they informed the Inquiry that they had a policy of obtaining consent for a hospital post mortem or stated that the clinician was charged with obtaining consent.

4.3 For the majority of hospitals, there appears to have been no policy pertaining to methods used or the information provided in requesting consent. Neither did they disclose any evidence that protocols existed for the amount of information to be provided to the next-of-kin when seeking consent. Medical professionals followed the custom and practice of those around them in the hospitals.

4.4 Some hospitals testified to using written consent forms during the relevant period. Most of these forms can be categorised as basic, meaning that they recorded consent to an examination, but this could not be described as informed consent. They do not refer to consent to the retention of organs and/or tissue, nor do they refer to the issue of a limited post mortem.

4.5 In general, most hospitals and health boards first grappled with the issue of informed consent to post mortem and organ retention in a concentrated manner when the controversy broke in 1999–2000, though some had introduced more detailed forms before that date, dealing with retention of 'tissue'.

5 Hospital Practices for Obtaining Consent to a Post Mortem

5.1 It is difficult to establish any patterns in the practice of the hospitals regarding the obtaining of consent. Hospitals within the same geographical area diverged on the methods used, while some acknowledged that the ways in which consent was requested varied from case to case.

5.2 Generally, the clinician who cared for the deceased person was the person responsible for obtaining consent. The individual who spoke to parents varied, however, with hospitals submitting that a range of personnel, including consultants, junior doctors or senior nurses would request consent. No predominant pattern emerges about the identity of the person who spoke to families about the matter.

5.3 Likewise, there is no predominant pattern showing that verbal consent or written consent to a post mortem was the norm across the hospitals surveyed. Indeed, some hospitals or groups stated that they had introduced written forms but admitted that verbal consent would, nevertheless, have been used in some cases. This practice was discouraged but accepted in a few exceptional cases subject to a policy of a written note being entered on the hospital chart and a signed form being sent in the post by the relatives.

5.4 Written consent forms were introduced in a majority of the hospitals surveyed at some point in the period under review, with more details given on the form in recent years. The consent form used by most hospitals up to recent years was basic and simply stated that the signatory gave permission for a post-mortem examination on his/her child. Such forms did not seek consent for organ retention. Neither did they usually mention the possibility of consenting to a limited post mortem, though this was expressly raised as a possibility in at least one hospital from 1997.

5.5 A written form of consent was introduced at Cork University Hospital (then Cork Regional Hospital) in 1979. This was based on a form of consent used in the United Kingdom under the Human Tissue Act, 1961. It specifically provided for the retention of tissue for laboratory study and for the treatment of other patients, and for medical education and research. On the evidence produced to the Inquiry, this represents the earliest introduction of a written consent form which informed the person that 'tissue' might be retained in the course of the post mortem. 'Tissue' was not defined on the form. A number of other hospitals also submitted that they addressed consent to retention of 'tissues' in the written consent forms used. Some hospitals explain that if the reference to retention of tissues was deleted on the form, organs were not retained for these purposes. This may be a suggestion that consent to organ retention was sought, though it appears that the meaning of 'tissues' was not explained to parents.

5.6 Although some hospitals used a written consent form, it was acknowledged that locum pathologists may have accepted verbal consent during the period under investigation. Consent was also obtained by telephone in some cases where the patient's family was not present in the hospital at the relevant time. Where verbal consent was sought, some hospitals acknowledge that it was not always recorded on the patient's chart.

6 Information Provided to Parents

6.1 The general practice was for the consultant with responsibility for the patient to obtain consent from the family. If the consultant were not available, the next most senior clinical person would do so. The person seeking consent made a subjective determination on how much information to provide to the family. Up to 1999 it was not the practice of clinicians at most hospitals to obtain consent to organ retention.

6.2 The pathologist would proceed with the post mortem on the basis of a request form from the clinician. This usually did not make any reference to whether or not consent from the parents had been obtained.

6.3 In relation to the information usually given to parents during the consent process, it was rarely reported prior to 2000 that information was sought by parents as to the technical nature of the post mortem. It became common practice by the late 1980s to specifically state that the body would be opened up, similar to having an operation, that there would be an incision, that the internal organs would be examined, and that there would be a cranial incision and examination. There might be specific reference to the heart, kidneys or whatever organ was the primary cause of concern, being examined. Although these discussions were not recorded, some hospitals noted that the nature and extent of the discussions changed over the years, becoming lengthier over time.

6.4 A number of submissions addressed the issue of the training of personnel for the task of requesting consent. Most staff gained experience from witnessing their peers obtain consent and thus developed expertise in clinical practice. As such, this appears to suggest that on-the-job training was the order of the day in requesting consent, and established habits were followed.

6.5 It is difficult to categorise the practices used by the hospitals. Some required only verbal consent until the late 1990s. Others had introduced written forms but did not refer to the retention of organs on those forms. There were inconsistencies in the practices adopted within health board areas and within hospitals themselves. No standardised approach is apparent. Moreover, few hospitals addressed the issue of what information was afforded to parents/next-of-kin when clinicians or other personnel made the request.

6.6 Hospitals have changed their policies and practices on the matter since 1999–2000. In most hospitals the clinician must now ensure that the family understands the reasons for the post mortem and an information leaflet is usually provided. This is recorded further in other sections.

7 Hospitals' Perceptions about the Expectations/Knowledge of Parents regarding the Post Mortem Process

7.1 There was a perception amongst the hospitals that families had little understanding of the post-mortem process. According to some hospitals, the next-of -kin would expect to be informed of the purpose and scope of the autopsy and the difference between a diagnostic and coroner's autopsy. But they acknowledge that there would generally not have been a great awareness of the issues pertaining to post-mortem practice and procedure until recent years.

7.2 A contrasting view is given by other hospitals, which state that they assumed that the next-of-kin understood that part of the post mortem involved the sampling of tissues and, on occasion, the removal of organs for microscopic examination.

7.3 Hospitals generally accept that information was not provided to families about the details of the procedure. The underlying reason advanced for this appears to have been a desire not to upset them with the details of the procedure. Requesting consent to post mortem is very difficult at a time of trauma for parents and next-of-kin. Prior to the controversy that arose in 1999–2000, hospitals state that pathologists were not aware that next-of-kin had particular expectations in relation to the removal, retention, storage or disposal of organs. Pathologists were aware, however, that families expected post mortems to be conducted quickly so as not to delay the funeral and they would also expect the body to be returned in a good condition.

7.4 Some hospitals stated that it was difficult to generalise about the expectations of parents, because some parents wanted minimal information, whereas others wanted more information. Hospitals state that senior clinicians could assess the expectations of families on a case-by-case basis.

7.5 A number of hospitals referred to the issue of trust as a factor that impacted on the expectations of families. Hospitals comment that relatives expected that their loved one was treated with respect and dignity at all times, and that a post mortem would be performed in accordance with 'good clinical practice'. Other hospitals also spoke of the expectation of parents that the post mortem would be conducted with dignity, sensitivity and respect.

7.6 Apart from that it was noted that where there was a possibility of hereditary transmission involved or where family members were at risk of developing a similar disorder, they would expect to receive genetic counselling and advice from an expert.

7.7 It is acknowledged in the submissions received from hospitals that the expectations of parents have changed over the time period covered by this report. From 1970-1980 parents may have expected to be informed of some of the procedures involved in a post mortem. Given the culture at the time they probably did not generally expect bereavement support or a discussion about the information obtained at post mortem, though this did happen on occasion. From 1980–1990 bereavement and terminal care support were sometimes provided for families as a response to new thinking in the area of bereavement. From 1990–2000 parents expected to receive information regarding the post mortem and some hospitals undertook to meet bereaved families to explain the cause of death and the post mortem to them, though this support was not always well-coordinated within the various departments of the hospitals.

7.8 It is difficult to avoid viewing times past without the application and benefit of hindsight. Moreover, it is difficult to apply the proper wider context of the particular time, given the cultural, technological, economic and other advances that have taken place since 1970. However, in general, hospitals acknowledge that the expectations of parents may have included the following:

- that a post-mortem examination would not be carried out unless they gave their consent
- that, if consent was given for a post-mortem examination, a post-mortem examination would be carried out
- that any post-mortem examination would be carried out by a suitably qualified person in an appropriate setting
- that the funeral of their deceased infant/next-of-kin would not be unduly delayed, or indeed, delayed at all
- that the body would be able to be viewed in the usual way, that is, any incisions made would not extend down onto the face or be apparent when the body was dressed

- that the parent/next-of-kin might wish to touch or hold their deceased infant following completion of the autopsy
- that their deceased infant would be treated with care and respect at all times whilst in the care of the hospital within the context of the post-mortem examination
- that the results of the post-mortem examination would be made available to them and discussed with them by an appropriate medical professional
- that the results of the post-mortem examination would have been accompanied by appropriate follow-up and referral, for example, to genetic counselling services
- that, for those parents who considered the issue, the body of their child would be returned to them complete with its organs.

7.9 Since 2000, parents may also have additional expectations to be provided with sufficient information to enable them to make an informed decision regarding the post mortem, retention of tissues, and disposal. Parents also reasonably expect to be given an opportunity to ask questions, to limit the post-mortem examination, to receive communication regarding the post-mortem results, and to have their wishes respected.

8 Was Consent Requested for Organ Retention?

8.1 The definition of 'human tissue' adopted by the Dunne Inquiry as 'human material' appears to have impacted on some hospital submissions, because all pathologists considered that taking tissue samples is an integral part of any post mortem, and some therefore believed that the consent given for post mortem necessarily included consent for the taking of tissue samples and organs if necessary. Consent forms used by some hospitals specifically referred to seeking consent for retention of 'tissues'. Some hospitals contend that seeking consent for retention of tissues equated to seeking consent for organ retention.

8.2 According to the submissions surveyed, express consent for organ retention was not specifically sought by hospitals. Until 2000, it was generally not the practice of hospitals to inform parents or next-of-kin of the full details of organ removal, retention, storage or disposal. Most hospitals considered that the consent to conduct a post mortem implied consent to retain an organ, and this was the prevailing standard practice of hospitals for the period from 1970 to 2000.

8.3 There was a general feeling on the part of medical staff that to give such detail in the absence of any evidence to suggest that it was required, or was necessary, or was common practice, would be considered cruel and insensitive to parents and next-of-kin. Most hospitals accept that parents would be unlikely to be aware of organ retention, and that even where there were follow-up consultations in relation to post-mortem results or subsequent pregnancies, these meetings did not prompt queries relating to retention of tissue or organs.

8.4 As regards coroner post mortems, hospitals submitted that consent for organ retention did not arise in such circumstances, so that it was not deemed necessary to seek consent. Hospitals viewed the retention of organs as a matter for the coroner to determine in such cases. In some hospitals pathologists occasionally retained organs at a coroner's post mortem for teaching purposes. Consent to this retention was not obtained.

8.5 All of the hospitals referred to the change in practice brought about by the controversy. In all hospitals, the matter is now addressed in a specific way with families by the provision of information and discussion with staff. Consent is sought for organ retention and the family make a decision on organ disposal prior to the commencement of the post mortem. This decision is implemented when the examination of the organs is completed.

9 Did Hospitals Retain Organs for a Period after Post Mortems?

9.1 Some submissions disagreed with the definition of 'organ' given by the Dunne Inquiry and stated that their retention practices were related to 'tissue' rather than 'organs'. For example, one hospital states that in 21 per cent of cases the brain was retained, and in 1 per cent of cases the spinal cord was retained. Other whole organs were retained in less than 1 per cent of cases. Tissue samples were retained in 89 per cent of cases in accordance with best practice guidelines.

9.2 Most hospitals stated that organ retention was confined to a small number of cases though the estimation of numbers or percentages is usually vague due to the absence of records of retention. There is also an apparent divergence in the approach of some practitioners evident from the submissions, both in their understanding of the necessity of organ retention and its frequency in practice. Some submissions take the view that where pathologists were not retaining organs or tissues they were not doing their job to the best of their ability.

9.3 All internal organs would commonly be removed during the post-mortem process and organs would be retained at the pathologist's discretion. Organs were retained for diagnostic purposes or for teaching if there was a complex defect or unusual lesions detected at autopsy. The most common organ retained was the brain.

10 Why were Organs Retained by Hospitals?

10.1 Diagnostic purposes was the primary reason advanced for organ retention by most hospitals. The organ may be retained to obtain a second opinion by a more specialised pathologist and/or for further extended examination where the cause of death was unclear or in doubt. In a paediatric situation it was easier and more practical to keep the entire lung for examination because it was so small to begin with. Some hospitals noted it was difficult to examine the brain in its 'fresh' state, so it would have to be retained for a period of time.

10.2 Although most hospitals submitted that organ retention was common practice, particularly in paediatric pathology, a small number of pathologists expressed the view that retention was unnecessary in most cases. In the hospitals at which these pathologists worked, the rate of organ retention was therefore relatively low. According to this minority view, although the organs, particularly the brain, would always be removed for examination, once tissue sampling of the organ was carried out the organ could be replaced in the body. This view is not reflected in professional guidelines and other statements of international best practice.

10.3 It was also acknowledged in some submissions that hospitals with national specialities would have retained a greater proportion of organs in those specialities than other hospitals. For example, hearts would be more frequently retained in a hospital that specialises in congenital heart disease.

10.4 A few hospitals stated that organs were retained for teaching and research, as two additional purposes of the practice of pathology. It has been stated that doctors may be educated as a result of autopsy findings and therefore it is not possible fully to separate diagnosis and education, although the primary purpose of the autopsy is neither education nor research. Others emphasise that the diagnostic efficacy of post mortems has hinged directly on contemporary and past research, and that it should be regarded as an ongoing process. In a minority of hospitals, organs were retained from post mortems for research both in Ireland and the United Kingdom. Consent was sometimes obtained for retention of 'tissue' for these purposes but organs were not referred to. In a small number of teaching hospitals organs were retained in pathology museums on an anonymous basis.

10.5 The necessity for organ retention has generally been considered best determined by the appropriate consultant pathologist according to the needs of each particular case, taking into account international practice at the relevant time. However, the absence of national guidelines in relation to the retention of organs contributed to a perception of inconsistency across pathologists and hospitals.

11 Storage of Retained Organs

11.1 Organs were fixed in formalin and stored in plastic containers. Containers were labelled and numbered so that they could be identified. Organs were generally stored in the pathology laboratories/departments, mortuary rooms or histopathology storerooms. During the retention period the pathologist and/or scientific staff in the pathology department would manage them and the clinicians had no role in this regard. According to most hospitals, organ storage was in accordance with health and safety regulations.

11.2 Organs were stored for the period required for examinations to take place. Thereafter, the organs would be disposed of as clinical waste. Estimates for the periods of organ retention varied between 2 and 3 months, while some hospitals stated that the retention period was determined by the pathologist's examination. They go on to state that the pathologist may retain organs for a longer period in some cases and it appears that, in some hospitals, organs were stored for a number of years rather than months. These instances would usually involve medico-legal, forensic or occupational health issues. Some hospitals provided no estimates of the amount of time organs were retained. In some hospitals the retained organs were not catalogued and became desiccated over time. A routine review of stored organs was not common practice.

11.3 In maternity hospitals more emphasis is placed on the fact that a woman's normal reproductive life spans 25 years or more. In the early 1980s, in keeping with advances in perinatal medicine and ultrasound diagnosis, some of the maternity hospitals began to retain organs for longer periods to try to elucidate causes for unexplained stillbirths.

11.4 In some cases organs have been sent to other institutions for further specialist examination and analysis. In other cases, the post mortem itself occurred at the other hospital. Hospitals now have a practice of retaining organs until families have expressed their wishes as to their disposal.

12 Return of Organs

12.1 Few hospitals addressed this issue. The prevalence of organ disposal via incineration at some time after the examination by the pathologists may explain this. A small number of hospitals have returned organs for burial since 2000 at the request of the families. Details are given of the arrangements made in this regard to comply with the family's wishes, with hospitals generally providing financial and bereavement support for the burial where required by the family.

13 Disposal of Organs by Hospitals

13.1 The hospitals' submissions recorded that the prevailing length for retention was until such time as the examinations by the pathologist were carried out. Thereafter, it appears that most hospitals disposed of the organs, though some were retained for lengthier periods. Disposal appears to have been within the control of the pathology department of the hospitals, with little or no medical or management oversight. There was generally no record kept of organ disposal and in some cases organs were stored for a number of years instead of being disposed of, probably due to administrative oversight. Methods of disposal used were burial and incineration, with incineration being the more prevalent form of disposal. Some hospitals had their own incineration facilities for some of the period under investigation and some hospitals used private companies or other hospitals to dispose of organs.

13.2 Following Department of the Environment regulations in 1989 and the establishment of the Environmental Protection Agency in the early 1990s some hospitals were forced to close their incinerators and had to make alternative arrangements. A number of hospitals contracted with a private company for disposal, and that company exported clinical waste to other countries such as the United Kingdom and Holland. A number of hospitals subsequently purchased burial plots in cemeteries to deal with situations in which the families chose not to make their own arrangements for burial of the organs. Cremation of individual organs was also facilitated in recent years where this was specifically requested.

13.3 Most hospitals submitted that disposal was carried out in accordance with applicable clinical waste procedures and Department of Health and Children guidelines. There were no specific guidelines from the Department of Health and Children in relation to the disposal of organs following post-mortem examination at any time since 1970. Guidelines have emanated from the Department in relation to the disposal of clinical healthcare waste generally, which encompasses organs. In 1994 the Department issued a policy document dealing with the Air Pollution Act, 1987 and EC Directive 91/689. In April 1996 draft specifications were sent to hospitals for dealing with the treatment or disposal of clinical healthcare waste, and in June and October 1996 the Department issued further communication relating to management plans for exports and imports of waste. A circular was also issued by the Department advising hospitals not to enter into contractual arrangements for the disposal of healthcare waste without prior consultation with the Department, and informing hospitals that the Department had entered into an agreement with a private company for the disposal of clinical waste. Further communication was issued in 1997 relating to contractual arrangements for collection and disposal of waste. A more detailed document called *Segregation and Storage Guidelines of Health Care Risk Waste* was issued in 1999.

13.4 Hospitals have responded to the controversy by providing families with pre-examination options for disposal of organs after the post mortem has been concluded. Where families want organs returned to them this is organised by the relevant hospital.

14 Maintenance of Records for Organ Retention

14.1 Formal recording of organs retained by hospitals was not commonplace amongst those surveyed. Generally the only formal records relating to the issue would have been within the post-mortem examination report itself. However, while the report usually states whether the brain was retained, it rarely records if an organ was retained for education purposes.

14.2 Few hospitals kept a register of retained organs. Furthermore, no standard practice for recording retention on post-mortem reports appears to have been operating because hospitals recorded organ retention to varying degrees in reports. Once again, hospitals have accounted for the change in practices and the implementation of national protocols since the controversy broke in 1999–2000.

15 What Information was Given to Parents following the Post Mortem?

15.1 Methods of providing information to parents after the post mortem varied. The hospitals addressed the issue of how post mortem results were communicated. Little or no information was provided on any other issues. All hospitals noted that the requesting clinician was supplied with a copy of the post-mortem report in hospital post-mortem situations. The prevailing practice in most hospitals was that the notification of the family was the responsibility of the clinician in charge of the case.

15.2 How the results were communicated varied, however, and no predominant practice is apparent from the submissions surveyed. Some hospitals stated that the clinician or medical team informed the families. In contrast, sometimes the practice was that the results were sent to the family's general practitioner so that he/she could inform the family. In some hospitals families were offered the opportunity to return to the hospital some time after their bereavement so as to discuss their child's illness and death with medical staff. These meetings became accepted as standard practice, although not all families took up the opportunity. When a post mortem had been carried out discussion about post-mortem findings usually took place at these meetings.

15.3 The 1990s saw significant changes in the level of information being provided to families after post-mortem examination. It became more common for consultants in some hospitals to provide parents/next-of-kin, at their request, with copies of the post-mortem report. As a result, some hospitals decided to alter the format of the post-mortem report so that the first section only was provided to parents, and not details of the anatomical dissection. This decision was taken on the basis that it was thought that giving parents the full report would be insensitive and would cause additional, unnecessary distress. A designated member of the midwifery or nursing staff also sometimes provided bereavement support services.

15.4 None of the submissions stated that the post-mortem report was given to families as of right. Submissions referred to a *request* for a copy of the report by families.

16 Coroner Post Mortems

16.1 Few hospitals addressed the practice and procedure of coroner post mortems in detail in their submissions for the relevant period. Some noted that the pathologist was independent of the hospital and was, therefore, acting as an agent of the coroner while performing the post-mortem examination. The general policy was for medical staff to contact the Garda Síochána, who then liaised with the coroner. In some cases the Garda contacted the pathologist.

16.2 Little information was provided about the discussions held with families regarding a coroner's post mortem. Instructions from a coroner to carry out a post mortem were invariably verbal (by telephone) and did not include an instruction in relation to organ retention.

16.3 Hospitals submitted that consent for organ retention was not sought in coroner post mortems because it did not arise or it was not deemed necessary to do so.

16.4 In relation to coroner post mortems, some hospitals noted that requests for the reports had to be made to the coroner's office. Information was given to families about results when the coroner's permission had been obtained to do so.

16.5 Some hospitals provided information about the practices now applicable to coroner post mortems. Several referred to the provision of information leaflets about the procedure, which began in 2000. Some ask families to sign a form indicating that they have been informed that a coroner's post mortem is taking place and that body parts may be retained. Hospitals require direct confirmation from the coroner of the direction to perform a post mortem before commencing the procedure, either by telephone call which is logged in the post-mortem diary, or by written direction.

16.6 Other hospitals make provision for the families to choose an option for organ disposal after the coroner's process is complete. Some provide for consultations with families in relation to organ disposal following post mortem.

17 Conclusion

17.1 As with Chapter Four, which deals with the accounts submitted by parents, this chapter sets out the hospitals' perspective on post mortems carried out during the period covered by the Inquiry. There was a large and unsurprising degree of consistency between the hospitals in relation to the technical performance of post mortems and the necessity for organ retention. Differences between the hospitals existed principally in relation to the form of consent used.

17.2 The practice in Irish hospitals since 1970 was, and is, to carry out post-mortem examinations either on the authorisation of the coroner or at the request of a clinician involved in the care of a patient during life. Hospital post mortems have been assumed to require the consent of the family of the deceased, though this is not set out in any legislative provision.

17.3 Post mortems are of benefit to the child's family in helping to complete the picture of why the child died, and may also be of value to future patients and medical professionals in increasing the level of knowledge relating to the condition from which the child died or the treatment the child received. As a necessary part of post-mortem examinations, pathologists use their professional expertise to determine whether or not to retain organs in order to assist in the diagnostic process. This is in keeping with best practice and international guidelines. However, revelations that organs were retained without the knowledge of the parents and families of the deceased child have caused immense distress and distrust amongst bereaved families. Although some parents understood what a post-mortem examination entailed and why it might have been recommended to them, the hospitals did not have a policy of informing parents of post-mortem practices or organ retention. This is not disputed by the hospitals.

17.4 It is clear from the evidence submitted to the Inquiry that organs were retained in some cases for longer periods than was necessary for diagnosis, and may have been used for education and training of medical professionals, or for research purposes in a small number of cases. Storage facilities were not always sufficient for maintenance of these organs and it appears that there was no effective protocol in most hospitals for disposing of organs no longer required for diagnosis. The common practice seems to have been to have 'clear-outs' of these storage facilities at regular or irregular periods, or at the discretion of the supervising pathologist. This is reflective of a professional pragmatism in relation to storage capacity, and a difference in perspective in relation to the symbolic significance of the organs.

17.5 A lack of care in the storage of these retained organs is apparent from the failure to maintain appropriate records of retention and disposal and may be explained by the different professional perspective pathologists had towards such organs. They did not appreciate the emotional attachment parents had to the child's organs. In many cases records are missing or incomplete and, even where post-mortem records are available, they commonly do not refer to organ retention or disposal. Educated guesses may be made as to retention based on the diagnosis entered on post-mortem records but this is clearly unsatisfactory.

17.6 Following the retention period, organs were commonly incinerated as healthcare waste either at the hospital itself, or transferred to other hospital sites, or in latter years transferred to private companies for disposal abroad. Though parents were outraged at the revelations of these practices and the categorisation of their children's organs as 'waste', the system of disposal employed by hospitals was not intentionally disrespectful to the children or their families. Hospitals were constrained by health and safety regulations in this regard and were obliged to consider organs as clinical waste.

17.7 Hospitals report changes in practice since this controversy arose in 1999. Hospitals, clinicians and pathologists are now aware of the importance attached by parents towards the organs of their deceased children and endeavour to ensure that parents are given all appropriate options in relation to the organs following the post mortem. Options available to families include, in some cases, postponement of the funeral until the organs can be reunited with the body; respectful disposal of the organs by the hospital at the family's request; return of the organs to the family at a later date for subsequent burial if they so wish.

17.8 It was the policy in all hospitals that consent should be obtained for diagnostic post-mortem examinations, though it is impossible to conclude whether or not this policy was always complied with, as records are no longer available in many cases. The means of obtaining consent varied between hospitals and over the years spanned by this report. Verbal consent may have been obtained and not recorded on the patient's chart, though some parents are clear in their recollection that their consent was not obtained at all. It was not the function of this Inquiry to investigate individual cases to attempt to resolve these factual disputes.

17.9 'Informed consent', as we know it today, was not obtained up to the 1990s or even later in some cases. This was due to many factors including the paternalistic culture of the time, and the context of grief in which the discussion about post mortem arose. In some hospitals verbal consent recorded on the patient's clinical notes was deemed adequate until the late 1990s, whereas in other hospitals a basic consent form was introduced in the 1970s. Detailed explanation of post-mortem procedures was not usually a feature of the consent process up to the 1980s and 1990s, with consent sometimes regarded as simply the formality of obtaining a signature. Where written forms were available, the language used was sometimes vague and misleading, particularly with references to 'tissue', which was not understood by parents to possibly mean whole organs.

17.10 Parents were not informed that it was common practice during post-mortem examinations to consider the necessity to retain organs for diagnostic, and sometimes other purposes such as teaching. The hospitals' view is that parents were not told or asked for consent to this practice because it was not in their best interests at the time of bereavement and it was also deemed implicit in the consent given to post-mortem examination that all necessary procedures would be carried out in order to reach a diagnosis, including retention of organs if appropriate. Parents were not told about the storage and subsequent disposal of organs for much the same reasons.

17.11 Whatever the justification advanced by the hospitals, the fact remains that parents were not informed or asked for their consent to retain organs from a post mortem carried out on their child. There is no real factual dispute on this issue. In the absence of legislative provisions to the contrary, clinicians either assumed that consent to post mortem included all that was necessarily involved in that examination, or took it upon themselves to give parents as much information as they thought the parents needed to know. The conclusion of this Report on the issue is that, though well motivated and within the accepted culture of the time, this does not provide sufficient justification for practices that were paternalistic and would now be unacceptable.

18 Recommendations

These recommendations are made in the knowledge that national protocols were drafted and adopted in 2003 following consultation with stakeholders. Some of these recommendations have therefore already been implemented in many Irish hospitals. However, in the interests of consistency and clarity across the hospital networks, it is deemed desirable to set out the recommendations here.

1   Clear national protocols must be put in place by the Department of Health and Children and Health Services Executive to deal with queries from families in respect of post mortem practices as well as the provision of standardised forms to be used on a national basis. The language to be used in such forms must be clear and comprehensible, and must avoid medical or legal jargon. Existing guidelines produced by the National Working Group on Organ Retention in 2002, and adopted by National Chief Officers in 2003 may be used as the basis on which to make any adaptations recommended in this Report. This must be done in consultation with relevant stakeholders.

2   Healthcare providers must ensure that health service employees are instructed in post-mortem policy and relevant procedures for giving information to parents. This must be included as part of the induction process for new entrants to the healthcare service.

3   Each hospital must have a bereavement liaison officer available to offer practical help and support to bereaved families and staff caring for those families. This officer must liase with the relevant pathology department and should have a good understanding of pathology practices so as to provide assistance to the family if required. Although it is the clinician's responsibility to discuss the post mortem with the parents, this may be done as part of a team approach with the bereavement liaison officer, who may provide appropriate follow-up support.

4   Post mortems must be viewed as a continuation of patient care and therefore part of clinical governance within the hospital. Although professional autonomy dictates the technical detail of the performance of the post mortem, responsibility for the administrative aspects of the process rests with hospital management who must make certain that protocols are in place to ensure all legal requirements as to authorisation and record keeping are satisfactorily complied with. This also

requires that an effective audit of post mortem practice be regularly undertaken to reassure the public that past practices cannot recur and that the hospital's policies and practices conform to current legal requirements.

5   An independent audit must be carried out of currently retained organs in all hospitals in the State. The Department of Health and Children and the Health Service Executive should engage in a public information campaign informing relatives that they may reclaim any currently retained organs within a 12-month period from the date of this Report. This should be organised and managed via a central enquiry line rather than by individual hospitals. Families who do not contact hospitals in this regard should not be approached with this information. Their right not to know must be respected, provided reasonable efforts have been made to disseminate information publicly.

6   If, after this 12-month period, organs remain unclaimed, they must be disposed of respectfully by the hospital in line with written policies. This must be done in accordance with health and safety regulations and will entail either burial in an approved hospital plot, or cremation. Conformity with policies and regulations must be demonstrated in accurate record keeping and monitored by periodic audit.

7   Accurate and detailed record keeping of retention and disposal of organs at post mortem must be maintained in all pathology departments in accordance with best practice guidelines. Physical disposal or return of organs to families must be carried out by technical services staff or the bereavement liaison officer respectively, in accordance with hospital policy and the wishes of the parent/guardian.

8   It is recommended that guidance be given by the hospital to families regarding burial or cremation of the organs and that they be advised to use an undertaker for this process. An information sheet setting out the necessary information must be given to families to whom organs are being returned.

9   Where organs are to be disposed of by the hospital in accordance with the wishes of the family, this must be done in accordance with health and safety guidelines established by the Department of Health and Children. These guidelines must ensure that the organs are treated with dignity and respect insofar as this can be facilitated by the safe and hygienic disposal method chosen.

10 The Department of Health and Children must engage in a public education and information programme to ensure that members of the public are informed as much as possible as to the post-mortem procedure, the value of retention of organs and tissue, the importance of pathology practices in our healthcare system, the value of post mortems in the education of medical professionals and in the carrying out of significant research, and the rights of families in this regard. Restoration of public confidence in medical practice, and specifically pathology practices, is vitally important to encourage a higher rate of post mortems in our hospitals.

11 Parents must be offered information as soon as possible following the post-mortem examination. If they seek to receive a copy of the post-mortem report, this request must be facilitated and any necessary explanations of medical terms provided by the treating clinician or general practitioner. Where possible, a follow-up meeting between parents and clinicians must be arranged to discuss the post-mortem findings in as much detail as the parents require. If necessary or desirable in the circumstances, the pathologist may also be requested to attend such meetings. Protocols must be put in place to provide a structure whereby parents receive a timely and appropriate response to their request for information.

12 Where a coroner's post mortem is required, parents must be so informed clearly and without delay. An information booklet setting out the powers and functions of the coroner, and the procedural aspects of the coronial jurisdiction, should be made available to the family. The appointment of coroner's officers is strongly recommended as a necessary facet of the provision of information to families.

Chapter Six

Pituitary Glands

1 Introduction

1.1 In addition to the question of whether organs were retained from post mortems carried out on their deceased children, in 2000 parents also became aware that pituitary glands may have been removed from their children without their knowledge or consent and supplied to pharmaceutical companies for the manufacture of growth hormone.

1.2 This chapter sets out the facts relating to the removal of pituitary glands from children undergoing post-mortem examinations in Irish hospitals. Although this Report deals only with paediatric post mortems and therefore concentrates on pituitary glands supplied from post mortems carried out on children, it is important to note that the supply of pituitary glands was not confined to paediatric cases. It is estimated that 90 per cent of the pituitary glands supplied in this country were removed at post mortems performed on deceased adults. The supply of pituitary glands for the manufacture of growth hormone was also common practice in other jurisdictions at the same time that it was taking place in Ireland.

1.3 This chapter sets out the general practice in relation to the storage and subsequent use of those glands by two pharmaceutical companies, Kabi Vitrum and Nordisk Gentofte, for the manufacture of human growth hormone. It was not feasible during the course of this Inquiry to correlate hospital post-mortem record numbers with consignment numbers provided by the pharmaceutical companies involved in this arrangement. The companies do not have any means of identifying the deceased from whom the glands may have been removed. This chapter is therefore concerned only with the generality of the practice and cannot address whether glands were taken in individual cases.

2 What is the Pituitary Gland?

2.1 The pituitary gland is located in the skull at the base of the brain and is responsible for the production of different types of hormones, including growth hormones. It influences height and also has other benefits in relation to bone and muscle building. In the normal person the human growth hormone is produced naturally during the course of life. The content of growth hormone in the gland depends on the size of the gland and the amount of growth hormone-producing cells in the gland.

2.2 The use of the human growth hormone, made from the gland and injected into patients, stimulated growth in young children who were deficient in the natural production of the hormone. Until the introduction of a biosynthetic form of the hormone in the mid-1980s, the only source of the pituitary gland was from dead bodies.

3 Retention of the Pituitary Gland

3.1 Pituitary glands were retained by the pathology departments of many hospitals at the request of pharmaceutical companies and used for the purpose of the manufacture of human growth hormone on a commercial basis. It was used in the treatment of a condition affecting children and known as short stature or, more technically, 'dwarfism'. The collection of pituitary glands occurred worldwide.

3.2 Justification for the practice was provided by some hospitals who regarded it as a humanitarian act. The practice of supplying pituitary glands to the pharmaceutical company developed over a period of time in the belief that it was necessary in the best interest of society. This was at a time when pituitary glands were in very short supply due to the absence of a synthetically manufactured substitute.

3.3 Hospitals viewed the provision of pituitary glands as common practice at the time because it was the only way of collecting material for the manufacture of growth hormone. Some hospitals seeking growth hormone therapy at that time stated that they were obliged to contribute glands in exchange for the treatment. In the case of Kabi Vitrum, there was no known relationship between the number of vials available for distribution in Ireland and the number of pituitary glands supplied to the company.

3.4 The use of the pituitary glands in this way was at a time when consent to a hospital post-mortem examination was regarded by clinicians and pathologists as giving an implied authority to do all that was necessary at that examination.

4 The Pharmaceutical Companies

4.1 From the evidence presented to the Inquiry, two international pharmaceutical companies were involved in the collection of pituitary glands from hospital pathology departments in Ireland in the 1970s and 1980s. These were: Kabi Vitrum (later known as Pharmacia and Upjohn and now by the name Pharmacia Ireland Ltd) and Nordisk Gentofte (now Nova Nordisk A/S). Kabi Vitrum collected glands at various hospitals including Our Lady's Hospital for Sick Children, Crumlin and the Children's University Hospital, Temple Street.

4.2 In the mid 1960s Nordisk Gentofte (now Novo Nordisk A/S) started to produce pituitary human growth hormone. The hormone was produced from human pituitary glands collected at post-mortem examinations throughout Europe and elsewhere. Its collection of pituitary glands in Ireland occurred between 1976 and 1988. In 1973, the growth hormone was registered in Denmark under the name *Nanormon* and from around that time was made available to children in a number of countries including Ireland and throughout the world. Nordisk Gentofte maintained a supply principle related to the post-mortem collection of pituitary glands worldwide including Ireland. For every pituitary gland collected from a country, the company would sell to hospitals in that country one capped vial of *Nanormon*. This was because the product was in short supply due to the difficulty of obtaining raw material for the manufacture of the product. The hormone was licensed in Ireland up to 30 September 1986.

5 Distribution of the Human Growth Hormone

5.1 Kabi Vitrum sold human growth hormone in Ireland and elsewhere under the brand name Crescormon®. It was a licensed prescription medicine in Ireland and a product authorisation was granted by the Department of Health and Children on 26 November 1976 to Kabi's Irish agent. An amended product authorisation was issued on 25 July 1978. The product was ultimately withdrawn on 25 April 1985.

5.2 Nordisk Gentofte was facilitated by a local distributor in Ireland, Leo Laboratories Ltd, who up to the mid-1980s carried out the collection of pituitary glands from hospitals in Ireland on behalf of Nordisk Gentofte. After this time Nordisk Gentofte carried out the collection by its own representative office.

6 Exclusion of Certain Pituitary Glands

6.1 Detailed written instructions were given by Kabi Vitrum and Nordisk Gentofte concerning the glands to be included in the consignments. A deceased person was not eligible for the post-mortem extraction of the pituitary gland if:

- the cause of death was hepatitis, sepsis, meningitis, encephalitis or multiple sclerosis
- the deceased had had dialysis or a transplant
- the deceased had signs indicating an addiction to self-injected narcotics
- the deceased had a macroscopically changed pituitary gland
- the deceased had been embalmed
- the deceased was suspected of being at increased risk of transmitting viral infections.

In addition, the post-mortem examination had to have been performed within 72 hours of death.

6.2 Kabi Vitrum submitted to the Inquiry that in addition to the specific exclusions referred to above, it specified during meetings with chief hospital pathologists that pituitary glands were only to be extracted from deceased patients upon whom a post mortem had been directed, and that the post mortem had to involve the opening of the skull for reasons separate from and independent of the collection of the pituitary gland. No documentary evidence was available to the Inquiry to corroborate this submission by
Kabi Vitrum and therefore no finding is made in this regard.

7 Withdrawal of Human Growth Hormone

7.1 The use of the human growth hormone derived from pituitary glands came to an end in April 1985 for Kabi Vitrum, and in October 1988 for Novo Nordisk, following concerns in the United States as to its safety and was replaced by a biosynthetic hormone, which had no connection with the human pituitary gland. The use of human pituitary glands has featured in the controversy over the development of Creutzfeldt-Jakobs disease and has been the subject of international investigation in that regard.

8 Payment for Glands

8.1 Kabi Vitrum paid a fixed nominal sum for the work involved in the extraction of each pituitary gland. These sums were intended to defray the cost of performing the additional work required during the post mortem to extract, remove and store the pituitary gland.

8.2 In 1978 the payment was IR£1.50 per pituitary gland collected. In about November 1981 the payment was increased to IR£2.50, and by 1985 the payment had risen to between IR£3.00 and IR£ 3.50 for each pituitary gland delivered.

8.3 The supply hospitals were often given equipment and tools necessary for the proper removal, treatment and storage of the glands. Where necessary a small, inexpensive deep freezer was supplied for the proper storage of pituitary glands until their collection. In addition, Kabi Vitrum also supplied items such as a histopathologist's lamp and textbooks.

8.4 Most hospitals had no documentation relating to the supply of pituitary glands or any payment that may have been received. Some stated they received textbooks or teaching slides. Another stated that payment was made to a research charity. In some hospitals a nominal handling fee was paid to the mortuary technician. The submissions suggest that monetary gain was not a factor in the supply of pituitary glands to the companies.

9 Collections

9.1 Periodic collections of pituitary glands were made by Kabi Vitrum every four to eight weeks at large centres and two to three times per annum at other smaller centres. Kabi Vitrum no longer possesses complete records of the number of pituitary glands collected at individual hospitals or the dates upon which they were collected. However, to the best of its ability in 2002, Pharmacia Ireland Ltd set out the total numbers of pituitary glands believed to have been dispatched for the production of Crescormon® from all hospitals from which Kabi Vitrum collected glands each year between 1977 and 25 April 1985. The figures show that over that eight-year period, a total of 6,418 pituitary glands was collected in the State by Kabi Vitrum.

9.2 According to its records, Nordisk Gentofte received its first pituitary glands from Ireland in May 1976. In the years 1976-1980, Nordisk Gentofte received less than 200 per year. From 1980 until 1988 Nordisk Gentofte received more than 500 glands per year. According to its records, the total number of human pituitary glands received from Ireland by Nordisk Gentofte at its production site in Copenhagen, Denmark, was 7,511. The amount of *Nanormon* supplied to Irish patients over that time period was greater than the amount of human growth hormone that could be extracted from these glands. From 1982 to 1986, the total number of vials supplied to Ireland was 31,300.

9.3 Nordisk Gentofte continued with the collection of a back-up stock of pituitary glands after Kabi Vitrum had discontinued its collection of pituitary glands in mid-1985. In 1988, Nordisk Gentofte received approval for its biosynthetic growth hormone product, *Norditropin*, and the production of *Nanormon* was phased out; 388 pituitary glands collected in Ireland in 1988 were therefore never used for the production of *Nanormon,* and remained, according to good practice and procedures, in frozen storage as a back-up stock in the premises of Nordisk Gentofte in Denmark. The back-up stock was retained in case the new biosynthetic human growth hormone *Norditropin* failed, or in case there was a continued need for pituitary human growth hormone in excess of the production of *Nanormon* that was in stock at the time Nordisk Gentofte ceased its manufacture. Of these 388 glands, 8 have numbers that may be hospital post mortem numbers. However, the company does not have the means by which to identify the deceased persons from whom the glands were removed, and the relevant hospital from which it is believed these glands were supplied does not have any records relating to the supply of pituitaries.

10 Supply Chain of Human Growth Hormone Medication

10.1 Kabi Vitrum supplied Crescormon® to its primary distributor in Ireland, Cahill May Roberts, on a consignment basis and pharmacies distributed the product on foot of prescriptions written for patients by qualified medical practitioners. Some or all prescriptions for Crescormon® may have been channelled through the General Medical Services system, through which the medicine was supplied free of charge to patients. There does not appear to have been any relationship between the number of vials of the medication available in Ireland and the number of pituitary glands supplied to Kabi Vitrum from Ireland.

11 Collection Period of Pituitary Glands in Ireland

11.1 Pharmacia Ireland Ltd stated that Kabi Vitrum collected pituitary glands from Irish hospitals between a date unknown in 1977 until 25 April 1985. It had been thought previously that Kabi Vitrum started collecting pituitary glands in 1974. The 1974 date was the date used in Pharmacia Ireland Ltd's statement on the matter in February 2000.

11.2 Novo Nordisk state that Nordisk Gentofte were supplied with glands by Irish hospitals between 1976 and 1988.

12 Irish Hospitals Involved in the Supply of Pituitary Glands to Pharmaceutical Companies

12.1 The arrangements with Irish hospitals were not based on formal written agreements but were developed over the years through personal contact between representatives of the hospitals and representatives of the pharmaceutical companies. For this reason, data are sometimes incomplete as recounting of information is dependent on personal recollection or correspondence discovered during preparation of submissions to the Inquiry.

12.2 The hospitals that stated they had extracted pituitary glands and supplied them to pharmaceutical companies were generally unable to provide precise details about the practice, the numbers of glands involved or the dates on which they may have been supplied. In the case of some of the hospitals listed below, the pharmaceutical companies have provided some details in the absence of any confirmation from the hospitals concerned. This is not an exhaustive list of hospitals involved in the practice. The pharmaceutical companies also listed other hospitals not covered by the terms of reference of this Inquiry as having supplied pituitary glands to them.

12.3 From the evidence submitted to the Inquiry, it appears that approximately 90% of pituitary glands were supplied from post mortems performed on adults. However, the hospitals were not asked in their original submissions to the Dunne Inquiry to compile statistics on post mortems carried out on children and the pharmaceutical companies did not know the identity of the deceased persons from whom the glands were taken. Therefore some of the hospitals listed hereunder may not have supplied pituitary glands from post mortems performed on children.

Hospitals that supplied glands:

- Tralee General Hospital
- Our Lady's Hospital, Navan
- Our Lady's Hospital, Drogheda
- Waterford Regional Hospital
- St James's Hospital, Dublin
- Midland Regional Hospital at Mullingar
- Midland Regional Hospital at Tullamore
- Midland Regional Hospital at Portlaoise
- St Joseph's Hospital, Longford
- Mayo General Hospital
- Letterkenny Hospital
- Sligo General Hospital
- Portiuncula Hospital
- Beaumont Hospital, Dublin
- St Laurence's Hospital (services transferred to Beaumont 1987)
- Our Lady's Hospital for Sick Children, Crumlin, Dublin
- Children's University Hospital, Temple Street, Dublin
- National Maternity Hospital, Holles Street, Dublin
- The Coombe Women's Hospital, Dublin

- Cork University Hospital
- St Vincent's Hospital, Dublin
- Galway Regional Hospital
- Limerick Regional Hospital
- St John's Hospital, Limerick
- Barrington's Hospital, Limerick
- North Infirmary, Cork

For most hospitals, it appears that pituitary glands were supplied during the late 1970s to the mid-1980s, though very few hospitals can provide any documentation in this regard.

12.4 The hospitals listed hereunder state that they had no involvement with pharmaceutical companies. Some of the hospitals surveyed provided no response to the question and reliance was placed on documentation submitted by the pharmaceutical companies.

Hospitals that did not supply glands:

- Blackrock Clinic, Dublin
- Bantry General Hospital
- St Mary's Orthopaedic Hospital, Cork
- Mallow General Hospital
- Rotunda Hospital, Dublin
- Cavan General Hospital
- Monaghan General Hospital
- Erinville Hospital, Cork
- South Infirmary/Victoria Hospital, Cork
- Roscommon Hospital
- Mater Private Hospital, Dublin
- St Columcille's Hospital, Loughlinstown
- Adelaide and Meath Hospital incorporating the National Children's Hospital

13 Was Consent Obtained?

13.1 No consent was obtained for the extraction and supply of pituitary glands. Although motivated to meet the medical needs of children suffering from growth hormone deficiency, this practice was inappropriate without the knowledge and authorisation of the parents of the deceased children from whom the glands were removed. Many parents would undoubtedly have consented to the extraction and supply of the glands if asked. The supply of pituitary glands by hospitals was done at a time when verbal consent to post-mortem examination was often regarded as giving implied authority to do all that was necessary at that examination. However, this argument of implied authority does not apply to the removal of pituitary glands, which was not a necessary facet of the examination.

13.2 In the case of one hospital that has made submissions to the Inquiry, its Ethics Committee discussed the retention of pituitary glands in 1980. Minutes of two meetings in 1980 were supplied to the Inquiry at which it was agreed to introduce a 'special authorisation form' to be completed by relatives of the deceased person. This form was not provided to the Inquiry and therefore it is unclear whether or not it was part of the general Autopsy Consent Form also mentioned in the minutes of those meetings, or indeed whether a specific authorisation form for pituitary glands was devised. However, it demonstrates that the appropriateness of obtaining consent for the practice was at least considered at the time.

14 Knowledge by Department of Health and Children

14.1 The National Drugs Advisory Board and the Department of Health and Children were aware of the distribution of growth hormone to Irish patients since the license for the product was issued in 1976. No concern appears to have been raised by the Department regarding the issue of consent for the extraction and supply of the pituitary glands used in the manufacture of this product until 2000.

15 Conclusion

15.1 The two pharmaceutical companies involved in this country in the collection of pituitary glands went to very considerable efforts to furnish information and documentation to the Inquiry.

15.2 The total number of pituitary glands collected by Kabi Vitrum in Ireland (based on a 2002 calculation) is 6,418, which includes glands collected from adult and children's hospitals. The Novo Nordisk A/S (Nordisk Gentofte) figure for pituitary glands received from Ireland by the company at its production site in Denmark between May 1976 and October 1988 is calculated as 7,511. The combined total indicates that 13,929 pituitary glands were collected in Ireland between 1976 and 1988 by the two companies. A small percentage of these glands were collected from post mortems performed on children. It is estimated that approximately 90 per cent were collected from post mortems carried out on adults, though it is impossible to ascertain what exact percentage is accounted for by such post mortems. Figures from each hospital cannot be ascertained with certainty.

15.3 These glands were consistently taken at post-mortem examination without any specific consent of parents or next-of-kin and without any statutory regime in place for so doing.

15.4 Overall, there was a paucity of documentation about the matter, which indicates a degree of informality in the arrangements between the hospitals and the companies. The lack of records about the numbers of glands supplied also indicates that the issue was not dealt with in a formal manner by hospitals.

15.5 The retention could only have been made with the authority of the pathologist in charge of the relevant hospital department. However, those retaining the pituitary glands did not intend to cause harm or distress. Their motivation was for a positive medical and public benefit, notwithstanding the lack of specific consent for retention and use of the glands.

15.6 The payment made was modest and was not a payment for the pituitary gland itself but for the additional work required in its recovery and storage, pending delivery to the pharmaceutical companies concerned. There was no known commercial motive on the part of any hospital or its staff in the supply of pituitary glands for the manufacture of human growth hormone. On the evidence to the Inquiry, pathologists did not profit personally in any manner from the supply of the pituitary glands to the pharmaceutical companies, given the sums of money involved and their application to educational or research purposes.

16 Recommendations

1   No human organs removed from a deceased child at post-mortem examination should be supplied by hospitals to any pharmaceutical company or other third party without the knowledge and authorisation of the parents.

2   Where such organs are supplied, arrangements should be clearly approved by hospital management and documented, and all information supplied to the parents on request.

3   The use of human organs derived from post-mortem examinations should be regulated by law. Use of organs for educational and research purposes is dealt with in Chapter Nine of the Report.

Chapter Seven

Disclosures in 1999–2000 and Hospitals' Responses

1 Introduction

1.1 In late 1999 the post-mortem practices in Our Lady's Hospital for Sick Children in Crumlin came under public scrutiny. Media revelations about the retention of organs at the hospital led to similar disclosures by other hospitals in 2000. The Department of Health and Children issued instructions to hospitals and health boards to provide for the needs of parents as speedily and sympathetically as possible, and to ensure that a policy of informed consent operated in all the relevant agencies. Counselling services were put in place and help lines established in order to respond to the concerns of parents and families. Where the families sought the return of retained organs, this was arranged by the relevant hospital.

1.2 Following the media revelations, parents contacted various institutions seeking information as to any post-mortem practices involving their deceased child. This chapter examines the issues arising from the parents' attempts to gather information as to the circumstances surrounding the post mortem of their child, and the ways in which the hospitals responded to those issues. Some of the information recounted in this chapter is taken directly from the submissions of parents as well as the hospitals' responses to the Inquiry.

2 Awareness of Organ Retention Issue and Contact with the Hospital

2.1 Parents became aware of the controversy through various electronic and print media. The various sources mentioned by parents in their submissions in this regard included *The Late Late Show* television programme in December 1999, news broadcasts on television and radio, newspaper reports and notices printed in the newspapers and magazines. In a few instances, parents were contacted directly by hospital staff about the matter.

2.2 The majority of parents contacted the hospital concerned in the days following the awareness that the issue may have affected them. Individual parents reported that it took them some time to summon up the courage to contact the hospital. Parents recalled that they worried about the effect on their families of receiving new information and they feared it would bring back the terrible grief they suffered at the death of their child. One parent expressed the fears she held about making enquiries because her husband had suffered a nervous breakdown previously.

2.3 Many hospitals recorded that they had set up help lines at some stage to answer queries by concerned families. Other hospitals appointed full-time liaison officers for a period to deal with queries or referred queries to a liaison officer working in another hospital. In a few instances, medical staff such as the director of nursing, a clinician or the pathologist dealt with queries. Some hospitals retained records of the responses to parents.

2.4 Examples of how some hospitals responded to the concerns raised by parents are given below. It is stressed that these are intended to be illustrative of the methods employed by hospitals generally.

2.5 Our Lady's Hospital for Sick Children, Crumlin

Subsequent to the media attention on the topic of organ retention on 6 December 1999, Crumlin Hospital bore the lion's share of enquiries at that time and in the following two years. It received a total of 706 enquiries, of which 559 had post mortems. Initially the consultant histopathologist at the hospital contacted each family within 24–48 hours and arranged to discuss each individual case with the family concerned, either by telephone where organ retention was not a feature of the case, or by meeting the family (usually within a week of their call) to explain the nature and purpose of a post mortem and the necessity for retention of tissue and organs in their specific case.

As a result of the volume of enquiries received by the hospital in the week of 6 December, Crumlin Hospital set up a Patient Support Unit to handle the enquiries it received from parents. The Unit was run by senior administrative staff and supported by a retired clinician, a clinical psychologist, the chaplaincy team and social workers. Other clinical consultants, members of the pathology department and medical records staff gave additional support. Two dedicated help lines were set up and a standard set of questions asked of each enquirer in order to establish the necessary facts. Due to the volume of enquiries, the consultant histopathologist could not meet each family individually and it was decided to refer the enquiries to the original consultant who had treated the child. This usually involved a meeting or telephone contact between the clinician and the family, followed up by written confirmation of the relevant information.

Crumlin Hospital states that its intention to provide a full response was hampered by the fact that the pathologist who had worked at the hospital for 28 years was deceased. There was a lack of documentary evidence of practices and procedures, the post-mortem reports rarely recorded the retention of organs unless the central nervous system had been referred to a neuropathologist for expert opinion, and there was also a significant time pressure imposed on staff to respond quickly to enquiries. Due to the lack of information recorded on the reports, the consultant histopathologist used his expertise and experience to interpret the reports to the best of his ability and to form an opinion as to whether or not organs had been retained. Information subsequently came to light in 2000 which caused him to reassess the usefulness of his interpretation of the post-mortem reports in circumstances where he did not have full information of the practices of his deceased predecessor. As a result he decided to discontinue the practice of providing an opinion as to whether or not organs had been retained. As a consequence of the difficulty in ascertaining the relevant information, sometimes information had to be relayed to families on a second occasion, and the hospital acknowledges that the families may have perceived this as a drip-feed of information.

Crumlin Hospital was perhaps unique in being the focus of attention for the media and the public in late 1999. Some families believed from inaccurate media reporting that the organ retention was carried out only in Crumlin, that post mortems had been carried out without families' knowledge, and some believed that organs had been used for transplantation without their knowledge. In dealing with the enquiries that were made to the hospital, social workers, clinical nurse specialists, pathologists, medical and support staff had to correct these misapprehensions as well as deal with the distress, hurt and anger caused and support the families who were trying to cope with upsetting information.

2.6 The Rotunda

When the revelations regarding organ retention practices began to be highlighted by the media in late 1999, the Rotunda Hospital confirmed to the Department of Health and Children that it retained tissues from post mortems. In early 2000, the Master issued a statement setting out post-mortem practices and inviting parents to contact a help line. The hospital placed a notice in newspapers in March 2000 inviting contact with the help line and apologising for any hurt caused to families. Calls were directed to the head medical social worker and clinical risk manager. The matron and master's offices also received calls at this time. An *ad-hoc* multi-disciplinary committee was formed to co-ordinate the hospital's response. The hospital received 240 enquiries up to March 2000. Initial letters were sent to families who had contacted the hospital and arrangements made for them to attend meetings with hospital staff. In some cases families requested meetings with a pathologist and this was facilitated by the hospital. A full-time bereavement support service was provided from July/August 2001.

2.7 The Coombe

The Coombe issued a public statement in February and March 2000 stating that organ retention may be a necessary part of post-mortem examinations, and that subsequent to examination, organs were incinerated by the hospital. The hospital set up a help line in March 2000. It received 130 queries, not all of which are relevant to the terms of reference of this Inquiry. Each telephone call was logged and callers were asked to confirm their query in writing so as to protect confidentiality. Each query was acknowledged in writing and searches were made to identify relevant records. Parents were invited to attend a meeting with a clinician/pathologist.

2.8 National Maternity Hospital, Holles Street

In December 1999/January 2000 the hospital set up a team of 50 individuals to deal with enquiries. This group was drawn from senior staff members from midwifery, management, nursing staff, chaplaincy, and social workers. A clinical psychotherapist was engaged by the hospital to train hospital staff in dealing with the issues that might arise. From January 2000 to April 2002, the hospital dealt with 818 cases where organs had been retained. A full-time bereavement liaison officer was employed by the hospital in September 2001 and works in close contact with social workers and the hospital chaplain to ensure that all bereaved parents are dealt with sensitively. Counselling is provided by the bereavement counselling services at the hospital in conjunction with clinicians.

2.9 Children's University Hospital, Temple Street

Temple Street received 193 enquiries during 2000. Extra staff were employed in the Medical Social Work department to deal with these enquiries. The hospital appointed a medical social worker as post-mortem co-ordinator to co-ordinate the hospital's response to the enquiries. On receipt of an enquiry a social worker contacted a consultant pathologist at the hospital to review the post-mortem report and clinical notes if available. From mid-2000, the practice was altered by facilitating a meeting between the post-mortem inquiry officer and the parents. In addition, the pathologist was available to meet the parents, if required. The hospital established an incident room and a freephone help line to deal with enquiries.

2.10 AMINCH

AMINCH state that they first received an enquiry in 1998 relating to post-mortem practices, and dealt with any queries on a case-by-case basis until 2000. Since that year a special projects office has been established to deal with queries and find out the relevant information for families who request it.

2.11 Overview of responses

Hospitals received varying types of queries, necessitating differing responses. Hospitals attempted to find relevant information for families. This was given to families in a variety of ways. Submissions from hospitals noted that information was provided through general practitioners or third parties where families so desired. Hospitals also communicated with parents themselves through phone calls, letters or meetings. In some instances, requests for information were passed on to the coroner or other hospitals. Counselling and bereavement counselling was offered and arranged for people who requested it.

Information and assistance was sought and provided about various matters, including registration of births and deaths, arrangement of baptismal certificates, whether consent was obtained for hospital post mortems, consent to coroner post mortems, whether organ retention had occurred and access to post-mortem results and reports. In some cases, information could not be accessed, such as instances where post-mortem reports could not be located.

3 Delay in Receiving Information

3.1 The swiftness of the responses to queries by concerned parents differed according to the hospital and the staff involved. Many parents found that they had to make repeated attempts to contact the relevant hospital before information was provided. Parents recalled making successive phone calls before receiving information. In some cases, hospital staff responded to queries by arranging a meeting with the relevant personnel to discuss the matter.

3.2 In a few cases, the time period between the initial contact and the receipt of information by parents stretched for months, with one family encountering a delay from May 2000 to February 2001 before having their queries answered, while another waited from February to July 2000 to receive answers. By contrast, some parents were provided with information within days. Any delays encountered in obtaining information increased the anguish for parents, with one set of parents complaining that the hospital concerned was not helpful in scheduling a meeting with the hospital representatives. Information provided was incomplete or misleading in some cases, thereby necessitating further contacts with the relevant hospital to secure more information.

3.3 As mentioned in Section 2 above, the complexity and breadth of some of the queries necessitated very detailed responses and follow-up contact. This may account for the delay encountered by families in some cases.

4 How was the Information Conveyed?

4.1 The information was conveyed by phone calls, letters and meetings. Families were generally given choices in relation to the method of communication. In some cases, families did not want telephone or written communication. Where telephone contact was acceptable to the parents, different hospital personnel made telephone calls at various times during the day. One parent recalled a telephone call at 8 pm from the hospital representative. Some telephone calls were made to parents at their places of work or while they were doing housework, with children in the vicinity. While some parents were content to receive the information as soon as possible, others viewed such communications as insensitive or '*a disgrace*', with one parent recounting that she fainted from shock after receiving the information via a phone call. Some parents recalled remarks made during such telephone calls as being hurtful and unhelpful and many felt that such information was not imparted sympathetically. One parent recalls being told that the parents had '*only buried tissue*'.

4.2 In other cases, an initial letter was sent to parents informing them of the general practice of the hospital and advising them that further information would be given to them. Some parents stated that they felt misled by such letters because they referred to '*tissue samples*', whereas parents were later informed that organs had been retained. Subsequent letters provided further information to parents about organ retention in their case. In some instances a list of organs was included with a letter about the topic, which was described as '*horrible, cold and unsympathetic*' by one set of parents.

4.3 In some cases, parents recalled that hospital staff were unwilling to convey the information on the phone. Instead the staff set up meetings about the issue with the parents. Parents had varying memories of meetings with hospital representatives. There was praise for the conduct of some meetings and parents were grateful to have somebody to discuss the matter with them. One parent recalled that she thought the hospital representative was forthcoming at the meeting. Other parents criticised the fact that they were asked to submit a list of questions to be answered at meetings, which caused parents to question whether the doctors were going to be '*open and honest*' about the matter. Another parent criticised the fact that four sets of parents attended a meeting with hospital representatives.

4.4 Some parents criticised the '*matter-of-fact*' manner in which the information was presented to them. Others submitted that staff were defensive in their dealings with them and felt that '*no straight answers*' were being provided to them. In those situations, parents reported that they had to ask a lot of questions to get the required answers, one parent said they had to '*drag answers*' from the doctor, and another parent related how they had to ask particular questions to get information. The parent recalled that: '*Now the atmosphere was if they were holding ... we were asking ... questions and they just didn't want to answer, you know. We just felt as if they were trying to hide something on us ... that they didn't want to tell us.*'

101

4.5 Parents left some meetings unhappy because of their perception that staff were not volunteering information and observed that hospital representatives at meetings read from reports but did not give them copies of the reports. Parents were shocked, stunned and upset by the revelations at the meetings. Some left the meetings in anger.

4.6 Several parents criticised the fact that the hospitals did not have records for the length of time that organs were retained, the date of disposal, who carried out the disposal, the location of the disposal and whether the organs had been incinerated or disposed of in some other manner. In one case the parents recalled that the pathologist in question had no records and no recollection of retention or disposal; they criticised his refusal to meet them. Another parent commented: *'One of the things I think about is the fact that nobody seems to know where [my son's] organs were incinerated. We were told it was not at the hospital, so where were they sent?'*

4.7 Others saw the lack of records as something that showed that the medical personnel thought they could *'take organs and do as they please'*.

5 Inaccurate Information

5.1 In some instances, hospitals had to communicate with the parents on a number of occasions because earlier communications had subsequently been proved inaccurate by further investigations. In those cases, parents reported that the distress caused by further information being communicated was heightened. Such information meant that the parents were trying to cope with revelations about organ retention when further information came to light, thus increasing their anxiety. It also eroded further any trust that the parents had in the hospital authorities to deal with the issues. One parent stated: *'I think that's what makes you think, well, maybe there's more coming because there's their lack of honesty.'*

5.2 In one such case, the parents held two meetings with hospital representatives. At an initial meeting, they were informed that *'slivers'* of tissue from organs may have been taken from deceased children but the hospital representatives denied that organs were taken. After subsequent media revelations about organ retention in that hospital, a second meeting was held where the hospital representatives informed the parents that their child's organs had, indeed, been retained. The parents felt that the hospital representatives *'gave us a raw deal'*. In another case, at one meeting parents were informed that the pituitary gland was taken. They recalled asking a lot of questions about organ retention during the meeting. Notwithstanding this, they were only informed about the retention of their child's heart at a later stage.

6 Explanation of Organ Retention Practices

6.1 No explanation was provided for the practices to many parents. Such explanations as were provided by hospital staff were brief, with hospital representatives stating that it was *'normal practice'* or *'standard practice'* or *'hospital policy'* to retain organs. Parents were dissatisfied with these explanations. Parents did not understand why retention occurred when they had known for a number of years the cause of death. This increased their anguish. One parent stated: *'I just cannot understand why they retained the organs ...They knew exactly what she had died from. If it had been the case that they could not identify what had gone wrong, that might be a different matter, but it is just not the case.'*

7 Support Offered to Parents by Hospitals

7.1 Each hospital developed its own methods for offering support to parents. Some parents reported that they were offered counselling by the hospital. Others acknowledged that the hospitals had paid for the costs of the burial of the organs of their child. In other cases, the parents had no further contact with the hospital once they had received the information they sought and had received their child's organs where that applied. In some of these latter cases parents did not want more contact with the hospital, whereas for others it was a further source of annoyance that the hospitals did not attempt to provide some support for them during the stress caused by the disclosures. One parent recalled that she had to leave by the back door again when she collected her child's organs and also stated that a prayer service was held, despite her wishes that there would be no such service.

8 Changes in Policy Regarding Post Mortems and Consent

8.1 All of the hospitals reported changes in the practices and procedures employed since the controversy broke in 1999–2000. The controversy brought about a change in the consent forms used, and their introduction where only verbal consent had previously been required. In the case of some hospitals, changes in policy and practice had already begun to be implemented before the controversy arose in 1999. For example, consent forms and protocols changed in Crumlin Hospital in 1997 and on a number of subsequent occasions.

8.2 Another factor that has assisted the standardisation of procedures is that the locations of post-mortem examinations have been centralised in some health service areas.

8.3 The Eastern Regional Health Authority produced guidelines for providing a quality response to families in relation to queries from post-mortem practices. These guidelines were endorsed by the National Liaison Group on Organ Retention in 2001 and shaped the development of the National Protocols and Guidelines for Organ Retention and Post Mortem Practices, which were adopted at the end of 2003. An implementation plan was drawn up to include the appointment and training of bereavement officers, standardised consent forms, arrangements for disposal of organs, and requirements for management of records.

8.4 The issues of organ removal, retention, storage and disposal are now discussed with families. In addition, families make the decisions regarding retention and disposal. Information leaflets and booklets are provided to families to assist them in making their decision, so that they are now informed about the details of the post-mortem procedure when the request for a post mortem is made. Parents are informed if organs have had to be retained and will be asked to indicate their wishes as to the disposal of the organs. The available options are generally a second burial, cremation, or disposal in a hospital plot. A service is sometimes performed at the hospital, attended by the social worker and chaplain if the parents so wish. When the post mortem report has been issued, a meeting is facilitated for parents with the clinicians and the pathologist at which the findings are discussed. Bereavement support is now commonly offered to families.

9 Conclusion

9.1 When parents became aware of the practice of organ retention in late 1999–2000, it became necessary for hospitals, some more than others, to respond quickly to enquiries in specific cases. Some hospitals received hundreds of enquiries from parents and other family members, while other hospitals received only a handful of calls. Although parents may perceive there to be inadequacies in the means by which their enquiries were dealt with by the hospitals, as a general rule hospital staff responded to the best of their ability at the time. This is in the context of some hospitals having difficulty locating documentary evidence relating to post mortems in particular cases, and the absence of a hospital protocol for dealing with situations of this nature. There is no doubt that in some cases mistakes were inadvertently made, inaccurate information unwittingly relayed, necessitating the subsequent correction of information in traumatic circumstances for the families. This undoubtedly caused a feeling of distrust and anger amongst affected families but may be at least partly explained by the hospital's wish to answer queries as quickly as possible so as to avoid further distress.

9.2 With the benefit of hindsight it may have been preferable for a moratorium to be imposed on the giving of information until all cases had been fully investigated internally and documented so as to ensure the accuracy of the information that was available. However, hospitals did not take this approach on the basis that delay could potentially cause further stress for the families. It was also the case that hospitals came under pressure to respond quickly from the Department of Health and Children, the media, and public representatives. The media environment at the time when this controversy arose was difficult for both hospitals and parents to cope with, given the sensitivity of the issues involved.

9.3 Irish hospitals did not anticipate the controversy that arose in late 1999. Although some hospitals had already begun a review of their procedures and had redrafted their consent forms before the controversy arose, most hospitals were nonetheless largely unprepared for the queries that came in late 1999–2000. In some cases contact was made by telephone call between the parents and the hospital. This was in response to the setting up of help lines to deal with queries. Parents were then usually given the option of response by telephone or post. If organs were still retained at the hospital, parents were offered a consultation with hospital staff. Due to the volume of cases to be dealt with, it was not possible for consultations to be offered to every person making an enquiry, as this would have seriously delayed the dissemination of information to the families.

9.4 Following the public reaction to the publication of organ retention practices, hospital managers introduced new policies and protocols dealing with consent for hospital post-mortem examinations. As stated above, the Eastern Regional Health Authority produced guidelines for responding to families in relation to queries from post-mortem practices. These guidelines were endorsed by the National Liaison Group on Organ Retention in 2001 and shaped the development of the National Protocols and Guidelines for Organ Retention and Post Mortem Practices, which were adopted at the end of 2003. An implementation plan was drawn up to include the appointment and training of bereavement officers, standardised consent forms, arrangements for disposal of organs, and requirements for management of records.

10 Recommendations

1   Clear national protocols must be put in place by the Department of Health and Children and Health Services Executive to deal with queries from families in respect of post mortem practices as well as the provision of standardised forms to be used on a national basis. The language to be used in such forms must be clear and comprehensible, and must avoid medical or legal terminology as much as possible. Existing guidelines produced by the National Working Group on Organ Retention in 2002, and adopted by National Chief Officers in 2003 may be used as the basis on which to make any adaptations recommended in this Report. This should be done in consultation with relevant stakeholders.

2   An independent audit must be carried out of currently retained organs in all hospitals in the State. The Department of Health and Children and the Health Service Executive should engage in a public information campaign informing relatives that they may reclaim any currently retained organs within a 12-month period from the date of this Report. This should be organised and managed via a central enquiry line rather than by individual hospitals. Families who do not contact hospitals in this regard should not be approached with this information. Their right not to know must be respected, provided reasonable efforts have been made to disseminate information publicly.

3   Each hospital must have a bereavement liaison officer available to offer practical help and support to bereaved families and staff caring for those families. This officer must liase with the relevant pathology department and should have a good understanding of pathology practices so as to provide assistance to the family if required. Although it is the clinician's responsibility to discuss the post mortem with the parents, this may be done as part of a team approach with the bereavement liaison officer, who may provide appropriate follow-up support.

Chapter Eight

Legal and Ethical Issues Relating to Post Mortems and Organ Retention

1 Introduction

1.1 This chapter considers legal and ethical issues raised by post-mortem practice and organ retention. It is important to stress that although comparisons are commonly made with the system in operation in the United Kingdom, the legal situation is markedly different there. Since 1961 a Human Tissue Act has been in existence in the United Kingdom, under which a post-mortem examination could legitimately take place as long as reasonable steps were taken to discover whether the relatives of the deceased raised any objection to such examination. Although this was not the same as 'informed consent', it was often interpreted in that way. The Bristol[21] and Alder Hey[22] Reports into organ retention must therefore be read in light of the existence of governing, though outdated, legislation. By contrast, Ireland has never had human tissue legislation and is governed, in the absence of such legislation, by common law principles.[23]

1.2 Contemporary medical ethics is a discipline in which a range of philosophical theories intermingle, from deontology (which focuses on the rightness or wrongness of an act in itself) to utilitarianism (which classically views the morality of an action as dependent on the extent to which it maximises happiness and enhances autonomy). Autonomy is the most significant value that has been promoted by contemporary medical ethics, and has dominated medical ethics discourse since the 1960s. The acknowledgement of this concept has led to the discrediting of medical paternalism and to the promotion of the patient as a partner in his/her healthcare. This, in turn, has led to the evolution of the doctrine of consent over the past four decades, though in a different way to its legal development.

1.3 As clearly demonstrated in the submissions and evidence given by parents whose children were the subject of post-mortem examinations, the issues of consent and control are paramount in their minds. They relate their hurt and anger at not being informed as to what was to happen to their child's organs, and at not having been given a choice as to the ultimate disposal of those organs. They also feel deceived by the manner in which information was finally given to them by the hospitals. This raises both legal and ethical issues relating to whether or not consent was necessary, and the extent to which information should have been provided to the parents. Consideration of these issues will demonstrate the different views of consent taken by lawyers and ethicists.

---

[21] *Learning from Bristol: the report of the public inquiry into children's heart surgery at the Bristol Royal Infirmary 1984–1995* CMND 5207

[22] The *Report of the Royal Liverpool Children's Inquiry,* 2001

[23] Common law operates through a system of precedent whereby legal principles are passed down through decades, and sometimes centuries, of judicial decisions and are accepted by courts unless the facts of the present case are different, or unless legislation has intervened to deal with the issue in the meantime.

1.4 Another issue raised by the practice of organ retention is that of rights over the dead body. We may generally think of ourselves as the 'owners' of our bodies, but in strict legal terms, this may not be an accurate statement. Respect for autonomy and for the freedom to make choices in respect of our bodies does not necessarily imply that we have property rights in them. Nor does the fact of parental responsibility mean that parents have ownership over the body of their deceased child. This is considered further below.

2 Consent

2.1 Throughout this report and the controversy that led to the establishment of this Inquiry, much attention has been paid to the ethical and legal concept of consent. This section of the report summarises what is meant by 'consent' and in particular 'informed consent' in the context of medical practice. The development of the law in this regard has been dominated by cases in relation to disclosure to individuals prior to making decisions as to their own health care, and therefore may not be seen as having immediate relevance to the issue under consideration in this Report. However, if there is to be a requirement that a form of consent should be obtained from parents/legal guardians prior to hospital post-mortem examinations, it is important to be aware of the parameters of what consent means in the medical context.

3 Respect for Autonomy

3.1 The value of consent in medical law and medical ethics is paramount as it serves primarily to preserve the autonomy and dignity of the individual. The central idea of autonomy is that one's actions and decisions are one's own, to be exercised free from external influences. This does not mean that one cannot be receptive to the views of others, but that one does not accept them unquestioningly. In medical practice it is important to recognise that patients may or may not want to have the necessary information about their medical problem, and may or may not want to be the one to make the important decision about what treatment to take. While many people may feel and act as autonomous individuals, some people act quite differently; their desire for information is less pronounced, their personal beliefs are less developed, relevant or strong, and their desire for control is more ambivalent. Therefore any process of consent should recognise and reflect the complex range of human experience and respect the concept of welfare as well as autonomy.

4 Changing Culture of Consent

4.1 Medical practice has traditionally been influenced by a paternalism characterised by non-disclosure by the doctor, and deference by the patient. Paternalism may be defined as the policy of restricting the freedom and responsibilities of one's dependants in their supposed best interest. The traditional Hippocratic Oath, sworn by generations of doctors, requires the doctor to 'prescribe regimen for the good of my patients according to my ability and my judgement and never do harm to anyone.'

Neither the Hippocratic tradition nor any of the ancient or even early modern medical ethics literature discuss any obligations of disclosure on the doctor, although concern did exist about how to make disclosures to the patient without harming him/her. Benevolent deception was the main practice in the nineteenth century with the patient's right to be informed being overruled by the duty to benefit the patient in cases where the information may harm the patient.

4.2 Up to the 1950s permission for surgery was sought from patients in a fairly rudimentary way that absolved the doctor of responsibility in cases of malpractice. The concept of 'informed consent' emerged in the 1960s in the United States when medical ethicists began to emphasise the importance of patient autonomy and began to question the presumption that a doctor is in a better position to assess benefits for patients than the patients themselves. Medical ethics came to be seen as a conflict between the old Hippocratic paternalism and a principle of autonomy. Within a short time autonomy had won the battle, and informed consent became the central focus in relation to all medical interventions. It has since been incorporated into Irish and English jurisprudence, to the criticism of some commentators who see it as unfortunate and prone to mislead.

4.3 Thus, the culture by which informed consent became a necessary pre-requisite in medical treatment is a relatively recent phenomenon, as is the accompanying focus on providing information. The history of medicine and medical research is full of examples of interventions and procedures carried out without consent, where this was considered perfectly legitimate by society at that time. For example, in an Irish Supreme Court case in 1954, *Daniels v Heskin*,[24] the court considered whether a doctor should have informed a woman who was suffering from post-partum discomfort that a needle had accidentally been left in her body following stitching after childbirth. A majority of the court rejected the notion of a general duty to disclose information to patients. Justice Kingsmill Moore said it 'all depends on the circumstances – the character of the patient, her health, her social position, her intelligence…and innumerable other considerations.' The issue of the patient having the right to know this information was not even considered. The accepted wisdom at the time was that because doctors knew more about medical matters, they were in a better position than the patient to know what was in the patient's best interests. This meant that giving the patient the information necessary to make consent meaningful, or the information required to make a choice, was simply not an option.

4.4 In the middle of the twentieth century other societal changes began to impact upon the culture of consent. The Nuremberg Code (1947) and the Declaration of Helsinki (1964) prioritised voluntary consent as an absolute necessity. This was, and is, in keeping with growing respect for autonomy and self-determination, and also served to promote public confidence in medicine and research. Other developments included a growing concern for issues of equality and civil rights, consumerism and an increasingly technology-driven healthcare system. Knowledge became the fundamental constituent of self-determination. The law also began to become involved in the relationship between doctor and patient and, having traditionally deferred to the profession, now began to move the legal notion of consent to a more central role.

---

[24] *Daniels v Heskin* [1954] IR 73

4.5 The most widely cited decision in modern legal jurisprudence in relation to the requirement for informed consent is an American case called *Canterbury v Spence* (1972).[25] In this case the Court held:

> True consent to what happens to one's self is the informed exercise of a choice, and that entails an opportunity to evaluate knowledgeably the options available and the risks attendant upon each. The average patient has little or no understanding of the medical arts, and ordinarily has only his physician to whom he can look for enlightenment with which to reach an intelligent decision. From these almost axiomatic considerations springs the need, and in turn the requirement, for a reasonable divulgence by physician to patient to make such a decision possible.

5 Modern Legal Foundation for Consent Requirement

5.1 The basic legal principle described above has now been accepted in most jurisdictions worldwide, though it is not regarded as absolute. The doctor retains a 'therapeutic privilege' not to provide information to a patient if he/she believes that the disclosure of the information would result in a serious deterioration of the patient's condition, or would render the patient incapable of making a rational decision.

5.2 The right to autonomy is not explicitly referred to in the Irish Constitution or the European Convention on Human Rights (ECHR). However, the right has been judicially recognised as being encompassed in these instruments. The right to autonomy has been held to be one of the unenumerated personal rights of the citizen, protected by Article 40.3.1 of the Irish Constitution, though in the few judicial decisions in point, the right has been interpreted as a limited one. The ECHR has been incorporated into Irish law since 2003 though it is presumed to add little to existing constitutional protections in this regard. The Commission and Court have found that the right of autonomy comes within Article 8 of the ECHR, which provides protection of the right to respect for private and family life, though this protection is not absolute. It is possible that the lack of an effective sanction for wrongful removal of tissue might be considered incompatible with Article 8 but this would be contingent on proof of transgression of the law by failing to get consent from relatives, and acceptance by the court that removal and retention of tissue at post mortem constitutes lack of respect for private and family life. The courts have not yet considered this.

5.3 The Council of Europe Convention for the Protection of Human Rights and Dignity of the Human Being with regard to the Application of Biology and Medicine: Convention on Human Rights and Biomedicine (Oviedo 1997) is designed to protect the dignity and integrity of human beings and to guarantee respect for their rights and freedoms with regard to the application of biology and medicine. Although Ireland has not yet signed the Convention, it is important to note that a number of Articles have possible relevance to the issue of organ retention.

---

[25] *Canterbury v Spence* 464 F 2d 772 (1972)

Article 2: 'The interest and welfare of the human being shall prevail over the sole interest of society or science.'

Article 5: 'An intervention in the health field may only be carried out after the person concerned has given free and informed consent to it. This person shall beforehand be given appropriate information as to the purpose and nature of the intervention as well as on its consequences and risks. The person concerned may freely withdraw consent at any time.'

Article 22: 'When in the course of an intervention any part of a human body is removed, it may be stored and used for a purpose other than that for which it was removed, only if this is done with appropriate information and consent procedures.'

5.4 Although the Convention is concerned with the protection of living persons, the principles may also be relevant to the removal and retention of organs post mortem. An additional protocol to the Convention was published in 2002 concerning organ and tissue transplantation. Some of the relevant articles state as follows:

Article 17 – Consent and authorisation: Organs or tissues shall not be removed from the body of a deceased person unless consent or authorisation required by law has been obtained. The removal shall not be carried out if the deceased person had objected to it.

Article 18 – Respect for the human body: During removal the human body must be treated with respect and all reasonable measures shall be taken to restore the appearance of the corpse.

5.5 A further Protocol was published in January 2005 dealing with biomedical research. Its provisions are concerned with research on living persons and give details of the information to be provided to research participants, and the requirement for consent.

6 Legal Doctrine of Informed Consent

6.1 The term 'informed consent' is often used to describe the process whereby a healthcare professional discloses necessary information to a patient prior to obtaining the patient's permission to go ahead with a procedure. Its purpose is to ensure that sufficient information has been provided to the patient to ensure that the patient is aware of the risks and benefits of the procedure, and its alternatives, before proceeding. In the context of consenting to one's own medical treatment one can confidently presume that an act is an informed consent if a patient or subject agrees to an intervention on the basis of an understanding of relevant information, the consent is not controlled by influences that engineer the outcome, and the consent given was intended to be a consent, and therefore qualified as permission for an intervention.

7 Is Informed Consent Achievable?

7.1 One of the difficulties in the area of consent is that there is often a substantial difference between the appearance of consent and the reality. If a patient is simply asked to sign a consent form it loses all significance, as it becomes just a formality that must be complied with for legal purposes to protect the doctor and the hospital from being sued. If, on the other hand, consent becomes too demanding in terms of what is to be disclosed to and understood by the patient, then it will never be achievable.

7.2 Some doctors misinterpret the obligation to obtain consent as a simple requirement to disclose facts and get a signature, rather than a process of discussion of facts and acquiring permission. In many instances the most inexperienced doctor is sent to 'consent the patient' as part of a formulaic process done to avoid legal liability, rather than a process in which the patient actually participates or controls. The junior doctor may not be able to answer reasonable questions from the patient and may have difficulty in explaining an unfamiliar procedure to a patient, particularly where the doctor has not previously performed or participated in the procedure him/herself.

7.3 The fundamental characteristics of the ideal of informed consent are that patients substantially understand both the nature of the procedure they are permitting and the fact that they are permitting it, in other words that they have a choice in the matter. Many patients seem to feel that they are simply being informed as to what is about to happen to them and that their signature is an acknowledgement of their having been informed. Pressure or coercion is never compatible with informed consent.

7.4 Many clinicians and other commentators criticise the ideal of informed consent on the basis of its impossibility, or at least impracticability. They reasonably point to the strain on time and resources in modern hospital settings, the difficulties involved in explaining complicated medical facts, and the unpleasant and often distressing nature of the subject matter. However, the *Charter of Rights for Hospital Patients* agreed by Irish hospitals in 1992 tells patients that, generally, treatment should only be given to a patient with his/her informed consent and the consent form should clearly state the nature of the procedure to be undertaken. Patients also have a right to be informed as to the nature of the illness or condition in language they can understand.

7.5 The *Guide to Ethical Conduct and Behaviour* (sixth ed.) issued by the Irish Medical Council in 2004 provides for implied consent to certain procedures by virtue of the fact that the patient has presented for treatment. It also stipulates that informed consent can only be obtained by a doctor with sufficient training and experience to be able to explain the procedure to the patient. In obtaining consent, the doctor must satisfy him/herself that the patient understands what is involved by explaining it in appropriate terminology. Patients are to be encouraged to ask questions, which should always receive a positive response from the doctor, and a careful answer in non-technical terms.

7.6 It is important to point out that the ideal of informed consent is not necessarily that the patient has *full* understanding of the medical facts, but rather a *substantial* understanding. Complicated medical information that may be difficult to comprehend may be explained in lay language, using common everyday analogies and explanations. Communication between doctor and patient should be regarded as a two-way process where the doctor listens to the patient in order to find out what information is relevant to his/her particular wishes and circumstances.

7.7 There is nothing about the consent process that requires written information to be given. In some medical procedures consent to minor procedures may be seen as implicit in consent given to a surgical or medical treatment. For example, when a patient is hospitalised for a surgical procedure, blood samples may be taken for analysis, medications may be given, and anaesthesia may be provided. In some cases written, or more commonly, verbal information will be given regarding these minor procedures, in others it will be assumed that the patient's consent to the surgery encompasses all that is necessary to facilitate that surgery and the patient's recovery.

8 Disclosure of Information

8.1 Given the limited human capacity to take in information, massive information overload is as likely to cause confusion and impair understanding as the provision of inadequate information. The ideal of informed consent does not require that all imaginable information be conveyed. Ethicists use a two-tiered standard to determine how much information should be given. Firstly, there are the 'core' disclosures. This is information that patients usually consider material in deciding whether to consent, and also the information that the doctor believes to be material about the proposed intervention. Unlike the legal position, the ethical focus is on what patients usually consider important, rather than whether or not they are reasonable in considering it to be important. These disclosures commonly relate to success rates, risks, side effects, alternatives, the doctor's experience of the procedure, and the costs involved.

8.2 The goal of achieving substantial understanding can only be realised on an individualised basis; simply because most people would understand something does not necessarily mean that a specific individual understands it. Therefore an additional second level of disclosure is required, that which asks what the specific individual considers relevant information. The only way for the doctor to discover what the individual patient considers relevant is by listening to the patient and participating in discussion rather than simply imparting information.

8.3 In relation to the legal test of what information must be disclosed to patients, there are traditionally two standards: the patient standard, and the professional standard. The former test would insist that the doctor reveal all relevant facts as to the proposed procedure; it is not for the doctor to determine what the patient should or should not hear. On this basis the patient should be as fully informed as possible so that he/she can make up her/his own mind in light of all the relevant circumstances. The quality of information supplied is to be judged from the perspective of the patient. Proponents of this test argue that it most fully satisfies the requirements of respect for autonomy, but even its advocates would usually accept that the doctor should be accorded a 'therapeutic privilege' to withhold information which would distress or confuse the patient.

8.4 On the other hand, the professional standard of disclosure takes the position that counselling and informing the patient are part of the clinical management of the patient. The extent and detail of the information supplied is a matter for decision by the doctor. The quality of the information supplied is viewed from the perspective of the doctor.

8.5 Irish law has traditionally taken the professional standard to be the appropriate one in deciding upon medical negligence actions. In the context of informed consent this means that if the doctor has followed the practice of his peers in deciding what information to disclose, he has complied with his obligation to his patient. However, if the actions of the doctor in giving information were inherently defective, the Irish courts might be prepared to judge that the doctor had not fulfilled his duty of disclosure prior to obtaining consent. It has also been decided that where the procedure is elective, in the sense that there is a choice to be made by the patient as to whether or not to proceed with the proposed treatment, a more stringent test of disclosure is required. Cases in recent years have moved towards a patient-centred test and have taken the view that where the patient has a choice to make as to whether to undergo a medical procedure, he/she has the right to make that choice with full knowledge of all material facts.[26]

9 Application to Post-Mortem Examinations

9.1 There is an argument that the law relating to consent does not apply at all to post mortems as the legal doctrine was developed in relation to interactions between doctors and living patients in the context of a proposed medical treatment. In the circumstances under discussion here, the patient is no longer alive, no medical treatment is proposed, the benefit is not to the patient him/herself, risks are not expected, the time within which the decision must be made is limited, and those who must make the decision may be extremely distressed. On this analysis, the law relating to consent is not applicable at all.

9.2 However, as pointed out by the Bristol Report, discussion of a post mortem to be carried out on a deceased child is sufficiently closely related in time and context to the care of the child that it could be said that the law remains the same. It might also be said that the child's parents become the patients as they are cared for in their bereavement by the medical and nursing staff of the hospital, and perhaps the duty is owed to them rather than to the child. This is particularly the case where a child has died shortly after birth and the mother remains the patient of the obstetrician who has a duty to advise her in relation to future pregnancies. There is no clear legal answer to this issue.

9.3 Consent is not required to be given where a post-mortem examination is authorised by a coroner within the terms of his powers under the Coroners Act, 1962. This report does not recommend any change in the law relating to this aspect of the Coroners Act as it is seen to be necessary in the public interest that the coroner be so authorised.

---

[26] *Geoghegan v Harris* [2000] 3 IR 536

9.4 The issue of a post mortem arises at a time of extreme grief. Nevertheless, a post mortem has to be completed as soon as possible in order to get the best clinical results. It is not possible to allow sufficient time for the grief to abate. Therefore, it must be discussed with sensitivity and openness for the clinician to discharge his/her duty. With proper training, clinicians should be able to communicate effectively and sympathetically with the necessary medical knowledge to inform the child's parents. Clinicians must understand the value and process of post-mortem examination in the clinical setting and also what it means for relatives. It is best clinical practice for clinicians to work closely with pathologists who can assist in determining which organs should be retained for the relevant purposes. They can also assist parents in providing details relating to the cause of death.

9.5 Many, though not all, parents feel that they must be informed of the details of each organ to be retained and the purpose for which it will be used. It is not enough for clinicians to tell such parents that they would like to examine the body after death and that this might involve taking tissue. Some parents need to understand what is involved in a post-mortem examination, including a description of whole body systems, removal of the brain, and the steps necessary to remove various organs. Other parents prefer not to know the details of the procedure but are nonetheless satisfied to allow the examination to proceed. Both sets of parents must somehow be accommodated in whatever information process is adopted. This is discussed further below.

10 Parental Authority

10.1 Under the Irish Constitution, *Bunreacht na hÉireann* 1937, the position of the family is recognised as predominant in terms of its place in society. Article 41.1.1 provides that 'the State recognises the Family as the natural primary and fundamental unit group of Society, and as a moral institution possessing inalienable and imprescriptible rights, antecedent and superior to all positive law.' Article 41.1.2 provides that the State guarantees 'to protect the Family in its constitution and authority, as the necessary basis of social order'.

10.2 Parents/guardians make decisions for their children on a daily basis, ranging from the clothes they wear, the food they eat, and the schools they attend. In the medical context, they are generally given wide authority to make decisions on behalf of their children though, in exceptional cases, legal provisions may be invoked to deal with situations in which parents breach their duties towards their children. In law, parental decision-making is limited to decisions that are in the child's best interests. Parents cannot, for example, give consent to a procedure to be carried out on their child for the benefit of themselves or the child's sibling. However, at least in the Irish constitutional context, the circumstances in which the State might intervene to overrule the decision of a parent are quite limited following the decision of the Supreme Court in *North Western Health Board v HW and CW*.[27] In that case the Court held by majority decision that the State could only interfere where there were exceptional circumstances, such as where the child's life was in imminent danger.

---

[27] *North Western Health Board v HW and CW* [2001] IESC 90

10.3 Therefore, while the child is alive, doctors and nurses must be careful not to infringe the autonomy and privacy of the family, though at the same time acting as an advocate for the child's interests. Getting the balance right is not an easy task. The Bristol Report acknowledged that although children's needs are ordinarily expressed through their parents, their interests do not always coincide. While alive, children must be listened to, provided with information that they want in an appropriate way, and encouraged to participate in decisions.

10.4 Difficult situations can arise where the parents of a child disagree on decisions relating to the child's treatment or other important issues. Where both parents are legal guardians of the child and agreement cannot be reached between them, an application can be made to the court to make the decision in the best interests of the child. Where one parent is the legal guardian, treatment may proceed on the consent of that parent alone, though best practice would indicate that if the other parent were also involved in the care and custody of the child, he/she should be involved in the decision-making process. The application of these principles in the case of a deceased child is more difficult.

11 Authorisation

11.1 As stated above, it is generally accepted that parents/guardians have the authority to make treatment decisions on behalf of their children, though these decisions may be challenged in exceptional cases. In relation to hospital post-mortem examinations, there is neither legislative guidance nor legal precedent in Ireland that outline parental authority in this regard. Despite this, it is self-evident that parents have a unique and continuing role to play in decisions relating to their children after death. Respect for this role demands that their permission be obtained for a hospital post-mortem examination.

11.2 In relation to hospital post-mortem examinations, the Scottish Report on Organ Retention[28] (2001) took the view that the language of consent is inappropriate here, for two main reasons. Firstly, there may be families who are content to allow the retention of organs taken from their relatives but who do not want or feel able to participate in a process akin to giving a fully informed consent to medical treatment in life. Secondly, since parents can only consent to procedures that are in the best interests of their child, and since it could be said that deceased children have no interests in law, parents cannot be empowered to give consent to a post-mortem examination to be carried out on their child. As pointed out by the Chairperson of the Scottish Inquiry, Professor Sheila McLean,

> The interests of others can clearly be enhanced by accurate diagnosis, sound medical research and the education and training of doctors, but there is no possibility of a benefit accruing to the specific child.

11.3 The Scottish Inquiry recommended that parents must have overriding authority in respect of post-mortem examinations to be carried out on their children. However, the means by which to recognise such authority is not through consent, but

---

[28] *Independent Review Group on Retention of Organs at Post-Mortem*, Final report, November 2001

authorisation. The Report takes the view that the use of the word 'authorisation' rather than 'consent' clarifies the scope of the decision-making powers of parents in these circumstances. It also meets the concerns of those parents who do not wish to receive information about post-mortem examination and/or organ retention, but who nonetheless do not object to these procedures being carried out. 'Consent' requires the provision and comprehension of information, whereas 'authorisation' does not impose this requirement. Parents may thus authorise procedures without having information forced upon them.

11.4 It is clear that parents are entitled, if they so wish, to receive information relating to the purpose of the post-mortem examination, the procedures to be carried out as part of that examination, and the retention of any organs or tissue pursuant to that examination. Their informational needs and decision-making authority must be prioritised and enshrined in legislation. The use of 'authorisation' as a means of empowering parents to maintain control of what happens to their child's body confirms their unique bond with their child, and facilitates their active involvement in all decisions relating to post mortems. Whereas 'consent' may be seen as a passive acceptance of a proposal put to the parents by someone else, 'authorisation' is a more active participation – the parents can choose, with the benefit of as much information as they require, whether to give someone power to do something in relation to their child. Without the exercise of their authority, the hospital post mortem will not take place.

11.5 The forms recommended by the Scottish Report invite the parents to consider initially whether they wish to be given further information about the hospital post-mortem examination. If they decide that they do not wish to have further information they may nonetheless authorise the performance of the post mortem examination and any action the hospital considers appropriate following that examination. They may choose to be informed later of the findings of the examination, or to request further information in the future. The alternative for the parents is to receive information about the post mortem, including retention of organs and tissue, and the preparation of blocks and slides. They may also authorise retention for approved medical research and educational purposes. Choices are also made available regarding the disposal of retained organs.

12 Property in the Human Body

12.1 One of the options for the recognition of the authority of parents in relation to the bodies of their deceased children is the property model. This argument would follow the line of thought sometimes expressed by bereaved parents to the effect that their children's bodies 'belong' to them, and that any removal or retention of organs was akin to 'stealing' what rightfully belongs to the parents. Other families find the language of ownership insensitive and abhorrent, as they prefer to identify with a sense of continuing parenthood, and see the child as a continuing member of the family.

12.2 The common law has rejected a property approach to the human body. Early cases seem to support the principle that there is no right of ownership in a corpse, though many commentators argue that the foundation of this principle rests on flimsy evidence from misreported cases. In any event, the principle of 'no property in the human body' has long stood the test of time and, although English cases are not legally binding on an Irish court, the common law principle is likely to be accepted by the Irish courts. This was pointed out in *AB & Ors. v Leeds Teaching Hospital*[29] referring to the decision of *R v Kelly*[30] below,

> However questionable the historical origins of the principle, it has now been common law for 150 years at least that neither a corpse nor parts of a corpse are in themselves and without more capable of being property protected by rights.

12.3 *R v Kelly* confirms an exception to this principle where work or skill has been applied to the corpse/body part such as to endow it with different attributes or commercial value. In such circumstances the application of skill would give a right of possession of the body to the person applying the skill. Applying this exception to pathology practice, there is a possibility that the law might take the view that, for example, the fixation of the brain gives that organ attributes or potential which are different to the unfixed brain. Therefore, the pathologist who applies his skill to this technique has a right of possession to the brain. However, in an earlier case in 1996, *Dobson v North Tyneside Health Authority and Newcastle Health Authority,*[31] the court held that there was nothing to suggest that the fixing of a brain was on a par with stuffing or embalming a corpse or preserving an anatomical or pathological specimen for scientific collection.

12.4 In the more recent *AB* case the judge addressed this point as follows:

> The principle that part of a body may acquire the character of property which can be the subject of rights of possession and ownership is now part of our law. In particular, in my opinion, Kelly's case establishes the exception to the rule that there is no property in a corpse where part of the body has been the subject of the application of skill such as dissection or preservation techniques. The evidence … shows that to dissect and fix an organ from a child's body requires work and a great deal of skill, the more so in the case of a very small baby … The subsequent production of blocks and slides is also a skilful operation requiring work and expertise of trained scientists.

12.5 The differing views expressed by the English courts on this point indicate the lack of clarity that exists in relation to whether or not the pathologist's act of fixing the organ transforms it into an item of property to which the next-of-kin might be entitled. It is similarly unclear whether or not the 'work and skill' exception would be applied in these circumstances in Irish courts but, as with the 'no property' rule itself, it is likely to be followed unless affected by legislative change. The interpretation of the rule in the context of pathology practice and organ retention remains undecided.

12.6 In any event, it is recommended that the language of ownership is not appropriate to the body of a deceased child. Whether or not one takes the view that the deceased person remains a 'person' in the eyes of the law, the use of concepts of property and ownership do not rest comfortably with notions of parenting and family.

---

[29] *AB & Ors. v Leeds Teaching Hospital* [2004] EWHC 644 (QB)
[30] *R v Kelly* [1999] QB 621
[31] *Dobson v North Tyneside Health Authority and Newcastle Health Authority* [1996] 4 All ER 474

The care and protection of children enveloped in the parenting role, the prioritisation of the family under the Constitution, and the privacy of the family unit, strengthens the need to recognise the clear authority of parents in relation to their deceased children.

13 Right to Possession of the Body

13.1 Although there is no property or ownership in a dead body, the common law does recognise a possessory right – the right to take or keep possession of the body in certain circumstances and for certain purposes. If it is necessary for the coroner to take possession of the body for the purposes of his investigation into the cause of death, he has an absolute right in common law to possession of the body until the investigation is concluded. Subject to this, the personal representatives of the deceased have a right to possession of the body until it is disposed of. This is derived from their duty to dispose of it. In the case of a child, the duty falls on the parents/guardians and they therefore have a right to possession of the body for burial purposes.

13.2 Even where there is a right in the next-of-kin to call for possession of the body for burial purposes, whether or not this right extends to all parts of the body has not been decided at common law. As the Bristol Report concluded:

> The common law is entirely unclear as to whether each and every part of a body which might be discovered, for example after an accident, or after burial of the rest of the body or every slide and tissue sample in a pathology examination, should be regarded as within the definition of 'the body', for the purposes of the duty to dispose. If the duty to bury does not extend this far, then it would follow that neither does the corresponding right to call for possession for the purposes of disposal. Thus, institutions in possession of archives or 'banks' of tissue, need not as a matter of law at least, give up that possession, even if the material has not 'acquired different attributes'. This appears so, even if the initial separation of the body part from the rest of the body was itself unauthorised.

13.3 The Bristol Report also recognised the necessity of giving detailed and specific information to parents but acknowledged that this would be painful for some parents already reeling from the loss of their child, while other parents will find the information to be helpful. The Report concludes that it is not possible to 'square this particular circle' and that 'there is a price to be paid for being informed'.

13.4 The suggestion of replacing the consent model with 'authorisation' as recommended by the Scottish Report appears to strike an appropriate balance between those who wish to exercise their right to know the relevant information, and those who wish to exercise an equal right not to know. This empowers parents whose child has died to make a choice as to how much information they wish to be given prior to making a decision in relation to a post-mortem examination. Given that much of the criticism of the procedures and practices of the past have been related to such choices not being given to parents, this may deal with some of those criticisms without forcing such information on those who would prefer not to hear it. Rather than have such a decision being made by the clinician, as was the case in the past, parents themselves are given the choice as to how much they can deal with at this time.

14 Conclusion

14.1 Many benefits are obtained from post-mortem examinations, both for families and for future patients. For those benefits to be properly obtained it is vital that parents are not excluded from the process. The Post Mortem Inquiry was established as a result of the distress, grief and anger felt by families when they discovered that the organs of their children, and other relatives, had been retained and disposed of without knowledge or consent. The overriding recommendation of this Report is that legislation be enacted to ensure that this will not happen again.

14.2 In a general sense, authorisation is always preferable to conscription as it is in keeping with respect for family life, privacy, and the emotions of the bereaved. Parental permission for the examination and any retention of organs must be given freely. Insofar as they request it, their authorisation must be based on clear and comprehensible information provided in a sensitive and supportive way.

14.3 It is inherent in the circumstances surrounding the communication process in this context that time may be limited, and parents will undoubtedly be grieving and in shock. In that sense, the process is very far from ideal in terms of imparting information and ensuring as far as possible that it is understood. In the past, it has been clinicians who have taken it upon themselves to decide the level of information to be given to parents. This has not always proved to be sufficient and has resulted in anger, distrust and suspicion in many instances where parents felt they were not told the full truth. Although it is painful to be told, parents have the right to honesty.

14.4 Parents must be recognised as partners with medical professionals in the task of making decisions regarding their children. Yet the difficulties are enormous. The parents are under huge emotional stress, and are being asked to make an important decision that they will have to live with for the rest of their lives. It is futile to simply go through the motions of reciting details to grieving parents, and obtaining their signatures on forms. A great deal more effort at communication is required if authorisation of the procedure is to be meaningful.

14.5 *Authorisation*, as described in the Scottish Report on Organ Retention outlined above, is based on recognition of the intimate bond between parents and children, the constitutional privacy of the family unit, and the right to prevent interference with that unit. It recognises the role that parents must be given to make decisions in relation to how their children should be dealt with after death. *Authorisation* implies an active decision-making function by the parents/guardians who are in a recognised position of power, and is therefore in keeping with a modern interpretation of the relationship between patients/carers and doctors as a partnership or therapeutic alliance. *Authorisation* allows those who do not wish to be given details about organ removal to nonetheless make a valid decision. It therefore empowers parents to remain in control of the post-mortem process while at the same time respecting their right not to be told the distressing details of it. Information is not being withheld from them, rather they are exercising their choice not to access such information and yet remain involved in the decision-making process.

15 Recommendations

1. The main aim of this Report is to place parents/guardians at the centre of decision-making and control in respect of hospital post-mortem examinations to be carried out on their children. However, for the reasons outlined, the doctrine and language of informed consent is inappropriate here and therefore is not recommended for use in such legislation. The alternative concept of *authorisation* is to be preferred. This is a stronger and more powerful recognition of the active role and choice of parents in decision-making in relation to post mortems.

2. Parents must be given the option of authorising a post-mortem examination to be carried out on their child on the understanding that this is being performed to provide further information as to the cause of death and the possible effects of treatment. Some parents may wish to authorise a post mortem without wanting to receive any further information or consultation. Their right not to receive this information must be respected. It must be made clear to them that they can come back with a future request for more information at any time. For those parents who choose this option, it must be stated on the authorisation forms that this includes authorisation of all actions necessary as part of that examination. The accompanying information booklet to be given to parents to read if they so choose must explain that this will include removal and sampling of organs, and may include retention of organs for diagnostic purposes. It must be made clear that organs retained at post-mortem examinations will not be used for any purpose other than diagnosis without the authorisation of the parents/guardian.

3. If they require further information prior to authorisation, parents must be told that the performance of a post-mortem examination involves the examination of the body of the deceased child. It includes the dissection of the body and the removal of organs, tissue samples and blood/bodily fluids. It is carried out to provide information about or confirm the cause of death, to investigate the effect and efficacy of a medical or surgical intervention, to obtain information regarding the health of another person/future person, and for audit, education, training or research purposes. Parents must be made aware that in certain circumstances it may be necessary to retain organs in order to complete the examination.

4. Parents must be given the option to authorise a limited post mortem. They may choose to limit the examination to particular organs but, in making that choice, must be informed that this will mean that samples will be taken from the organs being examined, and that information will not be available on other organs which may have contributed to the child's death.

5. Parents should also be informed of the potential benefits of retention in terms of education, training and research. If the retention period is short, they must be made aware that it may be possible to delay the funeral in order that the organs may be reunited with the body. In other cases, they must be made aware of their options in relation to disposal of the organs at a later date.

6. Legislation must be introduced as a matter of urgency to ensure that no post-mortem examination will be carried out on the body of a deceased child and no organ will be retained from a post-mortem examination for any purpose whatsoever without the authorisation of the child's parent/guardian, or the authorisation of the coroner in an appropriate case.

Chapter Nine

Use of Autopsy Material in Medical Education and Research

1 Introduction

1.1 This chapter examines the relevance of post-mortem practice to medical education and training, audit, and medical research. The benefits to patients that can follow from teaching and research on human tissue are undeniable. Many bereaved families affected by the organ-retention controversy are anxious to see the realisation of these benefits. However, the uses to which organs and pathology specimens have been put in the past have raised concerns with parents regarding the level of respect shown to their deceased children's organs, and the lack of information they were given about those uses.

1.2 There is significant concern amongst pathologists in relation to the use of surgically removed tissue and the extent to which archived blocks and slides of tissue retained as part of the patient's medical record may be utilised. However, the terms of reference of this Inquiry deal only with whole organs retained at post-mortem examinations, and therefore this Report does not address the use of surgical tissue from living donors. It is clear that this issue requires detailed and urgent consideration and legal clarification.

2 Uses of Autopsy Material

2.1 The taking of tissue from almost every organ of the body is an integral part of the post-mortem examination. The pathologist removes tissue in order to correctly identify and definitively confirm any abnormality suspected by naked eye examination. There may also be abnormalities not visible to the naked eye, which can only be detected by microscopic examination. Tissue sampling of organs is therefore a necessary part of the competent performance of a post mortem and essential to a thorough diagnosis. Most pathologists would regard a post-mortem examination carried out without such sampling as incomplete and unprofessional.

2.2 There may be circumstances in which the pathologist requires to retain a whole organ, commonly the brain or heart, for further detailed examination so as to ensure an accurate diagnosis. This may involve consultation with surgeons or other clinicians who treated the child, or it may necessitate referral to a specialist in another hospital.

2.3 Autopsy material may also be retained for purposes of audit, clinical governance and quality assurance. Audit is a necessary facet of hospital management as it serves to ensure the highest possible standards of patient care. The autopsy is the most effective way of scrutinising surgical and medical competencies in the hospital, and is in keeping with models of transparency and peer review of patient management. Case conferences are commonly held in many hospitals on a regular basis where diagnoses are reviewed with an interdisciplinary clinical team, including pathologists who may present both images and whole organs so as to facilitate discussion of diagnoses and surgical techniques. Quality assurance in pathology laboratories is essential to ensure the highest standards of testing and accuracy in diagnosis.

2.4 It has already been noted in this Report that in the past, organs were retained from hospital post mortems carried out on children without the knowledge or consent of the child's parents. Although the primary use of these retained organs was for diagnostic purposes, other use was also sometimes made of the retained organs. Historically, organs were sometimes anonymously preserved in specimen jars in pathology museums for teaching purposes. Organs were also used in research projects carried out by, or in association with, some hospitals and medical schools in Irish universities. Consent was not obtained for retention for either purpose until recent years, though a small number of hospitals had consent forms that specifically referred to the retention of 'tissue' for medical education and research. As discussed in other sections of this Report, this was not generally understood by parents to refer to retention of whole organs. Since 2000, practices have changed and consent is now specifically sought for organ retention for education and research purposes.

3 Medical Education and Training

3.1 Pathologists are registered medical practitioners who have studied medicine for six years and spent a further year in intern hospital training. They then follow a training course for a further six to seven years studying histopathology (study of cells and tissues) and autopsy pathology under expert supervision in Ireland and abroad. The Faculty of Pathology and equivalent professional bodies in other countries such as the United Kingdom and United States set out training requirements to be fulfilled prior to acquisition of specialist qualification. Pathologists may specialise in microbiology, biochemistry, or haematology (blood diseases) as well as histopathology. The majority of the work done by hospital pathologists relates to living patients who are admitted for tests and surgical treatment. The hospital pathologists who carry out autopsies are histopathologists. There are currently 73 consultant histopathologists listed on the Specialist Register of the Irish Medical Council as resident in Ireland, and 39 specialist registrars in training. There are a further 18 in positions of senior house officer. Each major hospital has one or more histopathologist(s) on staff.

3.2 The importance and value of medical education and training cannot be underestimated. Discussion of the way in which education and training of undergraduate and postgraduate medical professionals is structured is clearly outside the remit of this Report. However, serious concerns have been expressed to the Inquiry in relation to the decline in the post-mortem rate in Irish hospitals, and the consequent detrimental effect on education and training of medical practitioners and pathologists.

3.3 It is vitally important that medical students are facilitated and encouraged to observe post mortems in order to fully appreciate the progression of disease and the complexity of the human body in both its normal and abnormal condition. The basics of anatomy can be taught on cadavers that have been donated to medical science. These donations demonstrate a huge commitment to scientific and medical endeavour, and the generosity of such donors is gratefully acknowledged. The altruistic spirit of individuals and families who have provided this benefit to society should be recognised and applauded.

3.4 Pathology is an essential component of an undergraduate medical education and ideally requires students to observe autopsies and organs. However, due to the reduction in hospital post-mortem rates, many medical students and aspiring doctors do not see an autopsy in the course of their training. This may leave them uninformed and unprepared to explain post-mortem examinations if required to do so in the course of their career. Attendance at autopsies facilitates a better understanding of pathology and medicine by students, and also encourages respect for the dead.

3.5 Trainee pathologists require access to tissue and organs retained from autopsies and surgery in order to become sufficiently trained in diagnosing both common and rare conditions. Practical training in the complexities of dissection can only be realistically obtained through attendance and eventual participation in post-mortem examinations. Experience and discussion with treating clinicians form an important basis of competence in this speciality. Competent performance of an autopsy is a necessary and fundamental constituent of specialist qualification as a pathologist.

3.6 Organs retained over many years are sometimes preserved in pathology museums to allow visual inspection by medical students and are of huge value to teaching. Most medical schools at Irish universities maintain pathology museums. The size and content of these museums vary from college to college. Many of the specimens maintained at these museums are over fifty years old and none is identifiable. The museums are not open to the public. The collections are used to teach medical students and trainee surgeons in diagnostic and technical skills, and to ensure that they have reached appropriate levels of competency both prior to qualification and as part of continuing professional development during their careers.

3.7 The value of pathology museums for teaching purposes is incontrovertible. The specimens maintained at such museums play a major role in medical education and training of undergraduate and postgraduate doctors. However, consent to retention was not obtained from the families of the deceased for such use. No opportunity was thus given to them to donate these organs in the interests of medical science, as many would have wished. It is unclear from the documentation submitted to the Inquiry how many of the organs maintained in pathology museums are from post mortems performed on children.

4 Audit and Quality Assurance

4.1 Medical audit is a process of assessing the quality of health care. This may be done at an individual, local or national level but the objective remains the same. Audit is carried out to assess the structure, process and outcome in a healthcare setting and compare it with previously agreed standards or past results. It is an essential process in a healthcare system that prioritises quality and safety.

4.2 The relevance of post-mortem examinations to quality assurance and audit processes is abundantly clear. Despite advances in medical technology, in particular diagnostic imaging, numerous studies demonstrate continued discrepancies between clinical diagnoses and autopsy findings. It is self-evident that in circumstances where error rates and unsuspected findings are high, there must be a system for reviewing patient care and management in order to ensure the best possible quality of care for patients. The autopsy performs a critical function in this regard as it is the best means by which errors might be detected and standards consequently improved. In this sense the autopsy rate might be said to be an indicator of the quality of a hospital.

4.3 Quality assurance may involve the review of patient records to analyse the outcome of surgical procedures, or the use of a blood sample to ensure that accuracy levels in testing are maintained. Consent is not generally sought from living patients for retention of tissue samples as part of their medical record as it is taken to be implicit in consent for treatment. Consideration of the legal issues involved in the retention of tissue blocks and slides is outside the scope of this Report, which is focused on retention of whole organs at post mortem.

5 Research

5.1 The advancement of medical science depends on research, which may be broadly defined as the process by which new facts are established. Medical research ranges from traditional laboratory studies, to assessment of patient outcomes, to a statistical analysis of populations. There is often a blurred line between medical audit and medical research, both of which can have significant impact on future practice. This Report does not intend to address this long-standing debate.

5.2 Autopsies on individual patients or groups of patients with similar conditions provide insights into disease and responses to treatment. Such autopsies are fundamentally important in leading to greater understanding and recognition of symptoms of disease processes. The collection and use of biological samples from surgery and autopsy for medical research is invaluable. Medical research cannot progress without the use of such samples which are therefore of huge scientific significance. Their value to society is immeasurable.

5.3 To be acceptable, medical research can only be carried out according to legal and ethical requirements, which are imposed to ensure protection of the interests of all participants and researchers. The increasing scrutiny of medical research and clinical trials over the period spanned by this Report demonstrates a growth in concern and respect for the welfare and rights of participants, and a recognition of the fundamental importance of voluntary informed consent. Principles of respect for self-determination and the dignity of the human body are universal principles that do not depend on national legislation or legal precedent, and are inherent in numerous international declarations and conventions, most importantly the Declaration of Helsinki.[32]

5.4 In the European context, the most influential statements have been the European Convention on Human Rights, the Council of Europe Convention on Human Rights and Biomedicine (1997), and the additional protocols mentioned in Chapter Eight.

---

[32] World Medical Association. *Declaration of Helsinki: Recommendations Guiding Physicians in Biomedical Research involving Subjects* (1964, 2000)

Ireland has not yet signed the Convention. There has been a determined drive to respect human rights in the context of medical treatment and clinical research across the European Union, with an extensive public policy debate taking place in many European countries in relation to informed consent and the nature and appropriateness of regulatory models of research ethics review.

5.5 Clinical research involving trials of medicinal products on human subjects is subject to regulation through the EU Clinical Trials Directive, as implemented. This imposes a structure on the approval process for medicinal products across the EU, requires ethics committee review of such trials, and establishes binding requirements of consent. Regulation of research is not uniformly welcomed – some researchers view such oversight as an impediment to valuable research. However, regulation can also be seen as a means by which individual rights and autonomy can be safeguarded by the anticipation of dilemmas and difficulties. Further development of these arguments is outside the scope of this Report.

5.6 Research activity is generally now subject to ethical review, though the extent and quality of such review has varied over the years covered by this Report. In Ireland, the role of ethical review of trials on medicinal products is given to Research Ethics Committees (RECs), whose role and function has become more formalised since the implementation of the Clinical Trials Directive. Even prior to the Clinical Trials Directive, approval by an REC was usually considered a necessary precondition for funding, insurance and publication of research findings. RECs generally review research protocols with the following principles in mind: informed consent, freedom to withdraw without adverse consequences, benefit to participants, privacy and data protection. Despite the increased formalisation and regulation of the ethical review process, concern nonetheless exists in relation to research that falls outside the scope of the Directive, as well as the membership of RECs and the level of inconsistency in decision-making at local level.

5.7 Research on human tissue, including organs, has contributed to improvements in disease diagnosis and treatment. Scientific and medical literature is replete with examples of how research using human material has contributed to understanding of the causes of disease, as well as the development of cures and treatments. For example, children's organs were sometimes used in research projects aimed at investigating the cause of death of children who died of Sudden Infant Death Syndrome (SIDS, or commonly called 'cot deaths'). The organs of children who died from other conditions were also used in these research projects for comparison purposes in order to ascertain which organs were affected by SIDS. It is vitally important that such research be allowed and encouraged to continue and grow, and that the scientific value of pathology archives be promoted. However, in light of past practices, this must be done in a way that restores and stimulates public confidence, and balances the rights and interests of individuals with the public interest in ethical research.

6 Consent for Research

6.1 As discussed at various points throughout this Report, consent is widely regarded as one of the fundamental principles of medical ethics. It is emphasised in numerous research ethics codes and regulatory processes. For example, Article 22 of the Declaration of Helsinki provides that:

> In any research on human beings each subject must be adequately informed of the aims, methods, sources of funding, possible conflicts of interests, institutional affiliations of the researcher, the anticipated benefits and risks of the study and the discomfort that it might entail. The subject shall be informed of the right to abstain from participation in the study and to withdraw consent at any time without fear of reprisal. After ensuring that the subject has understood the information, the physician should then obtain the subject's freely given consent preferably in writing. If consent cannot be obtained in writing the non-written consent must be formally documented and witnessed.

6.2 Despite the emphasis clearly placed on the importance of consent in the research process, there is an argument that in relation to the use of human material, the concept of consent might be curtailed by an appeal to the public interest in research. The broader issues in this debate focus on rights of ownership over excised tissue, distinctions between surgical waste and post-mortem tissue, self-determination and utilitarianism. Concerns are commonly expressed within the research community that the imposition of a rigid consent structure will inhibit research, and that due consideration should also be given to the benefit of research to humankind. Various recommendations have emanated from professional bodies and legislative processes in the United Kingdom and Scotland, some of which rely heavily on the notion of anonymity and regulation as a safeguard against any undue interference with individual rights.

6.3 The Irish Council for Bioethics has published recommendations dealing with the collection, use and storage of human biological material in research.[33] While much of this report and its recommendations relate to material taken from living donors, there is also, *inter alia,* discussion of the importance of informed consent, and the use of pathology archives in research.

6.4 The Steering Committee on Bioethics (CDBI) at the Council of Europe has published draft recommendations on research on human biological materials, which will be submitted to the Committee of Ministers of the Council in 2006. The recommendations provide in Article 10.2 that information and consent or authorisation to obtain human biological materials should be as specific as possible with regard to any foreseen research uses and the choices available in that respect. Article 12 states that biological material removed for purposes other than storage for research should not be made available for research activities without appropriate consent or authorisation, and whenever possible, information should be given and consent/authorisation requested before biological materials are removed. Article 13 provides that biological materials should not be removed from the body of a deceased

---

[33] *Human Biological Material: Recommendations for Collection, Use and Storage in Research 2005.* Irish Council for Bioethics

person for research activities without appropriate consent or authorisation, and should not be removed or supplied for research activities if the deceased person is known to have objected to it.

7 Retention of Organs for Research

7.1 In the past, organs retained at post mortems carried out on children were sometimes used for research purposes without the consent of the child's parents. Some post-mortem consent forms referred to retention of 'tissue' for such purposes but although the clinicians understood this to include organs, the child's parents generally did not. The reasons why parents were not given this information and choice are outlined in earlier chapters of the Report.

7.2 Following consultation with stakeholders in 2002 guidelines were drafted by the National Working Group on Organ Retention and adopted by the National Chief Officers in 2003. An audit of conformity with these guidelines across all hospitals was outside the scope of this Inquiry. The guidelines provide that in discussion of a hospital post mortem with relatives of the deceased, the relatives should be informed that the pathologist might consider retaining organs for education and/or research purposes. In these circumstances specific consent is required. Relatives should be informed about the storage, use and ultimate disposal of the organs and the anonymisation of all samples.

7.3 In keeping with recommendations dealing with organ retention generally, in order for research to be undertaken on organs retained from a deceased child at post mortem, authorisation must be given by the child's parent/guardian. This applies to all post mortems, including those authorised by the coroner. The coroner's functions cease to exist once the investigation into the cause of death is complete. Therefore, further retention for any other purpose can only be done with the authorisation of the child's parent/guardian.

7.4 The process by which authorisation is given is a continuous one, dependent on good communication, disclosure of relevant information if required, competence and voluntariness. These components have already been discussed in Chapter Eight of this Report and apply here in equal force.

7.5 However, there are some potential problems where parents/guardians are invited to authorise the use of retained organs for research purposes. In many cases the research that may be undertaken on the retained organs in the future is not yet contemplated and therefore cannot be disclosed to the parents. An issue arises as to whether specific consent is necessary or appropriate in these circumstances at all, given the impossibility of predicting the research that may be undertaken in the future.

7.6 The Nuffield Council on Bioethics said in this regard:

> Expressions such as informed consent and fully informed consent are often used in medical ethics. They are somewhat misleading. Consent can be given to some course of action only as described in a specific way. Since the description can never be exhaustive, consent will always be to an action that is incompletely

described; moreover, the descriptions offered are often incompletely understood. This incompleteness cannot be remedied by the devising of more elaborate consent forms and procedures for patients, donors and relatives. Fully informed consent is therefore an unattainable ideal.

The ethically significant requirement is not that consent be complete but that it be genuine. Obtaining genuine consent requires medical practitioners to do their best to communicate accurately as much as patients, volunteers or relatives can understand about procedures and risks and to respect the limits of their understanding, and of their capacity to deal with difficult information. If all reasonable care is exercised, adequate and genuine consent may be established, although it will necessarily fall short of fully informed consent.[34]

7.7 It may be that a general form of consent may suffice which is unspecified, or a 'blanket' consent to use the organs for a broad category of research without necessarily knowing the details of each project that may use the organs in the future. However, if the language of informed consent is used in this context, it may be argued that such broad consent is insufficient as it is given in the absence of full and complete disclosure of the uses to which the organs might be put.

7.8 Those who argue for specific consent take the view that each time research is proposed in relation to the organ, the donor (in this case the parents of the deceased child) should be contacted for consent. In this way their wishes are fully respected in making choices as to what forms of research are acceptable to them and what forms are not. However, it must be recognised that it is not always possible or practicable to return to parents to seek new consent on each occasion on which it is proposed to carry out research using the donated organ. It may be that authorisation at the time of post mortem, the use of the organs on an anonymous basis, and a requirement for oversight by a Research Ethics Committee, would suffice to allay any fears that parents may have in this regard.

7.9 This Report is concerned to ensure that parents are as informed as they wish to be in relation to the retention and potential use of their child's organs. In relation to retention for diagnosis or educational purposes, the information given to parents can be as specific as the parents themselves require. However, in relation to future possible research uses of the organs, there would appear to be no means by which the information to be made available to parents at the time of the post-mortem examination can be specific.

7.10 The authorisation model proposed in this Report enables parents to control the amount of information they wish to receive, as well as controlling what they wish to be done to or with their child's organs. In this way they may choose the broad option of facilitating research to be carried out using the organs, without necessarily receiving details of the specific research projects. Alternatively they may choose to authorise research on specific conditions only, such as the condition from which their child died. They may authorise research on the basis that they wish to be re-contacted on each occasion on which it is proposed to use the organs for a research project. By

---

[34] *Human Tissue: Ethical and Legal Issues*. Nuffield Council on Bioethics, London (1995) para.6.19–6.21

giving parents these options, their decision in relation to how much information they would like to have and their wishes in respect of their child's organs are respected.

8 Conclusion

8.1 It is paramount that the highest standards of medical education and training be promoted and maintained for the benefit of our healthcare system. On this issue there is consensus. Patients, bereaved families and medical professionals share this common interest. The interests of educators and researchers do not diminish the interests of patients and families. There must be recognition that it is a shared goal, one that those outside the medical profession are encouraged to understand and participate in.

8.2 A model of partnership has supplanted the traditional prevalence of a deferential ethos to the medical profession. This modern culture of rights leads to expectations of consultation and mutual respect. This should not be seen as threatening the ability and flexibility of clinicians and researchers to continue to do their work. The authorisation process should not be seen as a hurdle that makes education and research more difficult. Public confidence in medical education and research must be revitalised and strengthened by openness and transparency in the system. The experiences of the past should be used to encourage higher standards of inclusiveness and shared understanding.

8.3 The conclusions reached in this Chapter apply equally to hospital and coroner post mortems following the discharge of the latter's functions. The coroner has no function or power to authorise the retention of organs at post mortem other than to establish the cause of death. When such cause has been established to his satisfaction, with or without an inquest, the coroner no longer has any powers in relation to the retained organs.

8.4 The parents/guardians of the deceased child must be given the choice to authorise the use of their child's organs for education and research purposes, and have the right to receive information on those choices as they require. Their authorisation of medical education and research to be carried out with their child's organs may provide some positive comfort to the parents in their bereavement.

9 Recommendations

1   Legislation must be introduced as a matter of urgency to ensure that no post-mortem examination will be carried out on the body of a deceased child and no organ will be retained from a post-mortem examination for any purpose whatsoever without the authorisation of the child's parent/guardian, or the authorisation of the coroner in an appropriate case.

2   The removal of organs from the body of a deceased child at post mortem is carried out as a necessary part of the examination of the body and diagnosis of the cause of death. It must be made clear in legislation that a post-mortem

examination includes the necessary removal of organs for this purpose. The retention of organs at post mortem may be necessary in certain circumstances in order to make an accurate diagnosis of the detailed cause of death.

3   It is recommended that public awareness of post-mortem practices be improved, including the necessity for organ removal, weighing and sampling for further tests.

4   In a coroners post mortem, the coroner may only authorise the retention of organs for the purpose of establishing the cause of the child's death. Retention following a coroner's post mortem for any other purpose must be authorised by the child's parents.

5   In any discussion about organ retention, parents must be given information about potential uses and benefits of retention for purposes of audit, education and research, unless they indicate that they do not wish to receive such information. It is recommended that organs may be removed and retained from the body of a deceased child at a hospital post mortem for purposes of audit, education and research, only where removal and retention for such purpose has been authorised by the child's parent/guardian.

6   It is recommended that authorisation of retention for research purposes may be general or specific. Choice must be given to parents as to what form of authorisation they wish to give. A general authorisation will facilitate the use of the retained organs for research purposes that are not currently foreseeable. A specific authorisation may limit the research use of the organs by prohibiting certain types of research being carried out with the organs. The authorisation form must enable full account to be taken of parents' views in this regard.

7   Where the purpose of organ retention is research, it is recommended that in addition to the requirement that retention be authorised, the research must be subject to ethical review by an approved Research Ethics Committee.

8   It is recommended that anonymised organs currently retained in pathology museums for teaching purposes should be maintained as a valuable educational resource. Any proposed inclusion of an organ in such a museum in the future must be specifically authorised and documented.

9   It is recommended that medical and nursing students be permitted and encouraged to attend post-mortem examinations. Legislation should provide for authorisation for such educational viewing to be sought from the parent/guardian of the deceased child or the coroner as appropriate. Guidelines must be drawn up to ensure that such attendance will be carried out in a controlled and respectful manner.

10 Information relating to post-mortem examinations and organ retention must be made available to bereaved parents in a comprehensible and sympathetic way. A bereavement liaison officer should be involved in these discussions so as to enable families to access the relevant information, and to reassure them that their decisions will be respected.

Chapter Ten

The Way Forward

1 Introduction

1.1 This Report has discussed the accounts given by parents of deceased children as to their experience of post-mortem practices and organ retention in Ireland from 1970 up to the controversy that arose in 1999 when organ-retention practices were publicised by the media. It has also examined the technical and practical aspects of the performance of post-mortem examinations in Ireland, the accounts given by some Irish hospitals of the post mortem practice prevalent in their hospital during the period under review, and the changes that have been made since 2000. Throughout this Report the following key issues have been clear:

- In the past, there was sometimes inadequate recognition or acknowledgement of the feelings parents have on the recent loss of a child, and the extent to which they feel the need to protect the child even after death.

- The failure to inform parents that organs might be retained as part of the post mortem carried out on their child caused huge distress and anger.

- The lack of information and choice in coroner post mortems is very difficult for some parents to accept.

- The level of information given, the standard of communication and the skill in supporting bereaved parents was often poor.

- The legal vacuum in relation to hospital post mortems is unsatisfactory, as neither families nor doctors know the parameters within which hospital post mortems can take place within the law.

1.2 The communication deficit that existed in the past must be corrected so that families do not feel marginalised in the system and instead are considered to be equal partners in the decision-making process relating to their child. Though hospital practices and policies have addressed many of these issues over the last five years, legislation is recommended to standardise and copper-fasten these changes.

2 Existing Legislative Provisions in Ireland

2.1 There is a dearth of legal provisions dealing with post-mortem examinations in Ireland with only the Coroners Act 1962, the Anatomy Act 1832 and the Registration of Births and Deaths Acts 1863–1996 providing even limited assistance in this regard. This distinguishes the situation in Ireland from that in existence during the same period of time covered by this Report in the United Kingdom where human tissue legislation has been in existence since 1961.

2.2 The Anatomy Act, 1832 provides a statutory framework for regulating schools of anatomy. At the time of its introduction, the legal supply of bodies was inadequate for the purposes of acquiring medical knowledge. This resulted in illegal trafficking of bodies. The Act provides for the granting of licenses to persons practising anatomy and for the appointment of Inspectors of places where such examinations are carried out. In relation to consent the Act provides that an executor, or other party having custody of the body, could permit an anatomical examination save in circumstances where the deceased, during his/her lifetime, had indicated that his/her body after death might not undergo such examination or where next-of-kin refused to consent to such examination. Even where a person during his/her lifetime had indicated that his/her body might undergo anatomical examination after death, this could not take place without the consent of next-of-kin.

2.3 The provisions of the Coroners Act, 1962 have already been detailed in Chapter Two. In addition to the summary of the Act set out there, it is noteworthy that the Act does not give specific statutory recognition to the role of State Pathologist. The function of state pathologist is covered by sections 33(2) and (3) of the Coroners Act, 1962. Insofar as relevant, Section 33(2) states as follows: 'A coroner may request the Minister (for Justice) to arrange (a) a post-mortem examination by a person appointed by the Minister of the body of any person in relation to whose death the coroner is holding or proposing to hold an inquest ...' Section 33 (3) states that 'it shall be the duty of the coroner to exercise his powers of request to the Minister under subsection (2) in every case in which a member of the Garda Síochána not below the rank of inspector applies to him so to do and states his reasons for so applying.' The Working Group on the Review of the Coroner Service recommended that coroners should be given the power to order a post mortem from the state pathologist on request from the Gardaí and without prior approval of the Minister, and that the rules and procedures governing these post mortems should be set out in Coroners Rules.[35] This Report concurs with that recommendation.

2.4 The first full-time state pathologist was appointed in 1974, with the post of deputy state pathologist established in 1997. The functions of the state pathologist include the following:

- Attendance at scenes of discovery of dead human bodies
- Removal of trace evidence from bodies for forensic examination
- Performance of external examination of bodies and autopsies
- Retention of samples, including organs, for further examination
- Production of reports for submission to the Director of Public Prosecutions and local coroners
- Attendance at criminal prosecutions to give evidence
- Attendance at coroner inquests
- Provision of instruction in forensic medicine
- Provision of advice on forensic pathology.

---

[35] *Review of the Coroner Service*, Report of the Working Group, para. 3.3.5

2.5 The Registration of Births and Deaths Acts 1863–1996 provide that all deaths occurring in Ireland should be registered, in the Registrar's district in which it occurred, as soon as possible but no later than five days after the death, except where the death has been referred to the coroner. The 5-day period may be extended to 14 days if the Registrar is notified in writing of the death and supplied with a medical certificate of the cause of death. A registered medical practitioner who treated the deceased within 28 days before the death must sign the medical certificate. If a doctor did not see the deceased within 28 days, or if the person died as a result of an accident or in violent or mysterious circumstances, the death must be referred to the coroner, in which case the death will be registered on foot of a certificate issued by the coroner to the registrar.

2.6 Historically all information on the certificates, other than the name of the medical practitioner certifying the death, was recorded in the Register of Deaths. The certificates were then sent to the Central Statistics Office in order to compile statistics on causes of death. The certificates were subsequently forwarded to the General Register Office for storage, and later destroyed after a number of years. The General Register Office has medical certificates from 1989 to 1996 and the Central Statistics Office has certificates from 1997. Certificates from the year 1993 were badly damaged by floodwater in 1998 and had to be disposed of. All certificates are now electronically scanned and indexed.

3 Professional Guidelines

3.1 In 2000 the Faculty of Pathology of the Royal College of Physicians of Ireland issued guidelines to the profession in relation to post-mortem consent and retention of tissue. The guidelines state that consent for a hospital post-mortem examination should be requested by a senior clinician, nursing officer or bereavement officer. Consent for teaching or research should be specifically sought and an information leaflet should be available with details of autopsies, funeral arrangements, disposal of retained organs, and death certification. Pathologists should make themselves available to families who require further clarification on details of the post-mortem examination.

3.2 The retention of blood, organ and tissue samples is clearly and strongly endorsed by the Faculty of Pathology as 'an integral part' of the post-mortem examination. According to the guidelines, retention must remain at the discretion of the pathologist performing the examination. Detailed examination of retained samples may prevent their return to the body prior to its release for burial. The Faculty distinguishes this from the situation in England where funeral arrangements generally run over a longer period of time, thereby enabling return of the organs to the body after examination. Families who are prepared to delay the funeral to facilitate the return of retained organs should be accommodated. The wishes of the family in relation to disposal of the retained organs should be adhered to as far as possible. This applies equally to coroner post mortems when the investigation has been closed by conclusion of the inquest, or death certification. The guidelines also include draft consent forms and information leaflets.

3.3 The Eastern Regional Health Authority produced guidelines for providing a quality response to families in relation to queries from post-mortem practices. These guidelines were endorsed by the National Liaison Group on Organ Retention in 2001 and shaped the development of the National Protocols and Guidelines for Organ Retention and Post Mortem Practices, which were adopted at the end of 2003. An implementation plan was drawn up to include the appointment and training of bereavement officers, standardised consent forms, arrangements for disposal of organs, and requirements for management of records.

4 European Tissue and Cells Directive 2004

4.1 The EU Tissues and Cells Directive 2004/23/EC was adopted by Council of Ministers on 2 March 2004. Member States are obliged to comply by 7 April 2006. The purpose of the Directive is to introduce high common safety and quality standards across the EU concerning the exchange of tissues and cells between States, and to secure protection for patients receiving tissue and cell treatments.

4.2 Basic requirements of the Directive include an inspection and licensing scheme, an adverse incident reporting scheme, and a documented quality assurance scheme. Tissue and cells used for industrially manufactured products and medical devices are covered by the Directive only as far as donation, procurement and testing are concerned. Other Directives cover other aspects. The Directive applies to tissues and cells including umbilical cord and bone-marrow cells, reproductive cells (sperm and eggs), foetal tissues, and stem cells (adult and embryonic). It excludes blood and blood products, human organs, and cells of animal origin. Autologous grafting, i.e. tissues removed and later transplanted to same patient, are not covered.

4.3 The Directive does not cover research using tissue and cells unless applied in clinical trials to the human body. It does not interfere with Member States' decisions as to use of stem cells, or to decisions as to meaning of 'person' or 'individual'. It states that the donation of cells from a living body must be preceded by a medical examination to ensure that the donor's health will not be affected. Donation from deceased persons must respect the dignity of the deceased, particularly by reconstruction of the body.

4.4 The Directive states that donation should be based on voluntariness, altruism, and anonymity. Donors must be given assurances regarding confidentiality of their donation and any related test results, and traceability of their donation. The Data Protection Directive 1995 applies to personal data processed in application of this directive.

4.5 The Directive provides that States must organise inspections and control measures to ensure that tissue establishments comply with the Directive. Personnel involved in tissue establishments must be appropriately qualified and provided with relevant training. Adequate tracing of tissue must be established through identification procedures, record maintenance, and appropriate labelling system. As a general rule, the identity of recipients should not be disclosed to the donor and vice versa. However, member states may provide for the lifting of anonymity in exceptional cases such as in gamete donation.

5 Human Tissue Legislation (UK)

5.1 Reference has been made in this Report to the human tissue legislation in the United Kingdom. The Human Tissue Act, 1961 came into force on 27 September 1961 in that jurisdiction. The purpose of the Act was to provide for:

- the use of parts of bodies of deceased persons for therapeutic purposes and purposes of medical education and research
- the circumstances in which post-mortem examinations may be carried out
- the permission for the cremation of bodies removed for anatomical examination.

5.2 Section 1(2) of the Act provides that the person lawfully in possession of the body of a deceased person may authorise the removal of any part from the body for use for therapeutic purposes or for purposes of medical education or research if, having made such reasonable enquiry as may be practicable, he has no reason to believe that any surviving relative of the deceased objects to the body being so dealt with. Section 2 deals with a hospital post mortem where there is no intention to retain tissue for therapeutic purposes, medical education or research. In this situation the examination is for the purpose of establishing or confirming the causes of death, or of investigating the existence or nature of abnormal conditions. The Act does not contain any criminal sanction for breach of its provisions.

5.3 Organ Retention Inquiries

The main findings of the *Bristol*[36] and *Alder Hey*[37] *Inquiries* have already been mentioned earlier in this Report and deal with the fundamental importance of communication and consent in the area of post-mortem retention of organs. Another report called the *Isaacs Report*[38] was commissioned following the discovery by the family of the late Cyril Isaacs that his brain had been retained following post-mortem examination, and used for research purposes. This was done without the family's knowledge or consent. The Report showed that storage and use of organs and tissue without proper consent after people had died were commonplace. Though the Report deals with coroner post-mortem examinations and organ retention in the context of deceased adults, the latter of which is outside the remit of this Inquiry, it is nonetheless worth summarising the main conclusions and recommendations of this report:

- The public was unaware of what happened at a post mortem and of the possibility of organ retention.

---

[36] *The Bristol Royal Infirmary Inquiry Report* 2000
[37] *The Royal Liverpool Children's Inquiry Report* 2001 (the Alder Hey or Redfern Report)
[38] *Investigation into events that followed the death of Cyril Mark Isaacs*, HM Inspector of Anatomy 2003

- Those who knew about organ retention did not discuss it with relatives and did not consider this to be unethical.

- Despite the radical shift in demand for information, many people still do not wish to be told the details of post-mortem examinations. Their right 'not to know' should be respected.

- The fact that a post mortem has been carried out for the coroner does not mean that the relatives consent to carry out research can be assumed once the coroner's need to retain organs has ended.

- The discovery that organs were retained without their knowledge has been the cause of great distress to some families. This has been exacerbated by uncertainty as to disposal of organs in cases where records have not been kept.

- The importance of research on retained organs cannot be underestimated and steps must be taken to encourage organ donation for research, but this must always be with the safeguard of informed consent by the relatives in every case.

- There is no system of quality assurance or audit of coroner post mortems, and there is confusion as to responsibilities.

- Though non-disclosure of organ retention may have been well intentioned, it is no longer acceptable or compatible with the culture of openness which must now prevail.

- It is essential that steps be taken to re-establish public confidence that research will only be undertaken with consent. Complete openness is required. Nevertheless, there will be some relatives who do not wish to be informed of the details. For those, unwelcome information must not be forced upon them.

- The recommendations contained in the Isaacs report are intended to introduce legal, administrative, ethical and other requirements designed to ensure that organs retained from coroner post mortems will not be retained for, or used in, teaching or research without the knowledge and consent of the relatives. It is also intended that the recommendations will help to restore public confidence in the post-mortem procedures and practices and thus enable organs to be used in beneficial research with full consent from relatives.

5.4 Human Tissue Act, 2004 (UK)

A new Human Tissue Act, which repeals the 1961 Act, will come into force in England, Wales and Northern Ireland in 2006. The Act has been lauded and criticised in equal measure in those jurisdictions. It aims to provide a framework for regulating the storage and use of human organs and tissue from the living, and the removal, storage and use of tissue and organs from the deceased, for specified health-related purposes and public display. The main features of the new legislation include the following:

- The Act makes consent the fundamental principle underpinning the lawful retention and use of body parts, organs and tissue. It does not cover *removal* of material from the living, which continues to be dealt with by the common law.

- It regulates removal, storage and use of human tissue, defined as material that has come from a human body and consists of, or includes, human cells.

- It lists the purposes for which consent is required – referred to as scheduled purposes. Consent required is called 'appropriate consent'. Penalties are imposed as a deterrent to failing to obtain consent.

- It establishes a Human Tissue Authority to ensure compliance. The Authority will issue good practice guidelines in statutory codes of practice and will also licence and inspect post-mortem activities.

Under the Act consent is required for 'Scheduled purposes'. These are as follows:

Part 1 – purposes generally requiring consent where the tissue is from the living/dead:
1 Anatomical examination. This requires witnessed consent in writing before death
2 Determining the cause of death, except where ordered by coroner
3 Establishing after a person's death the efficacy of any drug or other treatment, i.e. a hospital post mortem
4 Obtaining medical information about a person that might be relevant to someone else, such as genetic information
5 Public display; requires witnessed consent in writing before death
6 Research in connection with disorders or the functioning of the body
7 Transplantation.

Part 2 – purposes requiring consent where the tissue is from deceased persons:
8 Clinical audit
9 Education or training relating to human health
10 Performance assessment
11 Public health monitoring
12 Quality assurance.

There is an exception to the requirement for consent, which makes it lawful to use for scheduled purposes without consent human tissue already held in storage for a scheduled purpose on April 2006. Storage and use of existing holdings will be subject to good practice guidelines to be issued by the Human Tissue Authority.

6 Human Tissue (Scotland) Bill 2005

6.1 At the date of writing, the Human Tissue (Scotland) Bill was progressing through the Scottish Parliament.[39] The Bill contains three main strands: transplantation, modernisation of the Anatomy Act, and hospital post mortems. It also deals with retention of material from post mortems carried out under the authorisation of the

---

[39] Human Tissue (Scotland) Bill (SP Bill 42) introduced in the Scottish Parliament on 3 June 2005

Procurator Fiscal, whose office is similar in some respects to that of the coroner in this jurisdiction. The Bill was introduced following the publication of the report of the Independent Review Group on Retention of Organs at Post Mortem in 2001.

6.2 The basic principles underpinning the Bill are the need to respect people's wishes regarding post-mortem examination and retention of organs, and to provide clarity about the roles and responsibilities of those involved in post-mortem practice. A post-mortem examination is defined in section 19 of the Bill as follows:

> In this Act, 'post-mortem examination' means examination of the body of a deceased person involving its dissection and the removal of organs, tissue sample, blood (or any material derived from blood) or other body fluid which is carried out for any or all of the following purposes –
>
> (a) Providing information about or confirming the cause of death
> (b) Investigating the effect and efficacy of any medical or surgical intervention carried out on the person
> (c) Obtaining information which may be relevant to the health of any other person (including a future person)
> (d) Audit, education, training or research.

Save as discussed below, the provisions of the Bill in relation to post-mortem examinations do not apply to those carried out with the authorisation of the Procurator Fiscal.

6.3 The Scottish Review Group recommended the introduction of the concept of authorisation to replace that of consent to post-mortem examination.[40] The Bill accepts that recommendation by providing that the post-mortem examination and use of retained material must be authorised. Standardised authorisation forms and information leaflets are to be used across Scotland to ensure uniformity of approach in all hospitals.

6.4 The Report of the Review Group, and the Bill, draw a clear distinction between the retention of blocks and slides necessarily created at a post-mortem examination and which should be considered part of the deceased's medical record, and organs which should only be retained in exceptional circumstances and with specific authorisation. This distinction is based on the greater emotional significance generally attached to whole organs by families, as well as the potential clinical benefit to be obtained for the family from the retention of blocks and slides. In relation to samples retained following an examination authorised by the Procurator Fiscal, the Bill provides that they should become part of the medical record of the deceased and may be used for diagnostic and audit purposes without authorisation from relatives. Authorisation is however required for use of the samples for any other purpose.

6.5 Provision is made in the Bill for retention of tissue samples in existing holdings. If retained following post mortem authorised by the Procurator Fiscal before the coming into force of the Bill, the samples may be retained for education, training, and

---

[40] See Chapter 8, section 11 for further discussion of authorisation.

research purposes without further authorisation. For organs retained in similar circumstances, the Bill provides that they may be retained with appropriate authorisation, and the approval of a Research Ethics Committee if for a research purpose.

6.6 Penalties are imposed for non-compliance with the Bill. It will be an offence to perform a hospital post mortem or retain organs/tissue without authorisation or a reasonable belief that authorisation had been given.

7 The Way Forward for Ireland

7.1 This Report has presented the experiences of parents who have been affected by post-mortem practices and organ retention. Their grief and anger at the failure to inform them of the retention of their child's organs is palpable. Their shock and hurt at the way in which their child's organs were stored and disposed of was exacerbated by the difficulties many of them encountered in trying to establish whether and what organs had been retained and for how long. Many parents feel they have been let down by medical professionals, hospitals and the healthcare system in the lack of respect shown to them and their child.

7.2 Medical professionals have also been affected by this controversy. Many pathologists have been distressed at the way in which this issue has been portrayed, and some feel aggrieved that their adherence to the standards of their profession has led to criticism. Some clinicians have become reluctant to discuss post-mortem examinations with bereaved parents, leading to a serious decline in the hospital post-mortem rate.

7.3 Despite the problems of the past, parents and professionals should not be seen as taking opposing sides for the future. There is common ground on the need for legislative reform of both hospital and coroner post-mortem practice. There is consensus that respect for the wishes of the bereaved must be of paramount importance in this reform and that any legislation that may be introduced should be clear, consistent and transparent. The public must be encouraged to have confidence in the post-mortem system and must be satisfied that there are sufficient safeguards in the legislation to ensure respect for the wishes of bereaved parents. This will help to increase hospital post-mortem rates, which in turn will support medical education and research. As has been stressed throughout this Report, communication and authorisation are the key factors in the re-establishment of trust in the system.

7.4 Legislation dealing with hospital post mortems is required as a matter of urgency. The lack of clarity regarding the rights of parents/guardians of deceased children in this regard must be addressed in order to assure those affected by the organ-retention controversy and the general public, that communication, transparency and authorisation will be the hallmarks of the post-mortem system for the future.

7.5 There is inevitable overlap in this area between coroner post mortems and hospital post mortems. The clinical performance of the examination is largely the same. Some of the parents who made submissions to the Inquiry were distressed that their child had been the subject of a coroner's post mortem in which they had no control or no choice. As discussed in Chapter Three of this Report, it is essential that the coroner's jurisdiction to authorise a post-mortem examination in appropriate circumstances should be continued. It is vital that the independence of the office of coroner to investigate the cause of death be clearly understood as part of the administration of justice. It is not recommended that the system of authorisation proposed for hospital post mortems in this Report be extended to coroner post mortems, as this would be in conflict with the exercise of the coroner's functions. However, clear communication with the parents of the deceased child is necessary to ensure that they are informed as to, firstly, the reasons for the post mortem and, secondly, their options in relation to use or disposal of any material that might be retained as part of that examination.

7.6 The Review of the Coroner Service recognised that 'one of the weaknesses in the existing service lies in the lack of administrative support required to deliver optimal services to relatives'. The Review acknowledged the critical importance of continuing support and provision of information to relatives during the coroner's investigation, but pointed out that the lack of administrative support often puts impossible strain on the coroner's resources in this regard. It recommended that a new post of coroner's officer should be introduced at a regional level to support the services provided by the coroner.[41] The duties of this officer would include, insofar as relevant to this Report, liaison with pathology services and families, ensuring that families are kept as informed as possible about the current progress of the investigation and ensuring that appropriate support is provided for relatives through voluntary and statutory agencies. This Report strongly endorses this recommendation.

7.7 Once the functions of the coroner are complete and a cause of death certified, the coroner should notify the relevant pathologist that any further retention of organs from the post mortem are not authorised by the coroner. Arrangements should be put in place to ensure a clear line of communication between coroner and pathologist in this regard. Any further retention of the organs for clinical audit, education or research purposes must be authorised by the child's parents/guardians.

8 Recommendations

1. Consideration should be given to the implementation of the recommendations made in this Report to other post mortems, namely those carried out on babies who have died before or during birth, minors and adults. Although this Report does not specifically address post mortems in those groups, many of the recommendations may apply generically to all post-mortem practice. However, it should be acknowledged that these post mortems also raise distinct legal and ethical issues that were not within the Terms of Reference of this Report. If the recommendations in this Report are adopted, a Working Group should be established to ensure that appropriate adaptation in relation to those issues takes place. It must include membership from relevant stakeholders and family representative organisations.

---

[41] *Review of the Coroner Service,* Report of the Working Group (2000) para. 3.4.2

2. Legislation must be introduced as a matter of urgency to ensure that no post-mortem examination will be carried out on the body of a deceased child and no organ will be retained from a post-mortem examination for any purpose whatsoever without the authorisation of the child's parent/guardian, or the authorisation of the coroner in an appropriate case.

3. An appropriate legislative framework must be put in place to govern hospital post mortems. A regulatory model that facilitates guidelines to be updated when necessary to keep pace with medical and scientific developments is recommended. Legislation must clearly set out the purposes for which a post-mortem examination may be performed. In order to restore and maintain public confidence in the system, the legislation must set out clear safeguards for patients and their families, and encourage medical education and research. Penalties must be imposed for non-compliance with these safeguards.

4. Although not specifically addressed within the terms of reference of this Report, it is clear that human tissue legislation is urgently required to deal with issues relating to removal, storage and uses of human biological material from the living and the deceased. Provision should be made in such legislation to facilitate and encourage medical education and training, and approved medical research, while maintaining the principle of respect for the donor, the deceased person and the bereaved.

5. The recommendations of the Report of the Working Group on the Coroners Service must be implemented without further delay. A new Coroners Act must be enacted to clarify the legal duties and rights of coroners, and the procedures to be followed from the reporting of a death through to the holding of inquests. Clear structures must be established to deal with information to be provided to families, the appointment of a coroner's officer to liase with parents following a post mortem, and the provision of support to families through the inquest process.